in Fitzgerald has spent most of his life daydreaming about music
is drawn the following conclusions:

Nico's pronunciation of the word 'Clown' is the worst thing to
have happened in the 1960s
Bryan Ferry's dad seems like a lovely man
The only good songs about cars were written by The Beach Boys
- The plot of 'Down in the Tube Station at Midnight' by The Jam
makes no sense at all
- There'll never be a musician with a better name than Fab Moretti

artin Fitzgerald was born in London and currently lives in a convent
Nottingham.

D1435091

4 4 0054647 4

With special thanks to:

Andy McCrorie-Shand
John Moore
Paul Roberts
Harinder Singh
Stephen Wall
Chris York

RUTH *AND* MARTIN'S ALBUM CLUB

MARTIN FITZGERALD

unbound

First published in 2017
This paperback edition first published in 2019

Unbound
6th Floor Mutual House, 70 Conduit Street, London W1S 2GF
www.unbound.com

All rights reserved

© Martin Fitzgerald, 2017

The right of Martin Fitzgerald to be identified as the author
of this work has been asserted in accordance with Section 77 of the Copyright,
Designs and Patents Act 1988. No part of this publication may be copied,
reproduced, stored in a retrieval system, or transmitted, in any form
or by any means without the prior permission of the publisher, nor be
otherwise circulated in any form of binding or cover other than that in which it is
published and without a similar condition being imposed on the subsequent purchaser.

While every effort has been made to trace the owners of copyright material reproduced
herein, the publisher would like to apologise for any omissions and will be pleased to
incorporate missing acknowledgements in any further editions.

Text Design by PDQ
A CIP record for this book is available from the British Library

ISBN 978-1-78352-738-0 (trade pbk)
ISBN 978-1-78352-401-3 (trade hbk)
ISBN 978-1-78352-402-0 (ebook)
ISBN 978-1-78352-403-7 (limited edition)

Printed and bound in Great Britain by Clays Ltd, Elcograf S.p.A.

This book is for my mum, who never once told me to 'turn that racket off!'

Contents

Introduction

Towards the end of 2014, I finally signed up for a Spotify account and suddenly, in my house, I had access to the biggest record collection in the world. I no longer had to make choices and carefully consider which albums I should buy or where I would put them in an alcove of shelving that was already straining under the weight of previous purchases.

I could listen to anything – all via a tiny device that I held in my hand.

So, with the world at my fingertips, I obviously chose to listen to *Cassadaga* by Bright Eyes.

Bright Eyes had long been a blind spot for me and whenever I thought about rectifying this it seemed I was trying to catch up with something that had long since passed. Loads of my friends loved them, indeed swore by them, and that level of devotion intrigued me. Yet I'd opted out and decided that my life could do without this ultra-cool American band that made at least seven people I knew giddy.

Until I pressed play on an iPad while I was in bed.

Fast forward three weeks and I'm now the most enthusiastic Bright Eyes fan of 2014. So much so that I'm angry at the people, the so-called friends, who have let me wait so long to discover them. I approach Ruth, the most enthusiastic Bright Eyes fan I knew in 2004, and berate her for leaving me in this position.

'Ruth, why didn't you just sit me down ten years ago and *make* me listen to them?!'

And that's how it started.

Initially Ruth and I were just going to make each other listen to albums that we'd both missed and then have a coffee at work every Wednesday to discuss our findings. Then we thought we'd document it and, about twenty-three minutes later, we had an online blog called Ruth and Martin's Album Club.

The final piece of the jigsaw was when Ruth said, 'No one really cares about us, let's get a guest each week and make them listen to albums instead.' She then went further and decided that I was going to do all the work while she offered encouragement in between drinking gin and listening to Bruce Springsteen.

What started out as a small project between friends and some journalists we knew then took on a life of its own. Before long we were inundated with emails from a whole bunch of people who had found us online and wanted to be forced to listen to albums. We never actually met any of them, we'd just send a list of albums by email and ask them to pick one. In the case of Ian Rankin, I think I sent him about forty-seven emails because he's genuinely heard everything – apart from Madonna's debut.

In the main, the guests were people who were famous for other things but had a passion for music that their writing hadn't found an outlet for. Without planning it, that became an important factor for us – we were always keen not to be taken over by music journalists or become part of music journalism. We advised all guests to be personal in their writing and provide us with their own specific take on an album and their reasons for having avoided it. We weren't interested in reviews from a distance for albums that had been previously written about ad nauseam – we were interested in what *that* guest thought about in the time and place that they were encountering it. I think, looking back, this kept the project fresh and prevented us falling down a variety of nostalgic trapdoors.

The intros I wrote to each album also took on a life of their own.

What began as a 300-word piece written in bed snowballed into 2,000 words that were heavily researched in the five days before the last edition went out and the new one was due. I was reading a book a week and trying to sift through the story to find the little gems that interested me – stuff like The Jam leaving the studio at 6 p.m. every night so Paul Weller could watch *Coronation Street*. Or the fact that Flavor Flav was originally only in Public Enemy on the strength of his 'your mum' jokes.

Introduction

Again, more than anything, I was conscious not to rehash old ground. I wanted to try to give a freshness to these stories that sometimes focused on the minutiae that interested me, rather than the legacy and context that didn't. I also wanted to approach them with a sense of wonder and a lack of cynicism, to take the story back to the pre-fame days of the artist and chart their development.

In total, we produced eighty-one weekly editions between January 2015 and July 2016 – from Elvis to Kendrick Lamar and all sorts in between. We've included twenty-three of those editions in this volume, a cross-section of music from the last fifty years, and had a special illustration produced for each one.

Some guests loved albums and some guests *really* hated them, but it was all done in a spirit of 'it doesn't really matter'. Because it doesn't. This isn't 1,001 albums you *should* listen to before you die, a sentiment that has always puzzled me. This is more about the reasons why people opt out and what happens when you force them to opt in.

Oh, and it's about the stories too.

I hope you enjoy them.

Martin Fitzgerald
April 2017

1

Elvis Presley by *Elvis Presley*

1. Blue Suede Shoes
2. I'm Counting on You
3. I Got a Woman
4. One-Sided Love Affair
5. I Love You Because
6. Just Because
7. Tutti Frutti
8. Trying To Get To You
9. I'm Gonna Sit Right Down and Cry (Over You)
10. I'll Never Let You Go (Little Darlin')
11. Blue Moon
12. Money Honey

First time listener – Isabel Hardman

I'm the assistant editor at the *Spectator*, and write mostly about politics. When comment editors ask me to write about 'something else', they immediately regret it and never make such an offer ever again as the rest of my life is supremely middle-aged. I keep chickens, collect rare berry bushes, and like going for hearty walks or runs through the beautiful Chilterns.

Isabel's top three albums ever?

Here are three albums that I've thought of that I own in their entirety and will listen to in their entirety. I'm not sure if they are my favourites, but I've taken about five days to come up with an answer.

Ceremonials – Florence + The Machine
Listen – David Guetta
Days Are Gone – Haim

Before we get to Isabel, here's what Martin thinks of *Elvis Presley*

Do you want to know the maddest thing about Elvis Presley?

It's his real name.

Sounds made up doesn't it? Like an alter ego bestowed upon the King of Rock 'n' Roll. But it wasn't. He was always Elvis Presley.

As a ten-year-old who entered a singing competition, a loner kid who played hillbilly music at school and a teenager who sang blues songs in his neighbourhood – the whole time he was walking around called Elvis Presley.

Seems like an odd name for a nobody.

Aged eighteen he walks into Sun Studios, declaring that he'd like to record a song for his mother. It's a disingenuous statement, there are places all over town where he could record himself, at a cheaper price too. But it's here at Sun that he wants to be heard, that he wants to be noticed.

The receptionist, Marion Keisker, sees a shy, woebegone kid in front of her cradling a battered child's guitar. She asks him what kind of singer he is and he replies, 'I sing all kinds.' She asks him who he sounds like, and he replies, 'I don't sound like nobody.'

He may as well have walked in and said 'Hi, I've been sent from the future.'

Elvis records his first song, 'My Happiness', and Keisker listens, agreeing with the kid's assessment of himself. Yes, she could detect the influences, she knew what he'd been listening to, but he was right – he didn't sound like anyone else.

Sam Phillips, the producer and head of Sun Studios, feels the same. On hearing Elvis sing for the first time he simply nods and says he's an 'interesting singer'. He then tells Elvis to give him a call sometime and instructs Marion Keisker to make a note of his details, which she did – 'Elvis Presley. Good Ballad Singer.'

Really, that should have been that.

Elvis Presley had walked into a recording studio for the first time in his life and sung his heart out. And we'll get to this later, but he looked like Elvis too, by which I mean he looked bloody fantastic. It's hard to know what else they could have been looking for in a potential artist and, in all honesty, everyone at Sun Studios should have stopped what they were doing, recognised the good fortune that had come their way and directed all their efforts into the eighteen-year-old.

But they didn't. They did nothing. No call came from Sun Studios and Elvis becomes nothing but a cheap flirt – walking past the windows of Sun Studios on a regular basis, deliberately parking his car outside – hoping that he'll jog their memory and they'll give him a chance. But nothing. He goes unrecognised and unnoticed.

It's crazy when you think about it.

In January 1954, he decides to record another song at Sun, but this time he delivers a weak performance, affected by nerves, and nothing comes from it. Desperate, he gives up on the studio as a route to stardom and starts to audition for local bands. First up he tries out for the terribly named Songfellows and they tell him he can't sing. Next up, he auditions for a band led by a fella called Eddie Bond who tells Elvis to stick to truck driving because 'you're never going to make it as a singer'. Not one person, but multiple people, hear Elvis sing and basically say 'nah, he's rubbish'. It's at this point in the story I've often thought about inventing a time machine, going back to Memphis in 1954, and shouting 'WHAT IS WRONG WITH ALL YOU PEOPLE! HE'S ELVIS PRESLEY!'

But fortunately, common sense prevailed and everyone eventually stopped being so stupid.

On a trip to Nashville, Sam Phillips heard a song called 'Without You', a plaintive ballad that he thought, with the right voice, he could turn into a hit. He thought about the kid that had been stopping by for the last ten months and considered him a perfect fit for the purity and simplicity of the song. Phillips asked Marion Keisker to remind him of his name (how could he have forgotten?) and to invite him down to the studio.

'Can you be here by three?' she asked Elvis over the phone.

Whenever he recounted the story in the future, Elvis would say, 'I was there by the time she hung up.'

They worked on the song all afternoon, but Elvis couldn't quite get it right. Despite this, Phillips is now convinced the kid has something, a way of communicating with his voice that would make him a star. He asks Elvis to run through all the other songs that he knew, hoping to hit upon something, while watching through the control booth window. Yet something was still missing. The formula wasn't complete.

Phillips contacts a guitarist called Scotty Moore and tells him about the kid. He suggests that he hooks up with him to see if they can get something going. Scotty agrees and asks what the kid's name is. When he hears it's Elvis Presley, he says it sounds like something out of science fiction. He's right, it does.

Scotty Moore calls Elvis and arranges for an audition round his house with a bass player called Bill Black. Elvis turns up wearing a black shirt, pink trousers and white shoes. Despite this, they let him in and run through a bunch of songs. Neither Moore nor Black, his future band members, are particularly impressed. Black refers to him as a 'snotty-nosed kid, coming in here with his wild clothes and everything'. As regards his singing, he says, 'Well it was all right, nothing out of the ordinary. I mean, the cat can sing...'

Moore agrees – it was all right, nothing special, and he phones Phillips to give him the less-than-enthusiastic verdict. Phillips decides to give Elvis one more chance and suggests that all three of them come into the studio the next day.

And it's the same story. There's still something missing.

Until there isn't. Until they take a break from recording and Elvis picks up his guitar and starts messing around, singing a song from

1946 called 'That's All Right Mama'. Moore and Black start filling in, messing around too, completely uninhibited now the pressure is off.

Phillips hears them and sticks his head around the door.

'What are you doing?' he asks.

Their reply, which is absolutely brilliant, is, 'We don't know.'

It's the pivotal moment in the development of rock 'n' roll and no one knows what they're doing, it's happened by accident. Phillips gets them to start at the beginning and hits 'Record'.

And now there's nothing missing. It's full steam ahead.

Sam Phillips calls local DJ Dewey Phillips (no relation) and invites him to his house to hear the song. Both men stay up till 2 a.m. listening to it, over and over again. They're the only two men in the world who have access to Elvis's first single, they've discovered treasure, and they're simultaneously puzzled and excited by it. The song wasn't black, it wasn't white, it wasn't pop, it wasn't country. What could they do with it? Where would they go from here?

Dewey Phillips decides to play it on his radio show the next night and the response was instantaneous. Calls flood into the station and the switchboard lights up with a bunch of kids trying to find out more about Elvis Presley. The genie was out of the bottle. Elvis himself was in a cinema at the time – too nervous to hear his debut single being played on the radio and scared that people might laugh at him. Such was the response, though, that his mum and dad were dispatched to find him. Legend has it that his mum walked up one aisle in the cinema and his dad walked up another, until they finally found him in the dark and whisked him away to the radio station for an impromptu interview. What a scene that must have been:

'Come on son, don't worry about this rubbish film, you're about to become king of this thing called rock 'n' roll.'

'Oh.'

That night Dewey Phillips played 'That's All Right Mama' a total of eleven times on his radio show.

Overnight, Memphis had gone Elvis mad. And the strange thing, possibly the strangest of all, is that they don't even know what he looks like. All this adulation, all this hysteria, a song played eleven times on one radio show, and they don't even know what he looks like. Because he could have looked like anyone, but he didn't, he looked like Elvis fucking Presley. He looked like the most beautiful man ever, a man with skin so smooth he looked like he'd never shaved. For his whole life, in every era, he looked like he'd never shaved.

So imagine those people who were already sold by what they'd heard. Imagine when they saw him for the first time. He could have looked like anyone but he looked exactly like the young Elvis Presley.

The response was entirely predictable – a level of hysteria among teenagers that had never been seen before. I would recommend everyone watch his first national television appearance, on the Dorsey Brothers' *Stage Show*, to see why. He enters the stage as if he's been shot from a cannon and then proceeds to launch into 'Shake, Rattle and Roll' before improvising into 'Flip, Flop and Fly'. Is he nervous? Is he *supposed* to be nervous? He doesn't look it. He's only twenty, surrounded by people so much older, yet he's simultaneously dominant and assured – chewing gum between singing and breaking off to do those weird leg movements that caused so many young girls to go mad.

It wasn't that he was filling a gap in the market; he was offering a whole new market of his own.

Meanwhile, in the studio, he follows 'That's All Right Mama' with a string of other singles before reaching his turning point – 'Heartbreak Hotel'. If his previous singles were a consequence of 'messing around', this is anything but – it is a peculiarly moody song that his new record company, RCA, are reluctant to release, worried that it might not be a hit. But Elvis champions it and he is insistent. It becomes his first number one, his first of eighteen, and he never looks back.

Elvis Presley, his first album, is released in 1956. It's a collection of songs recorded between July 1954 and January 1956 that are mostly brilliant, save for a couple of appalling ballads and a truly dreadful version of 'Blue Moon'. It's in and out though, coming in at just twenty-eight minutes long.

But the cover. Look at him on that cover. Who's walking past that in a record shop in 1956 and not buying it?

In one image it says everything about what he has, what people had been missing, and what he would become. Lennon said that before Elvis there was nothing, Dylan said that hearing him for the first time was like busting out of jail. He had smashed down the door for everyone to follow, playing a guitar instead of a piano, being a star as well as a singer.

And whatever happened next, through his Lost in Hollywood years to his Stuck in Vegas years, there was always a healthy reverence, a sense that he was the one that started everything.

But more than that it was he, and only he, who could ever get away with simply being called The King.

So, over to you Isabel. Why haven't you listened to it? WHAT'S WRONG WITH YOU?????

Because I have a slight aversion to listening to things that people who know about music tell me I should listen to.

I tend to assume that the words 'critically acclaimed' mean I won't like something, and the same goes for films. At university I had a housemate who was obsessed with 'critically acclaimed' films and I hated every one of the ones I agreed to watch for being so poncey and boring, *Being John Malkovich* was a particular low point. I tend to like music and films that are rubbish and popular, whether it be chick flicks or Britney Spears. I watch films when I'm too tired to read, and listen to music when I'm doing something practical or walking to work. Both are crowded into other bits of my life, rather than being important in their own right.

Growing up, I was a weird but quite happy combination of bluestocking and tomboy (both terms that suggest girls should like lipstick not mud or books, but at least they give you a picture of the rather singular outdoorsy child I was). I was either curled up with a book or riding horses, climbing trees and making camps with my brothers in our garden – in a wonderfully isolated hamlet with a bus on Thursdays (it left at 7 a.m. and didn't come back). Music and films were a bit too buzzy for me. I've been to two concerts in my life: Justin Timberlake in homemade glittery T-shirts with a giggly group of girlfriends from sixth form and an Elton John concert with a family member who had free tickets. And I went to the Proms for the first time this year, even though I've worked in London since 2009.

I took a holiday job in HMV in my second year at university. They were desperate for more staff during the Christmas period and employed me even though I failed their music knowledge test spectacularly. I walked the shop floor and gave customers terribly bad advice on what albums to buy for their relatives for Christmas, based on things I'd seen while tidying the stock. I imagine a lot of people remember 2006 as the worst haul of musical Christmas presents they ever received as a result.

I do quite like music from the Olden Days, though: I loved the *A Hard Day's Night* film as a kid and the Motown classics were almost always on the hi-fi in our home.

I listen to Leonard Cohen when I'm cooking a big family meal as that's what my mother does and it doesn't feel right to be fussing over a large joint of meat without 'So Long, Marianne' playing in the background. My favourite song in the whole wide world is 'You Got the Love' by Candi Staton, which I fell in love with long before Florence got to it because it was at the end of *Sex and the City* and because it has terrific lyrics. I left my wedding to my best friend singing that song.

But most of the time I listen either to house music (I had to google my favourite artists to find out that the genre was called house, though, and I'm not sure I look or sound like someone who says they're into house. In fact, I only know David Guetta exists because a middle-aged Tory MP told me about him while doing a little dance to illustrate what sort of music it is) or pop-ish stuff. I could (and often do) listen to *Listen* by David Guetta all day, and similarly I love Chicane and Calvin Harris. I often play *Thousand Mile Stare* by Chicane while writing a column as it gets me in an intentional and focused mood. And then I do tend to download a lot of albums by female singers like Florence + The Machine, Lana Del Rey, Ellie Goulding and Haim. Or else I'll sing loudly and tunelessly along to *Joseph and the Amazing Technicolor Dreamcoat* which was my first ever CD and which I know off by heart from start to finish until my husband either leaves the room in great distress or pleads with me to stop.

I struggle to find out about new artists. I only ever hear music on the radio when *Desert Island Discs* comes on or the *Today* programme is doing one of its consciously cool slots. I periodically message my younger and cooler brothers asking for recommendations when I realise I'm still listening to stuff from 2012 and telling myself that it's very current. Or else I like a song that plays during my spinning class and I try to find out what it is once I've caught my breath at the end. Even Spotify passes judgement on me: the other day I tried its 'Discover' feature which recommends 'new' music based on what you're already listening to. It suggested a song from *FutureSex/LoveSounds* by Justin Timberlake. That album was released in 2006.

So the short answer to your question is that I haven't listened to Elvis because I am totally shambolic when it comes to finding music to listen to.

You've now listened to it at least three times, what do you think?

As an example of how shambolic I am, you can't get much better than the way I listened to this album. I listened to it three times, dutifully wrote up my thoughts and sent it to Martin. He was very kind, but said I'd listened to the wrong Elvis album. At least I now know a lot more about Elvis as a result.

Anyway, now I've listened to the *right* album and I've switched from singing tunelessly along to Joseph to dancing around my kitchen to this. 'Blue Suede Shoes', 'I Got a Woman', and 'One-Sided Love Affair' force you out of your seat. In fact, one of my sessions while listening to this album was at my desk while working, and it didn't work. I kept trying to put Chicane back on. It was a bit too noisy and jumpy. But it's perfect for cooking and cleaning. It's definitely not pretentious in the way that 'critically acclaimed' things normally are for me.

There were some songs that sound like the kind of crooning songs lots of people would love, but I could take them or leave them, to be honest. I got a bit bored during 'I'm Counting on You', for instance, and it reminded me of a less moving version of 'Valley of Tears' by Buddy Holly, which I do love. I also grew bored with 'Tutti Frutti'. I'm sure clever people would tell me that a) it's supposed to be repetitive and that b) I really don't have a leg to stand on given the stuff I normally listen to, but it *was* repetitive.

I found some keepers. 'I Love You Because' was really, really lovely. A gentle, slow, sweet song. I was humming 'Money Honey' for the rest of the day after I listened to the album for the first time. And my favourite was 'Blue Moon' as it was simple and his voice just sounded terrific and deep and gorgeous. But researching Elvis further, I found my favourite song of his on another album. I loved 'In the Ghetto'. It was more along the lines of the sort of heartfelt songs that I normally like, though they normally tend to be sung by female artists (not sure why).

Listening along, I realised how many of these songs have appeared in the soundtracks of the non-chick-flick films that I have managed to watch. They feel much more familiar than I was expecting. At the end of the first listen, I felt as though I'd heard just two songs: one was the sort of leaping around dancing song, and the other was a slower more thoughtful tune that I tended to get bored of. Of course, the whole point of Ruth and Martin telling me to listen to the album three times was that I was forced to notice the difference between the songs, and

Elvis Presley by *Elvis Presley*

I'm glad I did as I would have discarded it too quickly after one listen and never returned. I've realised that I like music that slots snugly into my life rather than that I have to make time and effort to listen to. *Elvis Presley* was the first album I've sat down and listened to without doing anything else at the same time. It felt odd.

I did like this album. Being totally unmusical and having never really immersed myself in music reviews or any of that sort of thing that involves actually thinking about music, I don't really know what to say about it. I feel a bit like the student in *On Beauty* who tells her art history lecturer that the reason so few students take his class is that no one's allowed to just say that they like the artworks. I like it, but there wasn't one song on there that I loved so much I had to play it again, right away. It was more the sort of album I'd very happily listen to while cooking, dancing merrily away as I moved around the kitchen with cheeks flushed from the heat of the oven and wearing my apron with chickens on that I put on when I'm doing Proper Cooking. And that tends to be old music – or *Joseph*. And for the rest of the time, I'm afraid I'll stick to meandering through music that MPs who are even sadder than me tell me I should listen to.

Would you listen to it again?
I've starred a number of songs from it on Spotify. Probably wouldn't listen to the whole album again. Unless I've got a lot of cooking to do.

A mark out of 10?
7.

2

What's Going On by Marvin Gaye

1. What's Going On
2. What's Happening Brother
3. Flyin' High (In the Friendly Sky)
4. Save the Children
5. God Is Love
6. Mercy Mercy Me (The Ecology)
7. Right On
8. Wholy Holy
9. Inner City Blues (Make Me Wanna Holler)

First time listener – Chris Addison

I direct some things, act in some other things, write still other things, and now and then do stand-up for coins and/or accommodation.

Chris's top three albums ever?

I really don't have a top three, but big moments for me in pop include:

The Smiths – *The Queen Is Dead*

Sugarcubes – *Life's Too Good*

The Leisure Society – *Into the Murky Water*

Before we get to Chris, here's what Martin thinks of *What's Going On*

When we announced this album on the blog the reception was unlike anything we've ever seen.

What typically happens is 50 per cent of people tell us the album is brilliant while the other 50 per cent tell us it's rubbish and they hope the guest gives it a right good kicking. But this week was different. It was 100 per cent pro-album – the first time that's ever happened.

And it wasn't just an expression of lighthearted joy either – it was weightier than that. There I was on Monday afternoon, trying my best to relax with a bag of Wotsits, when I was suddenly confronted with a load of tweets laced with reverence and implicit threat.

Here are just some examples:

@StuartBunby, who has an avatar of a chimpanzee playing baseball, said,

I really hope he likes it. It would be really good if we could all continue to get along.

I'll admit, the double use of the word 'really' scared me a bit and made me think that this Bunby character was a great deal more menacing than his surname suggests – i.e. not menacing at all because he's called Mr Bunby.

@John_p_d, who describes himself as a 'jazz lover', said,

I can't see how it would be humanly possible not to love this record.

Obviously I resisted the urge to reply with 'I can't see how it would be humanly possible to love jazz.'

And finally, @tillyv lived up to her Twitter bio ('Ambiguity alludes me') by saying,

Woah. He won't be able to write with the religious experience he is about to have.

I found this one particularly odd because one of the reasons the world is in such a mess is precisely because of people writing about the religious experiences they've had. But never mind. I decided not to pull her up on this because a) she seems nice and b) I'm not Ricky Gervais.

On Tuesday, I dragged myself away from twitter for a routine check-up at the dentist. Brian, the dentist, is a jovial sort and long-term reader of our blog who occasionally chastises me for telling silly jokes about the bands he loves.

Again, Tuesday was different.

He had me upside down in his chair, shone the bright light *right* in my face and, while prising my mouth open with what seemed like half of B&Q, said,

'You do know *What's Going On* is one of my favourite albums, don't you?'

It was a bit like that scene in *Marathon Man*, except Brian isn't a Nazi trying to escape his past.

Well, he says he isn't anyway.

So, with all these expectations, I struggled with what approach to take and was conscious that I had to do the album 'justice'.

With that in mind, here are some potential angles that I considered:

1) The father and son angle, with some amateur psychology thrown in for good measure

Any piece about Marvin Gaye is usually dominated by accounts of a ruthless father who used to beat him mercilessly as a child. Some people go even further and seek to explain his entire career as an attempt to simultaneously escape his father while also making him proud.

That may be true but it sort of ruins the jaunty opening.

With that in mind, I decided to move on and ignore the 'terrible dad spawns great artist' angle.

Sorry, terrible dads.

2) The Motown angle

I considered doing the entire piece on how Motown is easily the best record label ever and, with the possible exception of Chess, no one else even comes close.

In fact, it's so good that it's now an adjective in its own right and people quite naturally walk around saying 'I'm into Motown' in a way that no one has ever said 'I'm into Sony' or 'I'm into Bella Union'.

No doubt there's someone shouting 'I PREFER STAX, ACTUALLY!' at their computer right now, but surely that's just one of those weird things that people say – like salt and vinegar crisps belong in green packets.

Everything about Motown, particularly in the early days, makes me happy – they produced entertainers rather than singers; they recorded within hours of writing the song to capture the spontaneity; and they often ripped up their own release schedules because they were so excited about whatever brilliant song they just recorded.

Do you know what the first Motown record was that sold a million copies?

'Shop Around' by Smokey Robinson and The Miracles.

Do you know what 'Shop Around' is about?

It's about Smokey Robinson's mum pulling him to one side and basically saying, 'Before you get married, son, have as many girlfriends as you possibly can.'

What a woman. I wish my mum had said the same to me.

My love of Motown also explains my suspicion of northern soul. Why is everyone messing about with B-sides and rarities? Just put 'Needle in a Haystack' by The Velvelettes on and be done with it.

And why are we in Wigan? And why's everyone covered in talcum powder?

Sorry, it's not for me.

Finally, I love the fact that all you needed for a career at Motown was to be in close proximity to the recording studio. That was it. Just hang around and your time will come, like it did for Diana Ross and Martha Reeves – office girls who were put on the production line just because they were within reach.

'Excuse me Martha, can you stop typing for a second and come in here and sing "Heatwave" please.'

'Sure, no problem.'

'Great, and can you bring the Vandellas with you please.'

I'm fairly sure that if I'd been working there as a cleaner then I'd probably have had fifteen top ten hits by now and currently be on tour somewhere with the surviving members of The Four Tops.

That's how good it was.

Yet when you look at Gaye's career, it's complex and goes against the grain of the other artists. He starts out as a drummer, then gets marketed as a Nat King Cole-style crooner, before he decides to rebel against the company ethos. This basically involves smoking a load of weed, snorting a load of coke, and being a terrible pupil at the John Roberts Powers School for Social Grace where he was sent to be groomed.

He's also not helped by a stop-start discography that never quite takes off in the same way as The Supremes, The Four Tops or The Temptations. For every 'Can I Get a Witness' and 'How Sweet It Is (To Be Loved by You)' there's a string of forgettable songs that aren't hits. It's only really when he teams up with Tammi Terrell in 1966 that he has consolidated success for the first time.

Tragically, though, Terrell collapses in his arms on stage one night in 1967 and is later diagnosed with a brain tumour. She dies three years later, at the age of just twenty-four.

So, despite everything that I associate with Motown, the opposite appears to be the case for Marvin Gaye. His success is, at best, sporadic, and his personal life is littered with tragedy and unease.

Come the end of the sixties, with the label starting to fall apart, Marvin Gaye is still hanging on and looking for another move.

And he's just had his biggest hit so far – 'I Heard It Through the Grapevine'.

3) The political angle

One of the more interesting aspects of Gaye's career is how he became overtly politicised towards the end of the sixties in a way that other Motown artists didn't. Throughout his life he had personal battles with authority (his father, Motown), and as the decade wore on he embraced an emerging subculture that was defiantly anti-war and anti-government.

He tells of a time when he heard one of his own songs on the radio interrupted by a newsflash about the Watts Riots.

He tells of how his brother would come back from Vietnam with stories that would terrify and infuriate him.

Yet, all the while, Motown are still pushing him to 'entertain', to meet *their* expectations of who Marvin Gaye was.

He can't do it any more.

Instead, he starts wearing hoodies, grows a beard, and refuses to pay his taxes in case the government uses them to bomb Vietnam.

It's in this frame of mind that he starts work on *What's Going On* – an album that turned its back on a career of love songs and focused on the Vietnam war, spirituality, environmentalism and saving babies instead.

So here we are. Having considered the three obvious angles, I still felt dissatisfied. None of them seemed to adequately sum up the album and I felt there was still something missing.

For example, there's the James Jamerson story.

For those of you that don't know, Jamerson was the legendary bass player at Motown who played on practically all their hits. Naturally, Gaye wanted him for *What's Going On* so he tracked him down to a club and dragged him into the studio to record his part. There was only one problem – Jamerson was so drunk that he could barely stand up.

It didn't matter though. Jamerson lay on the floor, pissed out of his head, and nailed his part in one take. To this day it's one of the best bass lines ever and I'll never know how he did it.

So, yeah, at one point I considered doing 2,000 words on a drunk bass player.

And that was nearly that. I'd given up trying to find something that captured the essence of *What's Going On* and, instead, settled for what I had – some biography plotlines and a few daft jokes.

Par for the course, really.

Then I saw it.

In an interview just before he made *What's Going On*, Marvin Gaye said the following:

'I had to be an artist, and artists work in the privacy of their own imaginations.'

It was that final phrase that really struck me.

I couldn't stop thinking about it and it went round my head for hours. He'd come up with the perfect description for the creative process, one that explained why debut albums are often the best, why you should never cater for your audience, and why you should always ignore other people's expectations.

But more than that, he explained his own transformation.

He explained that *What's Going On* is as much about personal politics as it is about a wider context – the legacy narrative that now gives the album its weight.

He let you in on the secret of what happened and, in the process, reminded me that these stories are *always* best kept personal. So if you're asking me what I think of *What's Going On*, to do it justice, I would say its magic is in that phrase.

After twelve years and ten albums, Marvin Gaye finally discovered what he'd been looking for the whole time – the privacy of his own imagination.

So, over to you Chris. Why haven't you listened to it? WHAT'S WRONG WITH YOU?????

It takes me a long time to get round to things – the films of Billy Wilder, tax returns, writing this – and Motown was just another one of those foolishly neglected items on my very long list. When I was little most of the music in our house was classical. That came from my dad, the son of an Austrian woman who brought the Viennese love of chamber music with the suitcase of possessions she packed when she fled the Nazis. My childhood was all schnitzel and sauerkraut and septets. There was the occasional burst of pop too but only really through the records my mum had bought, which she seemed to have stopped doing once her children came along. It would be ten years until I'd hear of the existence of David Bowie. My first exposure to any kind of R&B was in the form of Boney M's 1978 *Nightflight to Venus*.

Charities have been started for less.

Leaving aside an early flirtation with the works of Queen, my own pop education began quite late under the tutelage of my school bus comrade Bob, who filled the vital role of Slightly Older Kid with Advanced Record Collection. He made me a copy of The Smiths' *Strangeways, Here We Come*, and since TDK D90s had two sides, slung in The Pogues' *If I Should Fall from Grace with God* too. These were a revelation. The energy of The Pogues, the sly gallows wit of Morrissey, the music from Marr the like of which I'd just never imagined existed, blew out a wall to my left and when the clouds of plaster thinned, there was this whole other world – whole other part of my brain, actually – a valley of possibilities, stretching away. I let slip Queen's hand and off into that valley I gambolled, writhing around in indie like an extra in a drug scene from a 1960s movie: The House of Love, The Sugarcubes, They Might Be Giants and the fey, pre-Roses la-la pop that Manchester put out (God, I loved The Man from Delmonte like only a weedy nerd could). By the time Madchester came along, I was an old indie hand in the right place at the right time.

For years after that I was pretty tribal about pop, as the gauche often are; I was an indie kid, all fanzines and certainty. That probably lasted about a decade until I met my wife, who is on every level a better person than me. She loves all the things I took pride in disdaining: soul, musicals, celery. And in a war of attrition over the last almost twenty years, she's got me round to the first two. (I will die before admitting celery is a foodstuff, mind.) Now among the thousands of LPs, CDs and downloads I own there's stuff in every genre. Except metal, which continues to elude me. But what all those lost years meant was that in spite of listening to (and loving) a great deal more of it in recent times, whole swathes of soul, funk, R&B and related sub-genres that would be bunged in the same grey slots in HMV have passed me by, including all but the title track of Marvin Gaye's *What's Going On*.

What's Going On by Marvin Gaye

You've now listened to it at least three times, what do you think?

God, the pressure. People love this, don't they? I mean, really fanatically love it as an album, an artefact, a milestone. God, the *pressure*.

I've been on a bit of an up and down journey with this one. See, that opening track is so strong, such a great piece of music, that I think I was waiting for an album of something similar – something that immediately grabs you, a constantly startling adventure in music, twists and turns and revelations at every corner. This is not that album. That first listen was a surprise. No, I'll be more honest: it was a disappointment. But that's the problem with the expectations we build up, isn't it? That's why so many critics level that utterly redundant opinion 'I would have preferred it if it was a bit more like…', the correct response to which is 'Well, it isn't, so suck it up and take it on its own terms, you solipsistic imbecile.'

So, having washed my expectations away, I went back to it and I must say I liked it a good deal better, which was exciting and pleasing and something of a relief because I'm a cultural coward and I'd hate to be seen as a dunce who can't appreciate A Classic. The third time I put it on, I was truly looking forward to being in its company again, but as the record turned… nothing. It just didn't take. To be absolutely straight with you, I got a bit bored.

I hope that we can still be friends.

Marvin starts out asking 'What's Going On' and neither having received a satisfactory answer nor being the kind of fellow to let a thing go, he investigates further with a song called 'What's Happening, Brother'. Actually, there's no question mark, so it's difficult to tell whether he's just reframed his original question or is now providing the answer to it. My guess is that it's a supplementary enquiry related to the first one since it starts with *exactly the same musical sequence the last song finished with*. Because what seems to happen after the belting opener is that Marvin noodles around for fifteen minutes or so asking vague questions over music that doesn't seem to change pace or go anywhere different to any great degree, making breaks at arbitrary moments when he's thought of another question. I find the meandering makes it hard to get hold of anything.

'Flyin' High (In the Friendly Sky)' and 'Save the Children' together sound like an extended improv looking for a hook, which is occasionally glimpsed before we lose all sight of it again. It's like variations on a theme without an actual, you know, theme. I liked 'God Is Love' and 'Mercy, Mercy Me (The Ecology)' better. They seemed to have more of a shape, the latter even surviving the addition of a saxophone, an instrument which when blown with any vigour rarely doesn't sound like a pig trapped in a barrel. And 'Inner City Blues' is simply great. It has more purpose than anything since the title track, marching forward on the hookiest of hooks. It's simpler at its core than a lot of the other tracks and perhaps that's why I like it. Maybe here's the focus I've been subconsciously looking for; the song seems to develop, rather than wander.

I hope that we can still be friends.

I hesitate to say this, but there just don't seem to be as many ideas here as there are songs. STOP! NO! LISTEN! I'm aware that I'm hearing it forty-five years after the event and that in fact any of the extraordinary, ground-breaking musical things Marvin Gaye may well have done here will have been so appropriated and re-used over the time since that it's impossible for me to see them clearly from my vantage point. I know someone who hates Monty Python because before he saw any of their work he'd seen a million thudding sixth-form acolytes attempt to synthesise their genius, their turns of phrase. So by the time he got to Python itself, it was ruined for him.

That could well be happening with me and this album because, oh look, here are the strings I find so cheesy and awful in disco and here's the jazz flute that I've hated since 1970s Italian kids' cartoon *Mr Rossi* and the sound of 'Right On' has been parodied so often in blaxploitation/cop spoofs that it's hard to take it seriously, but maybe I'm just looking the wrong way up the tube. Even so, it's the only way I can look.

I hope that we can still be friends.

I also know that this album is supposed to be an explosive political statement and so I'm chary of not liking it for reasons of cultural sensitivity and – more importantly – the aforementioned cowardice. Yet the songs are so frustratingly vague. He starts with the general thesis that there's something going on and then goes on to specify only that some of the things that are going on are going on with drugs and other things that are going on are going on with children.

Following that is a quick sidebar in which he's keen to point out that none of it is God's fault before he's right back to it, noting that something's also going on with 'The Ecology'. He's really no more specific about the problems than this. I have started to suspect that if I were to buy the deluxe reissue of this album, I'd find tracks that didn't make the original cut called 'Seriously Mate, Right?' and 'Cuh. Life, Eh?' His obvious sincerity is not in any doubt and I'm certain that at the time it was released this was something quite extraordinary, but I want my explosive political statements to be all fire and revolution and lyrical petrol in a musical bottle, Marvin, get out of second gear! But yet again, I'm falling into the idiot's trap of measuring this thing by my own expectations, so let's take the lyrics on their own terms. Here's a segment of 'Save the Children':

> Oh what a shame, such a bad way to live
> All who is to blame, we can't stop livin'
> Live, live for life
> But let live everybody
> Live life for the children
> Oh, for the children
> You see, let's save the children

Let's save all the children
Save the babies, save the babies.

I mean, I can't say I disagree with him. In fact, I loudly applaud the whole notion, but it just doesn't come as any great revelation, you know, the idea that we should *really try* to save the babies. To be brutally plain, you could absolutely take those lines and alternate them between two old men nursing Guinness at a bar, drunkenly agreeing with each other over and over.

ARTHUR: Live life for the children.

PETEY: Oh, for the children.

ARTHUR: You see, let's save the children.

PETEY: Let's save all the children.

ARTHUR: Save the babies.

PETEY: Save the babies. Have you any scampi fries back there, love?

I confess I'm being slightly harsh to hammer the point, but as great statements go it does all feel a bit undercooked.

I hope that we can still be friends.

But look, I don't like not liking this album since it's so important to so many people I know (plus cowardice etc. etc.). I'm comforted that a friend of mine who is an enormously knowledgeable classical music buff took until he was in his fifties to get his head round Mozart; maybe I just haven't found the key that unlocks *What's Going On* yet. So let's focus on the positive: I did really enjoy it the second time I heard it and if you incorporate the fact that I adore the title track and 'Inner City Blues' is fabulous, then I enjoyed it at least 60 per cent of the time I was listening to it. Which also means that I very well might enjoy it again. The best things grow on you, don't they? Apart from athlete's foot – that one's the exception. So that's what I'm taking from this: an acquaintance that if worked at might one day become a firm friendship.

I really do hope that we can still be friends.

Would you listen to it again?

I definitely will. Late at night with whisky next, I think. But I won't listen to it as A Classic, just as some music. See what happens if I come at it from that angle. See if it can breathe a bit more out from under the weight of everyone telling me how good it is.

A mark out of 10?

I enjoyed 60 per cent of my listening, so 6. For now.

3

Straight Outta Compton by N.W.A.

1. Straight Outta Compton
2. Fuck tha Police
3. Gangsta Gangsta
4. If It Ain't Ruff
5. Parental Discretion Iz Advised
6. 8 Ball
7. Something Like That
8. Express Yourself
9. Compton's n the House
10. I Ain't tha 1
11. Dopeman
12. Quiet on the Set
13. Something 2 Dance 2

First time listener – Tim Farron

Tim Farron is Leader of the Liberal Democrats and Member of Parliament for Westmorland and Lonsdale in the Lake District. He was born in Lancaster and before entering politics he worked at Lancaster University.

In his spare time Tim enjoys walking in the countryside with his wife Rosie and their four children, and watching his beloved Blackburn Rovers attempt to return to the Premier League.

Tim's top three albums ever?

Steve McQueen – Prefab Sprout

The Clash's first album (but the US version because it's got '(White Man) In Hammersmith Palais' and 'Complete Control' on it)

Since I Left You – The Avalanches

Before we get to Tim, here's what Martin thinks of *Straight Outta Compton*

Here's the story of N.W.A., told over four meetings.

1) Prologue – 1985

Consider the following:

Los Angeles is spread over 465 square miles and has 8,400 police officers.

New York is spread over 321 square miles and has 39,110 police officers.

If you boil that down, it means that Los Angeles has to maintain law and order with 103 fewer police officers per square mile. The odds don't seem right, do they? How can such a small police force effectively cover such a large area?

The answer was simple – they were brutal, they intimidated the streets. They would say, generously, they were preventing crimes before they happened, laying down the law whether it was broken or not. Yet the truth was less about police work, or justice. They were sending a message.

Indeed, their own police chief, Daryl Gates, once said the following:

'Casual drug users should be taken out and shot.'

That's not an overheard remark, or a slip of the tongue, that was a comment made before the US Senate. The Los Angeles Chief of Police, in front of the country's elected representatives, actually said that casual drug users should be taken out and shot.

And no one did anything.

If there was one particular district in LA that was singled out for special treatment from the LAPD it was Compton. Unemployment and poverty were widespread there, and the largely African-American population was in the grip of a crack cocaine epidemic that was destroying nearly everything in sight.

The police decided to resort to extreme measures to solve the problem – they acquired a tank and flattened properties in a perfunctory search for drugs and criminality. On one occasion Nancy Reagan cheerfully sat in on one of the raids.

She ate a fruit salad as the tank knocked down the walls of someone's home.

After finding just one gram of crack, she was quoted as saying:

'I saw people on the floor, rooms that were unfurnished… all very depressing. These people in here are beyond the point of teaching and rehabilitating. There's no life, and that's very discouraging.'

And no one did anything.

2) The first meeting

Jerry Heller had brought Elton John and Pink Floyd to America. He'd represented Van Morrison, ELO, Marvin Gaye, The Who, Journey, Creedence Clearwater Revival, The Four Tops and Black Sabbath. Yet, in the mid-eighties, he'd run out of talent and found himself loitering around LA trying to catch a break.

His friend Lonzo approaches him in 1987:

'Hey, Jerry. I got this Compton guy keeps saying he wants to meet you.'

'Yeah? A rapper?' Jerry asks.

'Nah. He's like a street guy, got a lot of big ideas. He says he wants to start a record store or something.'

Jerry's heard it all before. Forty-seven and lacking whatever enthusiasm he once had, he tells his friend to spare him the story and move along.

But he doesn't. Over the next weeks and months, Lonzo keeps chasing Jerry about the kid from Compton:

'Hey, man. You gotta see this Compton guy. He's on at me all the time about it.'

Heller became simultaneously exasperated and intrigued. On the one hand, he ignored his friend while, on the other, he knew that playing hard to get was a deliberate move and only the most determined would get through his defences. The kid from Compton, whoever he was, was playing his part to perfection by refusing to give up.

Finally, Lonzo approached Heller again.

'Listen, Jerry. The guy says he'll pay me for an introduction to you.'

Heller's ears pricked up.

'How much?'

'Seven hundred and fifty,' Lonzo replied, 'and to be honest I could use the money.'

It wasn't the money that swayed Heller, or a sense of duty to his friend. He just appreciated the initiative, the fact that some kid he didn't even know was prepared to offer $750 just to meet him.

Heller gave in.

On Tuesday 3 March, 1987, a car pulled up outside Heller's business premises and out stepped a short kid wearing wraparound sunglasses and a Raiders cap.

Lonzo introduced them: 'Jerry, this is Eric Wright, aka Eazy-E.'

Easy said nothing, just pulled out a roll of notes from his sock and paid Lonzo his finder's fee on the spot. Heller watched on, charmed by the fact that the kid didn't once move his lips while he was counting the money.

Heller asks, 'You want to play me something?'

Eazy speaks for the first time.

'Sure.'

He played him 'Boyz-n-the-Hood', '8 Ball' and 'Dopeman' and Heller thought it was the best thing he'd heard in years.

Eazy then began to talk.

'I want to start my own label. A place where an artist could work without anyone looking over his shoulder, telling him what he could and could not do – a free environment, no rules, no catering to any taste other than the artist's own.'

Heller asked him if the label had a name.

'Ruthless Records,' Eazy said.

Heller asked him if his group had a name.

'N.W.A.,' Eazy said.

'What's that mean, "No Whites Allowed"?' asked Heller.

Eazy laughed for the first time during the meeting.

'Sort of,' he said.

3) The second meeting

Heller spins through his Rolodex, his life's work flicking before him. He needs a friend, someone to help him distribute. He finally arrives at Joe Smith, chairman of Capitol Records – nicknamed The Gentleman.

Heller visits the Capitol Building, optimistically designed to look like a stack of hit singles, and excitedly enters Smith's office.

He played him 'Boyz n the Hood'.

Smith was horrified.

Heller then flipped it over and played 'Dopeman'.

Smith was still horrified.

'Stop, stop!'

There was an uncomfortable silence between the two men. And then Smith gave his verdict:

'Jerry, what makes you think anyone is going to buy this garbage? Who's going to listen? Tell me, who's going to play this? No radio station in the world.'

Heller tried his best to convince Smith. He reminded him of The Stones, The Sex Pistols and a whole host of other bands that seemed 'too much' to one generation but never enough for another.

Smith held his ground.

'This crap is never going to make it.'

He then offered Heller a million dollars, just for the rights to the name Ruthless Records.

'It's a great name. Really, I'll have my girl bring in the chequebook.'

'I don't want to sell the name. I want to sell the music,' insisted Heller.

'Never. It'll never sell.'

Heller left the office dejected and gave Eazy-E the bad news.

'The gentleman at Capitol said no.'

Eazy absorbed the information, without a hint of reaction.

'That's cool,' he said. 'Fuck 'em.'

4) The third meeting

Heller was desperate. Everyone had turned their back on him and he was running out of options. In a move befitting the situation, he set up a meeting with Priority Records.

Who was the biggest act on Priority at the time?

A cartoon group called The California Raisins who mostly sang Motown covers.

Heller walked into their offices, this time accompanied by Eazy-E, and played 'Straight Outta Compton':

'You are now about to witness the strength of street knowledge.'

The people in the room were silent.

Straight outta Compton
Crazy motherfucker called Ice Cube
From the gang called Niggas with Attitude

It was a shock to the system for a label used to dealing with animated dried fruit.

Heller then played 'Fuck tha Police':

Fuck tha police coming straight from the underground
A young nigga got it bad cos I'm brown

The people in the room were still silent.

Then Heller went in, business to business. He used all his old tricks and tried to convince them that Priority was the best 'fit' for N.W.A. Yet the executives just sat there in silence. They still hadn't spoken since they heard 'Straight Outta Compton'.

Finally, Eazy interjected. He'd watched the whole performance from the corner and felt it was time to say something:

'Why don't you at least come down and hear the band play?' he asked.

'OK,' they replied.

Eazy-E knew he had them.

5) The final meeting

It could never last. The tension, and the attention, brought on by success started to tear it down within a couple of years.

Ice Cube, the band's lyricist, had left amid accusations of being ripped off.

Dr Dre, the producer, was being courted by record labels that, all of a sudden, were ready to listen.

'We got to work this shit out,' Dre says as he picks up the phone to Eazy.

Eazy doesn't say anything.

'This is important,' Dre pleads. 'You want to get with me up here?'

They arrange to meet at the studio, two old friends from Compton trying to work out how they can keep this thing together. When Eazy arrives, though, Dre isn't there. Instead, Suge Knight walks in, flanked by bodyguards holding baseball bats.

Eazy knows he's been set up.

'You got to sign this,' Knight says, holding up a contract that releases Dre from his commitment to Ruthless Records.

Eazy doesn't move.

'You see that white van parked down there on the street?' Knight continues. 'We got Jerry Heller tied up in the back of that van, gun to his head, blow his goddam fucking brains out.'

Eazy doesn't move.

'We can get your moms too. You want us to?'

Eazy signs.

It was the end of N.W.A. They'd sent a message of their own, but now it was time for the start of something else.

6) Epilogue

On 3 March 1991, three African-American men were driving along the freeway in the San Fernando Valley. A police car noticed the driver was speeding and started to pursue him.

The driver started to panic.

He was on parole for a previous robbery conviction and was concerned that this could be seen as a violation. He'd also drunk some alcohol during the evening and wasn't sure whether he was over the limit or not. Rather than taking any chances, he decided to put his foot down and outrun the police. The pursuit raced through residential suburbs, with multiple police cars joining the hunt and a helicopter hovering overhead.

Eventually, they cornered the car and ordered the passengers out of the vehicle.

The first to emerge, Bryant Allen, was kicked, taunted and threatened.

The second to emerge, Freddie Helms, was hit on the head while lying on the ground.

Finally, the driver emerged – Rodney King.

He laughed, he smiled, he waved to the helicopter overhead.

The police officers forced him to the ground, kicked him six times and struck him thirty-three times with their batons while, unbeknown to them, the entire incident was being filmed from across the street. King was eventually arrested and taken to hospital where he was treated for a fractured facial bone, a broken right ankle and an assortment of bruises and lacerations.

During his treatment, a nurse watched as the police officers that brought him in laughed and bragged about how many times they'd hit him.

But then the film of the incident went public.

America saw how the LAPD policed its streets and was rightly horrified. There were calls for both justice and calm. The police had to be arrested, the men who were seen to be so guilty had to be punished and brought before the law that they themselves had bent out of shape.

On 22 April 1992, a jury of ten whites, one Latino and one Asian acquitted the police officers. They were free to go.

And this time, the people did do something.

So, over to you Tim. Why haven't you listened to it? WHAT'S WRONG WITH YOU?????

N.W.A.'s *Straight Outta Compton* is a classic album, one of those albums you must listen to before you die.

So, question number one is: given that I am a self-proclaimed music nerd, why did I never buy this record and why have I never knowingly listened to it all the way through before?

Well, I'm not completely sure. Maybe because there are only so many hours in the day and you can't listen to everything? Maybe because rap is not my thing? But then again I bought, love and still listen to De La Soul's *3 Feet High and Rising*… but De La Soul are safe and cuddly, so maybe *Straight Outta Compton* is too edgy, sweary, violent and misogynistic for a tame chap like me? Actually, that might well be it… but perhaps the main reason is that I felt it wasn't for me.

Forgive me, but I've always had a problem with David Cameron saying that he likes The Smiths, in particular that he likes *The Queen is Dead*. There's a line in 'Panic' that goes, 'the music they constantly play, it says nothing to me about my life…' I don't want to be an inverse snob, but The Smiths do not sing to David Cameron about anything in his life at all. What Morrissey sings cannot possibly resonate with him. I'm a northern working-class bloke, an angsty eighties teenager. The Smiths say plenty to me about my life.

Now, for some music that doesn't matter. Even fairly avant-garde or groundbreaking stuff like The White Stripes, Cocteau Twins, Blur aren't setting out a manifesto or representing anyone or anything. There isn't an ideology simmering away there, they aren't speaking of their particular life experiences, offering a personal sense of belonging to those who share that identity and that's absolutely fine – and I love all three of those bands, by the way, and for what it's worth, I would have no complaints if the PM liked any of them; indeed he has my blessing!

But N.W.A. have a simmering ideology, a boiling one even. They speak about their lives, they share their identity. There is fury in this album which is as authentic and sincere as it is foul-mouthed and misogynistic. But I'm not straight outta Compton, I'm straight out o' Preston and what I knew about N.W.A. is that they said little to me about my life... which is absolutely OK, but I simply – in my over-earnest way – felt that I would be insincere, inauthentic, a wannabe, a fake, if I got into N.W.A. So I listened to all the Madchester stuff instead.

So, excuses over...

Over the years I've come to accept that music is music and that I should stop being so up myself and just listen to stuff!!

You've now listened to it at least three times, what do you think?

It's a good piece of work. To misquote Public Enemy, you can believe the hype. This is an important and influential album but it is also a great musical accomplishment. It's full of energy, sincerity and lyrical intelligence. It's also pretty funky, decent tunes. The last track, 'Something 2 Dance 2', is preceded by several other tracks that you can most certainly dance to. In fact, listening to the album I have flashbacks of being at university in Newcastle dancing to a few of these – in particular track four, 'If It Ain't Ruff', which has a knowingly jazzy feel to it.

Much of the rap that I'd listened to in the eighties was about the samples that underpinned the rap as much as the words themselves. This album is well produced, it's full of good tunes and clever mixes, but the words are king. All music is derivative, there's nothing new under the sun, but my first impression is that the lyrical focus of this album owes more to Gil Scott-Heron than to earlier rap artists. Only Gil Scott-Heron didn't swear so often, he appeared to respect women and he had a few solutions to the problems he identified. And I now sound like my dad…

So let's get my criticisms out of the way. The swearing is ridiculous – it sounds like a pastiche of itself. I couldn't help laughing at it, thinking of Chris Morris's 'Uzi Lover' from *Brass Eye* or the appallingly toilet-mouthed Rude Kid from the pages of *Viz*.

Worst of all is the way women are spoken about. The language is more than misogynistic – it is a blanket treatment of women as sex objects and nothing more. Some will say that we have to accept this as social realism and all that – and again I don't doubt their sincerity – but to be angry at society and authority, or to celebrate hedonism, doesn't require such a loveless, graceless and damaging assault on womankind.

Oh, and I should point out that much as I admire Eazy-E, Dr Dre and Ice Cube, the Liberal Democrats take a rather different position to them on law and order…

That may all sound pretty damning, but on balance I have to say I liked the record.

The opening burst of the title track, 'F*** tha Police', and 'Gangsta Gangsta' leave you very clear over what these guys are about! Self-referential, dramatic backdrops, fresh, brave, resonant of early punk, hedonism with a bit of nihilism… and no Chic bass lines.

Having established themselves, N.W.A. then seem to feel free to let the tunes elbow their way in. 'If It Ain't Ruff', 'Parental Discretion', 'Something Like That' and 'Express Yourself' contain laid-back grooves, the occasional recognisable sample and an odd piano loop.

The rest of the album focuses again heavily on the rhymes and the lyrical content. Ice Cube's rant against women in 'I Ain't tha 1' contains the delightful line, addressed to his female companion, 'I got what I wanted – beat it', which I suppose makes this track the closest thing N.W.A. get to a tender love song...

'Compton's n the House' sounds clichéd but only because I've heard so many copying this kind of impressively egotistical attack on wannabes, copycats and also-rans over the last twenty years. It's easy to forget that this isn't a cliché, we are listening to the originals. We finish with 'Something 2 Dance 2'. Great track, and incredibly well produced... indeed the album is a great piece of production as well as a great musical work.

Music is all about connections, about 'what does this remind me of?' The album this one reminded me of the most is The Sex Pistols, *Never Mind the Bollocks*. They share the same air of desperation, of churning out a shocking but brilliant piece of work almost as if they had no choice to do anything else. And both albums were influential beyond compare. Both albums made music accessible – and the making of music affordable and comprehensible. To me, almost everything worthwhile in music in the last forty years owes something to the Pistols. *Straight Outta Compton* is certainly worthwhile, and it owes plenty to Johnny Rotten and co.

Would you listen to it again?

I would listen to it again, but not with the kids around...

A mark out of 10?

I'd give it 8 out of 10 artistically, but for my personal enjoyment of it more like 6 out of 10.

4

Madonna by Madonna

1. Lucky Star
2. Borderline
3. Burning Up
4. I Know It
5. Holiday
6. Think of Me
7. Physical Attraction
8. Everybody

First time listener – Ian Rankin

Ian Rankin writes the Inspector Rebus novels. He says they are international bestsellers, which may explain how he manages to spend so much money in bars and record shops.

Ian's top three albums ever?

VERY DIFFICULT THIS. But right now, on this very day:
Solid Air – John Martyn
Let It Bleed – Rolling Stones
Unknown Pleasures – Joy Division

Before we get to Ian, here's what Martin thinks of *Madonna*

The Madonna edition as an 800-metre race.

Off we go.

In the summer of 1978, Madonna leaves her home in Michigan and flies to New York for the first time. She's twenty years old.

In terms of her biography up to this point, all you really need to know are the following five pieces of information:

1) At the age of five she is traumatised by the death of her mother.
2) She develops a difficult relationship with her father, and practically all other forms of authority.
3) She's educated at a strict Catholic school. Nuns everywhere. All that stuff about original sin, all that stuff about *the* Madonna, and she's sitting there – actually called Madonna.
4) She's a straight 'A' student. She's *really* smart.
5) Madonna doesn't just want to be a star – she knows she's going to be a star.

That's all you need to know and, while I haven't got time to really dwell on any of it (it's a race you see), the last point is worth briefly expanding on.

When you look at the people that made it, that *really* made it, the defining characteristic seems to be that they always knew they would. Prince saw his dad perform when he was five years old and wanted the same for himself – by the time he's ten he's dancing on stage with James Brown. Elvis Presley walked into Sun Studios as a kid and, when they asked him who he sang like, he said 'I don't sing like nobody'.

You can confuse this for ambition, or determination, but I don't think it is. They just knew – and Madonna, more than anyone else, knew all along.

So, back to New York.

She's arrived to take advantage of everything the city has to offer and make her name as a dancer. Wearing an out-of-season winter coat, with just $35 in her pocket, she gets in a taxi and tells the driver to drop her off in the 'middle of everything' – a great destination. So he takes her to Times Square, where she wanders round, head spinning, in awe of what she sees before her. The sheer spectacle of New York for the first time – what John Cheever called 'the invention of giants'.

By the end of her first night she has a boyfriend and a place to stay. She's nothing if not resourceful.

She takes a series of odd jobs to get by, eats at irregular hours (mostly fruit) and starts to get the lie of the land, looking for an opportunity to launch herself.

The opportunity arises, in November, when she auditions for the highly respected Pearl Lang Dance Company.

Where everyone else turns up like an extra from *Staying Alive*, the substandard but infinitely more fluorescent sequel to *Saturday Night Fever*, Madonna arrives looking positively post-apocalyptic, wearing a T-shirt held together by safety pins and ripped fishnet stockings.

She immediately stands out.

And then she dances for them – all technique and wild abandon, delicately held together at the seams. After the audition, Pearl Lang herself walks up to Madonna, as if to get a closer look. She puts her hand up to her face and whispers – 'My dear, you have something special.'

Madonna's reply is instant – 'I know.'

I should warn you at this point that if you haven't fallen for Madonna's charms yet, you probably never will. Although, saying that, there's considerably more to come.

At the start of 1979, she decides that being just a dancer isn't enough and that it could take five years for her to be accepted into a major dance company. And then what? She's just another dancer in the group. That won't do at all. On top of her frustrated ambition there is also a more immediate concern – she needs money. So in an attempt to diversify and keep a roof over her head, she turns to nude modelling.

She visits a fella called Anthony Panzera, who has a studio on West 29th Street.

He recalls that she walked in looking like a 'boyish tramp', like something out of a Dickens tale. In the completely undiscerning world of nude modelling he is about to turn her away.

'I was hoping for someone a little less boy-like,' he says.

Sensing that she is about to be rejected, she immediately takes off her blouse, exposes her breasts, and says to him, 'Do boys have these?'

She then takes off the rest of her clothing and, now in charge, says, 'Just tell me where to pose.'

Panzera looks up, in awe of what he sees before him, and says, 'What's your name again?'

'Madonna,' she says.

Imagine hearing that, in a world before *this* Madonna became famous. What a name. She may as well have stood there and said 'the Virgin Mary'.

But it gets better.

'No last name?' asks Panzera.

Madonna walks over to his desk, with all the attitude of an impatient naked woman, and puts him in his place once and for all.

'Do I look like I need a last name to you?'

Ruth and Martin's Album Club could do a thousand albums but I don't think I'll ever tell a story better than that.

You somehow hope that all the people that she travelled through on the way to stardom could one day get together and reminisce about their encounters. The taxi driver telling everyone about the time she told him to drop her off in the 'middle of everything'; the pornographer who says 'yeah that's nothing mate, let me tell you about the time I asked her if she had a last name.'

But back to the story. There's the bell. Four hundred metres to go.

Unsurprisingly, Madonna quickly realises that being a nude model isn't quite what she had in mind either. So she branches out again – this time as a singer.

After a short stint as a member of a group called The Breakfast Club she comes to the conclusion that 'groups' aren't really for her and she'd rather have the control and spotlight of a solo singer. Accumulating talent wherever she goes, always acting as her own best advertisement, she acquires a network of musicians and songwriters that will help her achieve her dream.

In 1981 she records her first series of demos, including the song 'Everybody', and takes it to Danceteria – one of the hottest clubs in New York.

She walks up to the DJ, Mark Kamins, and says:

'This is a great song. It's called "Everybody". People will love it.'

She then tells him how handsome he is and kisses him full on the lips.

Kamins plays the song the next night and the place goes nuts. The response is so good, unlike anything Kamins has seen, that he passes the demo tape on to Michael Rosenblatt – an ambitious executive at Warners. He in turn plays it, likes it, and as soon as he meets Madonna in the flesh, offers her a record deal.

At last, it's happening. At the age of twenty-four she is about to take off.

There is only one problem. The deal has to be finalised by Seymour Stein, president of Warner's Sire Records, and he's in hospital recovering from heart surgery.

Madonna though.

She's not bothered. She insists that Rosenblatt gets the tape to Stein in hospital, even though he's lying in bed with a drip in his arm. He does what he's told, of course he does, and Stein hears the demo and flips out in his hospital bed. He demands to meet her straight away and even gets his barber to come to the hospital to cut his hair. He wants to look his best, he wants her to know that she is signing a deal with someone who won't be dead in six months.

Madonna walks into his hospital room, completely oblivious to the fact it's a hospital room, and says:

'The thing to do now is to sign me to a record deal.'

Stein sits up in his bed and says, 'Well, you had one before you even walked in the door.'

Relieved, excited, but nevertheless confident, always confident, Madonna approaches the bed, extends her hand, and says, 'Nice doing business with you, Mr Stein.'

Remarking on her ruthlessness, Stein would later say that if the shortest way home was through a cemetery on Friday the thirteenth, she would take it.

Still, the deal is done and in 1983 Madonna releases her debut album – a signpost of what was to come. 'Lucky Star', 'Borderline', 'Burning Up' and 'Holiday'.

'Just one day out of life – it would be, it would be so nice.'

In the hands of a man that could come across as suicidal, but in the hands of Madonna it's anything but.

Two hundred to go. The race for the line.

What follows for the rest of the eighties is nothing short of astonishing, one of *the* careers in popular music. The songs, the videos, the outfits – you remember them all. The Gaultier, who could forget the Gaultier? Why is she never the new Bowie? Why is she never the new Dylan? Song after song, hit after hit, reinventing herself, and defining the decade. Striding all over it like a musical version of the *Attack of the 50-foot Woman*.

They say she's a feminist icon and she is – she had the boys dancing behind her on stage, she dated the famous men and then pushed them to the back of her photograph. She had control and power – she earned the right to be honest.

They say she's a gay icon and she is – she said 'fuck that' to tragedy and victimhood at a time when the gay community moved the same way and stood up. They embraced each other and moved on together, confidently.

Remember when she released *The Immaculate Collection*?

I can see the record company now:

'Ha, I get it. Immaculate Collection. You're called Madonna. I get it. Very funny.'

I can see Madonna now:

'It's an immaculate collection.'

And she's right, it's not a pun. It's the defining document of all this, the best of the best ofs, the greatest of the greatest hits. It doesn't even have 'Dress You Up' on it. Or 'True Blue'. Or 'Dear Jessie'. I don't often swear when I do this but, fuck me, that's a back catalogue if songs of that quality don't make the final cut.

Me though.

I loved The Fall, Sonic Youth, The Smiths. But I adored Madonna – the complete and total glory of her. In a record collection of shrinking violets and 'musicianship', she stood out. On a bedroom wall covered in posters of fringes and cardigans, she stood out. And you forget. Before dance music happened to her in the nineties, she *was* dance music in the eighties. She was all the dances – something for the start, the middle and the end of the night. Something for everyone. With 'Crazy for You' she soundtracked about 85 per cent of first kisses I ever had. Does she know that, do you think? All those parties. The kids in living rooms, hallways, disjointed on the stairs – all 'Crazy for You' in the eighties, all the kids that she travelled through as they grew up.

And that's what she was, the artist that I grew up with. In school, college and university. At home too. Madonna was everywhere, Madonna was glory – the first pop star I ever fell in love with.

Heart racing.

Hitting the line.

Eyes closed. Crazy for you.

So, over to you Ian. Why haven't you listened to it? WHAT'S WRONG WITH YOU?????

Madonna was one month shy of her twenty-fifth birthday when her first album came out – which makes her seem a late-starter compared to today's fresh-faced batch of pop star wannabees. Me? I was twenty-three in 1983, and things weren't exactly working out.

I know this because I used to keep a fairly accurate diary. The day *Madonna* was released into the world (27 July) saw me in a job at a tax office in Edinburgh, earning the princely sum of fifty-three quid a week net. It was over a year since I'd graduated (Upper Second Class Honours, thanks for asking) and I was living in a bedsit in Arden Street,

Marchmont. I had applied for funding to do a PhD but had recently taken receipt of the rejection letter. I was getting pretty used to those, as they were arriving thick and fast for the short stories I was sending out into the cold, heartless bastard of a UK media world. Friends kept moving away – one was about to head to London and a job with a £6,500 p.a. salary – not that I was obsessed with money, you understand.

I was applying for jobs anywhere that would pay better than the tax office, cycling home of an evening to open the official-looking letters telling me to jog the fuck on. And the bike itself (bought for twenty-five quid second-hand) was playing up.

There's no indication in my diary that I was listening to much music at that time. The only LP I bought in July was *The Beatles 67-70*. I'd stopped watching *Top of the Pops* and didn't buy singles. At high school, I'd moved between prog and the likes of Status Quo and Alex Harvey. Then punk came along and by university (1978–82) I was into the more industrial and gothy stuff – Joy Division, Throbbing Gristle (I was a fan club member), The Cure and Bauhaus. Throughout, there had been David Bowie and Eno, The Rolling Stones and John Martyn. But disco?

Disco?

Just as Charlie didn't surf, Ian didn't dance, not since those sweaty schooldays with the constant fear of rejection as you approached the girl seated the other side of the assembly hall. And if she did deign to accompany me for three minutes of Sweet or Mud or The Rubettes or The Osmonds… Oh, the horror. The horror. For the fact of the matter is, I danced like an ungainly banshee, really throwing myself into it. Eventually I would notice my partner backing away from the flailing limbs and flapping bell-bottoms – *probably not getting a snog later then*, I would think to myself, not for the first time. Punk, when it came along, was OK. In fact, it was great. I could pogo, robot and dying-fly with the best of them. But discos and nightclubs would almost never see me darken their dimly lit doorways, unless they were hosting a pal's birthday or wedding.

I did have a few disco twelve-inch singles in my collection – Chic and Donna Summer maybe, stuff with good production values and interesting arrangements. But that was about it. And as a twenty-three-year-old, I had left bubblegum pop music behind long ago.

No reason then why I would have known about Madonna, certainly not until *Like a Virgin* or the film *Desperately Seeking Susan* (which I did see with my girlfriend in 1985). But in July 1983 I wasn't in the mood for getting into any groove or enjoying good times on anything fans of Madonna might classify as a holiday – though I did manage a wet week in Ireland.

But put away that tiny violin, dear reader, for my situation was about to improve markedly. On 16 August a call from the *Scotsman* newspaper informed me that I'd won second prize in their short story contest. My prize was a Sinclair Spectrum computer and paid publication in their weekend supplement. And a further month later, the Scottish Education Department had a change of heart. I'd be going back to uni after all – with three years' funding to do a PhD. So I could chuck in the tax office and wipe my arse on the job applications.

But was I cheered up enough to warrant a saunter on to the dance floor? Nah, I'd still have been murder.

You've now listened to it at least three times, what do you think?

She would go on to better things – we all know that. She would reinvent herself, devour different influences, and become something altogether bigger than the music she made. But would you know it from this first outing? Very doubtful, I'd say. If I'd heard this in 1983 I would have dismissed it as a lightweight outing by someone with a tinny voice and not enough ideas, someone who might manage a couple of hits before disappearing off the radar.

'Insipid' is one word I've used in my scrawled notes. Maybe the sterile early-eighties production has a lot to do with it. All those synths and simplistic electronic beats. The wakka-wakka guitars and twanged basses. Yes, I suppose I can imagine people dancing to it after a few too many drinks. Yes, I can see how the numbingly unimaginative lyrics and rhymes might speak to those just out of puberty. 'Starlight, starbright, first star I see tonight … You may be my lucky star, but I'm the luckiest by far.' If you say so, missus, but it's hardly the most revolutionary opening to one of the great careers in pop culture.

She sounds like a pert enough pixie throughout, though she was probably a full decade older than many of her immediate or soon-to-be fans. Cruelly, the version of the album available to me on Spotify is a reissue of some description, which may explain how 'Borderline' comes to be elongated to seven minutes, with one of those tedious fills in the middle, the kind that bedevilled 'extended mixes' and 'DJ versions' of the era. Remember that four-minute song you liked? Then try an added three minutes of half-arsed post-production, usually involving even more motorik drum machine and the odd thwock on a bass string. By the time you leave the dance floor, your hair will be plastered to your face and your clothes will need wringing out – a look guaranteed to endear you to the opposite sex.

And the thing is, 'Borderline' is one of the better tunes here. It has a proper hook, one you don't mind being attached to. But it leads on to 'Burning Up' and various other vanilla showcases for a voice that has the subtle allure of a cheese-grater. And the words… words about needing to be adored, about needing your infatuation to be reciprocated, about the devastation of rejection. Appealing, perhaps, to that teenage audience. OK, maybe even to folk in their twenties. But I'm fifty-five now and just find it tedious. The songs start to resemble photo-stories from *Jackie* magazine and its ilk, with interchangeable characters and emotions. As soon as you hear her sing the word 'attraction', you know that 'reaction' and 'satisfaction' can't be far behind.

'These tears I cry for you are so hopeless.'

Well, cheer up then and let's go for that cheap package break in the sun, because:

'It's time for the good times, Forget about the bad times...'

Leonard Cohen she ain't. She feels pre-programmed and pre-packaged, which again may have something to do with the arid, inorganic studio methods and mechanisms of the age. It doesn't sound to me like music to be played in your bedroom when a few chums have dropped round. It sounds... disposable. That Madonna herself was to prove anything *but* disposable is hugely to her credit. She would make very good records and high-calibre videos. She would act, set the fashion world on fire, be the name behind a book called *Sex*, give as good as she got in interviews and – eventually – become one of those artists you watched out for, because whatever she'd done now, it wouldn't be boring, even if she ended up flat on her matador arse.

I get that. I just don't get it from this first album.

'Let the DJ shake you, Let the music take you.'

Thanks for the offer, Madge, but I think I'll sit this one out.

Would you listen to it again?

I'd rather not. I found much of the experience quite painful.

A mark out of 10?

3 (but 7.5 for everything she did afterwards).

5

Nevermind by Nirvana

1. Smells Like Teen Spirit
2. In Bloom
3. Come as You Are
4. Breed
5. Lithium
6. Polly
7. Territorial Pissings
8. Drain You
9. Lounge Act
10. Stay Away
11. On a Plain
12. Something in the Way
13. Endless, Nameless

First time listener – Alex Massie

Alex is the Scotland editor of the *Spectator*, a columnist for *The Times* and a contributor to various other publications including the *Scottish Daily Mail*, the *Scotsman* and *Foreign Policy*. He mainly writes about politics and accepts that it looks unlikely that he'll ever fulfil his childhood dream of being cricket correspondent for the *Daily Telegraph*. The world is a cruel place.

Alex's top three albums ever?

Live at the Old Quarter – Townes van Zandt
Blue Kentucky Girl – Emmylou Harris

Workers Playtime – Billy Bragg

Before we get to Alex, here's what Martin thinks of
Nevermind

In 1986, Kurt Cobain wrote a song about Spam (the pork-based meat product, not unwanted emails) and told anyone who would listen that, one day, he was going to release a record that would make him as famous as U2 and R.E.M.

It's difficult to imagine anyone looking at the troubled, often homeless nineteen-year-old believed a word he said. Chances are they walked off and told themselves that he was a loser and Monty Python had already cornered the extremely niche 'songs about Spam' market.

Fast forward a year, and his ambitions seem even more unlikely.

In 1987 the would-be superstar finally gets his own place: a derelict shack in Aberdeen, in Washington state. Eager to make the place his own he adds a few personal touches – posters on the wall of his favourite bands and a bath in the living room full of turtles. Not one to waste a huge amount of time on housework, he drills holes in the bath so he doesn't have to clean it out, the holes acting as a drainage system straight through to the floorboards. How lovely.

It's also around this point that he starts to take LSD because there's a grocery strike in Aberdeen which cuts off the supply of alcohol. Faced with the option of driving miles to Olympia or crossing a local picket line, neither of which he can be bothered with, he opts to take a load of acid instead.

Oh hang on, I've forgotten his pet rat Kitty. Yeah, he has a pet rat too. Of course he does.

There's an incident around this time which perfectly illustrates the state Cobain was in.

One day he comes home and sees a spider on the ceiling. Deciding that he has enough animals in the house already, he summons Kitty the Rat and instructs her to kill the spider. Kitty, not fluent in the ramblings of a twenty-year-old Kurt Cobain on acid, just sits there.

Taking matters into his own hands, he gets a can of Brut deodorant from his bedroom with the intention of spraying the spider so hard in the face that it eventually dies.

But, when he walks back into the living room, he accidentally treads on Kitty's head.

Heartbroken, he wraps Kitty up in some dirty underwear, takes her out to the front yard and clubs her to death with a piece of wood, putting her out of her misery for good. Imagine seeing that as you go for a stroll: a twenty-year-old Kurt Cobain, in his front yard, hitting some pants with a bit of wood.

He then goes back into the house, screams 'Fuck You!' at the spider and goes to bed where, according to his journal, he lies awake waiting for the spider to crawl all over his face.

In less than four years, he will release a record that will make him as famous as U2 and R.E.M.

And this is how he does it.

He somehow manages to convince Krist Novoselic, a six-foot-seven bass player, to form a band with him, and they add Aaron Burckhard, the first in a series of drummers. What these two see in Cobain at this stage is anyone's guess, but never mind (no pun intended), Nirvana is formed. They rehearse a bit, play a few poorly attended gigs in front of people with mullets, and then decide to make a demo tape with a local producer who thinks the singer's name is Kurt Covain.

The demo recorded, Cobain sends it off to his favourite record labels, who either think it's rubbish or can't remember receiving it. Someone at SST says it's 'alternative by numbers'. Thankfully though, the producer sends a copy to a local independent label called Sub Pop, where it receives a favourable reception. So much so that they get in touch and ask the band if they'd like to record a single.

So far so good. In less than a year since he killed his rat by mistake, Cobain is about to make an actual record with an actual record company.

And then the drummer gets promoted to assistant manager at the

Burger King in Aberdeen, and decides to dedicate himself to his new career instead.

Refusing to let Burger King ruin his dreams, Cobain gets some bloke called Dave Foster to play drums and they record 'Love Buzz' – their first single. Cobain is so excited that, when it's released, he listens to the local radio station all day waiting to hear it. Annoyed they never play it, he phones up the station and requests his own single. Of course he does. Finally, a few hours later, he hears it while driving and pulls over with a great big 'that's my song they're playing on the radio' smile on his face.

Sub Pop then suggest an album to follow up the single.

So far so good. If there ever was a plan, it seems to be working.

And then the new drummer gets arrested for beating up the mayor's son and is put in jail. Cobain fires him and brings back Burckhard, the original drummer, who realises that making an album might be better than working in Burger King after all. But then he gets arrested for driving without insurance in Cobain's car, so he gets fired too. Honestly, I could write this whole piece about Nirvana's mad drummers.

Next up on drums is Chad Channing. At this point Nirvana also become a four-piece when they recruit guitarist Jason Everman, who happens to have the money to pay Sub Pop the $600 they need to record the album. Not that he was being used or anything.

While writing the album, a pivotal moment occurs which points the way to so much of what happens next. Cobain listens to the *Meet the Beatles* album seven times on the spin and, immediately afterwards, writes his first pop song.

He takes it to the rest of the band and they say, 'That's great, what's it called?'

Cobain says, 'I dunno.'

The band say, 'What's it about?'

Cobain says, 'It's about a girl. I know, I'll call it "About a Girl".'

You can see why people called him a spokesman for his generation.

Nevermind by Nirvana

Bleach, the first album, is subsequently released to good reviews, particularly in the UK, and Nirvana hit the road, playing over a hundred shows in 1989. While obviously a massive achievement for the Kurt Cobain we met at the start of the story, it's important to state here how much Nirvana were just another American band that made loads of noise and look liked psycho lumberjacks. When they toured the UK with TAD in October of 1989, me and a couple of mates had tickets to see them at the Astoria but couldn't even be bothered to leave the pub around the corner, so we missed them. One of them where you've had a few and the gig becomes an inconvenience. Lol @ me and my mates.

When Nirvana return to America and realise they've spent what little money they've made, they start to think the whole 'being in a band' idea was maybe a waste of time after all. So they start looking for work. At one point Cobain, along with Novoselic, sets up his own cleaning company called Pine Tree Janitorial and produces a load of flyers with drawings of them both pushing brooms around. Imagine that. They advertise all around Olympia and, thankfully, no one calls them. Thankfully because, if they had, this story might have ended with Nirvana setting up a highly successful cleaning company in northwest America.

But it doesn't. They decide to make another record instead.

Nirvana wouldn't be Nirvana unless they fired a couple of people first though. Jason Everman is first to go because Cobain decides there's room for only one person playing guitar and looking cool. Next is Chad Channing, after Cobain decides that he's not a very good drummer and is affronted when Channing suggests that he would like to contribute his own songs to the band. The last thing Cobain needs is a highly ambitious drummer who eventually wants to write his own songs.

So they replace him with Dave Grohl.

Apparently when Grohl was first in a room with Nirvana, he was so shocked by what he saw that he said 'What, that little dude and that big motherfucker?' Meanwhile, Cobain's first impression of Grohl, noted in his journal, reads, 'This new kid on the block can't dance as good as your MTV favourites, but he beats the drums like he's beating the shit out of their heads.' Upon such words, the now legendary lineup is formed. They've found their man and can stop firing people for a bit.

Cobain goes for it.

Realising that the likes of U2 and R.E.M. aren't messing about with a small label like Sub Pop, he decides to throw them in the bin and tout his band around the major labels with a tape of new songs. A flurry of interest is duly generated which leads to them signing with Geffen. Deal signed, album on the way, they return to the UK to play Reading Festival in 1991, where I, eventually, see them for the first time. They're sixth on the bill on the Friday afternoon, just below other 'era-defining' bands like Chapterhouse and Pop Will Eat Itself.

And then on 10 September, just a couple of weeks after that performance at Reading, they release the first single from the album – 'Smells like Teen Spirit'.

So far so good.

And everyone knows what happens next. Geffen originally hoped that *Nevermind* would sell 250,000 copies in total but, by the turn of the year, it's selling 400,000 copies a week. Nirvana has made the loudest pop album ever, an album of single syllables that reveals itself best on the first few listens. Trust me on the single syllable thing. The first twenty-two words of 'Come As You Are' all have one syllable. The chorus of 'In Bloom' has thirty-eight words, and thirty-six of them have just one syllable. It's mad, as if they've been written by a child – albeit a really talented angry child that knows the occasional big word and shouts a lot. Even the drums and the bass are in single syllables. It's probably why Nirvana songs worked as ringtones on Nokia phones in the nineties when the Sonic Youth ones very much didn't.

And it went on to sell thirty million copies. Cobain had done it. This most unlikely of winners had done it.

Nevermind by Nirvana

I loved Nirvana, I *really* loved them, but so much of what is said now seems bizarre to me. All that stuff about Cobain being a spokesperson; all those other bands that weren't Nirvana but somehow get thrown into their orbit. Those pictures where he looks dead sad and those where he plays with guns. Somehow, as is often the case with these stories, the glory has been lost in the retelling. In the Amy Winehouse film that signposts her death from the first scene; in the Cobain film that trawls his childhood in a search for 'meaning'. 'Back to Black'. 'Nevermind'. The big choruses, the way you felt when you first heard them and didn't know what happened next. That's the glory and somehow it's been lost.

Which is a shame, because it's the best part of the story.

In 1986 Kurt Cobain wrote a song about Spam and told anyone who would listen that, one day, he was going to release a record that would make him as famous as U2 and R.E.M.

And in 1991, after accidentally killing his rat, firing a load of drummers and failing to get Pine Tree Janitorial off the ground, that's exactly what he did.

This most unlikely of winners had done it.

So, over to you Alex. Why haven't you listened to it? WHAT'S WRONG WITH YOU??????

Because it's music.

I don't really do music. Except country music because that's whisky poetry, really. Before I drowned my iPod, 80 per cent of the stuff on it was country. You know, Townes and Johnny and Waylon and Emmylou and Dolly and Hank and Merle and all the other guys and girls in the gang. I had a spell when I was deeply in love with The Smiths and have retained a fondness for Billy Bragg but, really, that's about it for music recorded in the last thirty years.

Music and me fell out at an early age, you see. I was expelled – for insolence – from recorder class aged five. Later, there was a compulsory singing evaluation to see whether we should be in the school choir. We had to sing 'Once in Royal David's City'. My audition was terminated at 'Roy'.

As teenagers, incarcerated in an exclusive educational penitentiary, we'd sit up late swilling illicit home-brew, smoking roll-ups and listening to Serge Gainsbourg. When we weren't playing bridge, that is. Insufferable, I suppose, but there you have it.

Anyway that would have been the same year Nirvana made their mark. The year my mother gave me a fetching dressing gown for Christmas, I think.

So I don't think I was Nirvana's target audience and little – nothing, actually – has since caused me to reconsider that view. I can't pretend their absence from my life has caused me any great inconvenience.

Basically, you can sum up what I know about them in three words: Seattle, Grunge, Dead. If I think really hard about it I can remember that they had a song called 'Smells Like Teen Spirit' and that Mr Nirvana was, for a spell, married to a big, dirty girl of the type for whom Brendan Behan would have felt a certain tenderness.

That's enough, isn't it?

You've now listened to it at least three times, what do you think?

This is an assignment that deserved to be taken seriously. Consequently, I listened to this album in each of life's three states: sober, drunk and hungover. Sober was the worst, I assure you. I mean, expectations were low but it's easy to cope with not liking the music, rather harder to endure the fact that it is so crushingly, crashingly boring.

Most of the songs sound exactly the same and the ones that don't are even worse. Take 'Endless, Nameless' for instance. On paper, the lyrics offer some momentary promise. Sure, it's cod late-period Beckett – 'Silence/Here I am/Here I am/Silent/Bright and clear/It's what I am/I have/Died' – but there are worse things to impersonate than that. But the music – to use the term in its loosest sense – appears to involve nothing so much as recording a motorcycle crashing into a ten-tonne truck. Fine if you like that sort of thing, I suppose, and if you do it is the kind of thing you like. But there's six minutes of this. It's the sort of music they should play in dentists' waiting rooms just to warn you of the horrors ahead.

Still, those are some of the better lyrics. 'Something in the Way' begins by being like something Ringo Starr might have written but then you realise the inspiration is actually Adrian Mole – 'It's OK to eat fish/'Cause they don't have any feelings'. OK. Music should have a higher goal than simply rebuking or trolling Yoko Ono.

'Smells Like Teen Spirit' has its moments, I guess, but shouting 'entertain us' over and over again reminds me that it's basically what would have happened if you'd given Harry Enfield a guitar. It's all very Kevin the Teenager, which works well as a joke but loses its appeal the moment you realise, Christ, these people actually want to be taken seriously. As for lyrics like 'I found it hard/It's hard to find' I mean, come on, get tae fuck. This is writing in the same way that rearranging fridge magnets is writing.

And the sound! Sweet Mary, mother of God, the sound. Most of the time setting fire to an aardvark would produce a similar sensation. The more he shouts and screams – and there's a lot of shouting and screaming – the worse Cobain sounds. Smells like teen spirit, perhaps, but it sounds like he's got throat cancer.

The best bits are the quiet, introductory bits but then the guitars start grinding away and everything just becomes a wall of noise. 'Lithium' and 'Lounge Act' are a bit better but most of the songs are ruined by never-ending, banal choruses. Choruses that are whiny whiny whiny when they're not busy being whiny and shouty shouty shouty.

And that, in fact, is another problem with *Nevermind*. It is soaked in self-pity, which is rarely an attractive state. Sure, you may object, but that's because it's an album about teenage angst or something and, OK, perhaps it is but Cobain was twenty-four when it was released and old enough to have known better.

It's all one note too. Not, perhaps, literally, but certainly figuratively.

There's precious little light and shade, no sense of movement or development. Grace, obviously, is impossible. It's just one damn thing after another, all performed in a dreary monotone that makes you wonder if Cobain is secretly as bored of it all as the listener swiftly becomes.

I wanted to like it and not just out of contrariness but, in the end, claiming to have enjoyed the experience is a dishonesty too far. Sure, there's the occasional good bit of guitaring – hooks, I believe they're called – but that's not enough to sustain the entire enterprise.

An enterprise that is, ultimately, just dull. Bad music is entirely forgivable but dull music is much worse than that. It rains a lot in Seattle and you can tell that from this album. It's the sound of bored teenagers trapped in a garage waiting for the rain to stop. Which it never does. If that's the effect they were striving for then, fine, it succeeds on its own terms and bully for Kurt and the boys. But the novelty of all that passes pretty bloody quickly. Bored teenagers are never much fun. They should shut up and do something useful. Like, read a book.

Would you listen to it again?
I hope not.

A mark out of 10?
3.

6

It Takes a Nation of Millions to Hold Us Back by Public Enemy

1. Countdown to Armageddon
2. Bring the Noise
3. Don't Believe the Hype
4. Cold Lampin' with Flavor
5. Terminator X to the Edge of Panic
6. Mind Terrorist
7. Louder Than a Bomb
8. Caught, Can We Get a Witness?
9. Show 'Em Whatcha Got
10. She Watch Channel Zero?!
11. Night of the Living Baseheads
12. Black Steel in the Hour of Chaos
13. Security of the First World
14. Rebel Without a Pause
15. Prophets of Rage
16. Party for Your Right to Fight

First time listener – Lord Stewart Wood

Stewart Wood is a Labour member of the House of Lords, and used to be a member of Ed Miliband's shadow cabinet. Before that he was an adviser to Gordon Brown, first at the Treasury and then at 10 Downing Street. He taught and wrote about politics at Oxford University for fifteen years, and is now writing about it again.

Stewart's top three albums ever?
Minstrel in the Gallery – Jethro Tull
Straightaways – Son Volt
Sheet Music – 10cc

Before we get to Stewart, here's what Martin thinks of
It Takes a Nation of Millions

It's March 1987 and Public Enemy are driving to Manhattan to play a concert in support of their debut album – *Yo! Bum Rush the Show!*

Let me quickly introduce you to the band making the journey that day.

First up, there's Carlton Ridenhour, aka Chuck D.

Chuck grew up on Long Island, his formative years framed by the Black Panther movement, the Vietnam War and that James Brown period of really long songs with hardly any lyrics.

He ends up studying graphic design and starts doing flyers for a local DJ collective called Spectrum City, who throw the best parties in the neighbourhood. Well, nearly the best parties. Chuck often finds himself dancing with a girl, about to make his move, only for some idiot to come on stage and rap over the beat, totally killing the mood. Annoyed that his love life is being ruined, he decides his only option is to go on stage and do the MC thing better than everyone else.

So he does, and he is so good that Spectrum City recruit him as their front man, change their name to Public Enemy and sign to Def Jam Records.

There you go, an entire enterprise born out of sexual frustration.

Next up, there's Professor Griff and the S1Ws.

Professor Griff is Public Enemy's Minister of Information –

charged with disseminating the group's pro-black politics throughout the media. He's also in charge of the S1Ws (Security of the First World), who serve the dual role of being the band's dancers and onstage muscle. I say dancing, it's more like a combination of military drills and martial arts performed while holding plastic Uzis.

It totally works though and more bands should do it. The Corrs, for example, would be vastly improved if some of them had guns.

Then we have Terminator X, the band's pioneering DJ. His real name was Norman Rogers so you feel he definitely benefited from the whole name change thing more than anyone else.

Last, but definitely not least, we have Flavor Flav – a trained chef and someone who could play about fifteen instruments. He also shouts 'Yeah Boyeee!' at practically every opportunity and is often seen wearing a clock around his neck. How did he join Public Enemy? The story goes that he met up with an early incarnation of the group and told a load of great 'your mum' jokes, so they decided to recruit him as their hype man.

I know, he joined Public Enemy on the strength of his portfolio of 'your mum' jokes. It's probably my favourite 'how I joined the band' story ever.

NB: I had a friend at school called Kevin who would always win every 'your mum' battle with the following line – 'Your mum's got sideburns on her hips'. Now, all I'm saying is if Kevin was on Long Island in the mid-eighties it probably would have been him in Public Enemy, and not Flavor Flav. Last I heard of him, about fifteen years ago, he was in a band called Mum Cuss.

But anyway, back to Public Enemy. They're about to do their first ever gig in Manhattan, in support of their debut album.

And it doesn't quite go to plan.

As soon as they walk onstage with their guns a voice booms from the crowd:

'Get them clowns off the stage!'

The owner of the heckle isn't just anyone, it is none other than

Grandmaster Melle Mel of the Furious Five, a legend from the first wave of hip hop and one of Chuck D's heroes.

'We're supposed to be stopping the violence! That shit ain't hip hop.'

Not a great start then.

They carry on with the gig but, to make matters worse, the music just doesn't resonate. It sounds dated and distinctly unradical. To be fair to them, their debut album was recorded a year before and, had it been released then, things might have been different. However, Def Jam's parent company, CBS, was preoccupied with the *Live 1975–85* Bruce Springsteen box set. As a result, everything else was pushed back. In the fastest moving genre in music, prone to massive technological developments, Public Enemy had recorded an album that would have sounded great in 1986 but sounded old in 1987. And it's all Bruce Springsteen's fault. The bastard.

Shortly after their Manhattan debut, Chuck D hears Eric B and Rakim's 'You Know You Got Soul' and that annoys him even more. Its Funkadelic sample and effortless delivery was more nuanced, and subtler, than Public Enemy's bombastic sound of 1986. He described it as the 'most incredible rap record he'd ever heard' and was furious he didn't have anything to go up against it. It further convinces him that he needs to do something radical, that Public Enemy needs to change tack.

So this is what they did, this is how they created 'Rebel Without a Pause'.

Flavor Flav, primarily in the band because of his jokes, programmed a beat into a rudimentary drum machine – a much faster beat than anything on their debut. Added to that are samples from James Brown, Chubb Rock, The Soul Children and, er, Jefferson Starship.

They then needed an intro, so they sampled a section from a Reverend Jesse Jackson speech where he says he 'don't know what the world is coming to'.

Neither do I Jesse, people are sampling Jefferson Starship.

Finally Chuck D and Flavor Flav add their vocals – the former delivering a barrage of radical politics while the latter adopts a 'brother from the corner' perspective who doesn't know whether he should be egging his partner on, or trying to calm him down. That's basically the crux of the song for me, that someone in the band is so shocked by what they're hearing that he keeps interrupting it to express his concerns, before finally deciding to just go with it. Imagine a version of 'Tomorrow Never Knows' where Paul McCartney interrupts every now and again and says 'Bit mad this, isn't it John?'

I was at school when 'Rebel Without a Pause' was released and, within days, loads of kids were bringing in tapes and playing the song to each other, trying to learn the rap. It was impossible, like trying to construct a 147 break. I was particularly terrible, always getting stuck part way through the first verse – the equivalent of two reds and a black. There was, though, a real sense that it was unlike anything else around in 1987. I remember it vividly, as if it was yesterday – the kids in my class listening to it during break and on their way home, trying to get to grips with it. You didn't even need instruments, which was just as well, as we didn't have any.

I don't remember any other song from that time in the same way.

It was aggressive, honest and catchy. It was called 'Rebel Without a Pause' and they were called Public Enemy. They had a logo of a black man as a target and, on stage, they looked like an army. It's tempting to say that ticks a lot of boxes for a sixteen-year-old but, to be honest, it still does and I'm now 45. I don't think any other band has ever quite got their look as right as Public Enemy did.

With the success of the single, realising they'd now found their lane, they get to work on their second album – *It Takes a Nation of Millions to Hold us Back*.

I always leave room for the guests to talk about the album so all I want to say is 'Night of the Living Baseheads' sums up the whole thing for me.

It's a song that details the effects of the crack cocaine epidemic on

African-Americans in a way that makes you simultaneously grasp the problem while dancing around as if you're on crack cocaine. Honestly, it's quite an achievement.

That's the album right there though, and that was *the* new politics in 1988. Articulation – one thing linked to the other, the message and the music. When they came to England, they were unrelenting, coming onstage and screaming 'Fuck Thatcher' to a bunch of kids who wanted to hear exactly that. And I mean exactly that – no metaphor, no 'Shipbuilding', no 'Waiting for the Great Leap Forwards'. Just 'Fuck Thatcher'.

And afterwards they made you dance.

Over the next few years they release a series of acclaimed albums, staying in their lane, and ushering in a golden age of hip hop. More than that though, they break out from the confines of their community and confront other audiences, whether they're wanted or not. They tour with the likes of Anthrax and U2 and, in the most bizarre booking since Showaddywaddy shared a bill with Einstürzende Neubaten, they even supported the Sisters of Mercy.

Eventually, though, their popularity waned as a creative force and band members started going their separate ways. Professor Griff turned out to be a terrible Minister of Information after all and was fired for anti-Semitic comments. Terminator X, on the other hand, retired to run an ostrich stud farm in North Carolina. Flavor Flav is still a member, but you're more likely to see him on reality TV these days. A few years ago I stumbled across him on a show called *The Farm* where he was having an argument with Keith Harris and Orville. As I said, separate ways.

So what you're left with is the one constant, the one that never lets you down – Chuck D, a true radical and as good a front man as you'll ever see.

Looking back, it seems a huge act of self-sacrifice to base your entire band's career on a political stance. It's difficult to see how they could have ever diversified, how they could move out of the framework of protest and become a different band. It's like Dylan deciding that the 'Times They Are a-Changin'' Dylan is the only Dylan you'll ever need.

You can see why he never wanted to be limited in that respect, how he had the luxury to move on.

Likewise, you can also see, and admire, that Chuck D still feels that the times haven't quite changed enough.

So, over to you Stewart. Why haven't you listened to it? WHAT'S WRONG WITH YOU?????

I suppose the main reason I didn't listen to Public Enemy in 1988 was because their lead singer wasn't a man in an overcoat and long beard standing on one leg playing the flute.

That's not quite true, but almost.

Music then, as now, is the most important thing in my life other than (some subset of) the people I love. It's my constant companion, my touchstone for all that is good, beautiful, groundbreaking and energising about life. But when I was twenty I was fussy about music. I liked music that was packed with ideas, musically and lyrically – 10cc, Jethro Tull, Joni Mitchell, Peter Hammill. I wanted music that challenged and stretched me. I liked to be mentally exhausted or emotionally drained by the end of side two. I needed half an hour to decompress after hearing Tull's *Thick as a Brick* until I was thirty-four.

Of course all these desiderata should have led me towards Public Enemy in 1988. But my dimensions of challenge were actually very conservative, anchored in the narrow range of music I already loved. I wanted the virtues of jazz without actually having to listen to jazz. I wanted more intricate melodies, more sophisticated harmonies, more dabbling with time signatures, more complex instrumental arrangements. And counterpoint. I wanted more counterpoint than is healthy for any human being. I couldn't get enough. And for some reason I just thought hip hop didn't have it. (I was wrong of course. *It Takes a Nation* has buckets of it.)

Let me be brutally honest: I was a white boy from rural Kent whose taste in music was even whiter. I bought Roachford's album in 1989, but I'm not sure that counts as a full-throated embrace of music outside the white mainstream. When I heard music at a party I wanted to score it rather than dance to it.

The signs of branching out beyond Jethro Tull and Van der Graaf Generator were definitely there. My university housemate Dave (who was cooler than me, though I'm now significantly cooler than him) played De La Soul's *3 Feet High and Rising* constantly while we were doing our finals in 1989, and I remember opening my bedroom door so I could eavesdrop on it. And a few years earlier I'd loved Grandmaster Flash's *The Message*. But, for reasons I can't quite recall, they felt like one-offs, not musical discoveries that opened the door to new things. Maybe it all comes down to the same shyness that stopped me asking the girl I fancied when I was seventeen out for a Chinese.

Looking back I guess it is true that, for all my adoration of music, I had yet to make the two great discoveries of real music lovers: 1) that if you truly love music you will find things to truly love in a wide range of music; and 2) that whether you like country, soul, blues, pop, funk or rock, somewhere in the mists of time there is a record that is a messy musical soup from which all the good stuff springs. And I bet you if that record was ever discovered you'd hear Chuck D, Hank Williams, Bobby Bland and a bloke in a long beard playing the flute, getting on like a house on fire.

You've now listened to it at least three times, what do you think?

I read that Chuck D said his intention with *It Takes a Nation* was to create an 'aural missile'. That's a pretty apt description of how it felt to me. Hearing it for the first time was like being on a rollercoaster. It was massively energising. And it's fast – deliberately faster than a lot of rap and hip hop, apparently, which makes it urgent and insistent. I felt I'd be letting Chuck down personally if I didn't give it my full attention.

Many of the things I'd heard about hip hop are there in generous helpings. The lyrics have lots of boasting, responses to critics, claims to be misunderstood. There's arguing with people who don't like them, a hat-tip to Farrakhan and I think a bit of arguing amongst themselves. And it is gloriously angry: about shitty music, being accused of plagiarism, shitty TV, drugs, shitty DJs, unjust war, shitty journalism, white America. 'I got a right to be hostile, man, my people are being persecuted.' I love the anger, though I listened to it with a sneaking suspicion that someone like me is still part of what was making them angry twenty-seven years ago.

But there's also lots of great things in there I didn't really expect. The opening line ('London, England, consider yourselves warned') made me think they were a band that wanted to speak to the world and not just the East Coast (by which I mean New York, not King's Lynn). And when I followed the lyrics on second hearing, I laughed a lot. You have to when you hear Sonny Bono rhymed with Yoko Ono, and 'school of hard knocks' with 'Clorox' and 'Xerox'. In 'She Watch Channel Zero' (my favourite song) the case against his girlfriend watching bad TV is that he wants to watch the Superbowl: 'We got a black quarterback, so step back'. Love it. There are lines I'll remember forever, such as: 'You can put that in your "don't know what you said" book.' My favourite is 'Your singers are spineless as you sing your senseless songs to the mindless', a remark which even if it wasn't aimed at Black Lace's 'Agadoo' certainly should have been.

The big surprise for me musically was the gorgeous, dense overlay of samples, riffs, discovered sounds and interruptions throughout the album, ingredients that reminded me of what George Martin did for The Beatles. The whole album feels raw but beautifully sculpted ('organised noise' as Hank Shocklee called it), and the production is incredibly clean and powerful. Some of the songs are stuffed with musical ideas in the way an album like *L* by Godley & Creme is overflowing with invention (I know, I know – everyone makes that comparison, but sometimes you have to state the obvious). The sheer range of sounds is striking, from the funky riff in 'Caught, Can We Get a Witness?' that reminded me of a chase scene from *Starsky & Hutch*, to the German electronica influences in 'Terminator X to the Edge of Panic'. And an album that samples James Brown, Isaac Hayes and Stevie Wonder alongside Queen, David Bowie and Slayer is not to be sniffed at.

And then there's Chuck D. I think I'm slightly in love with Chuck after hearing the album three times. He has a voice brimming with authority, passion and warmth. I could listen to him all day. He could rap about reform of planning regulations and I'd be enthralled. I have to admit, Flavor Flav didn't quite do it for me as much. He felt like the slightly chippy mate of the cool boy in your class at school, and each time a new song began I found myself hoping it was one of Chuck's.

By the time I was on to my third listening, I'd stopped paying as much attention to the poetry of the lyrics and was just enjoying the album as a trunk of funk. I found it exhilarating to have the album in my headphones on the tube. The attitude and the swagger rubbed off on me somewhere near Green Park, and I felt a wave of irrational happiness that I didn't expect.

A couple of songs left me a bit cold. 'Party For Your Right to Fight' is a disappointing end to the album. And don't get annoyed with me, but half an hour into the album I longed for a tune. Or more accurately, I wished that the same extraordinary imagination the band brought to sampling, arrangements and lyrics could also be brought to melody and harmony. I guess that wouldn't be hip hop, more prog-hop. But these categories don't mean anything really, do they? And if they had a go at it I bet it would be amazing.

One last thing. I'd appreciate it if someone could tell me what 'cold lamping' is. I'd like to think it's Flavor Flav's account of something David Cameron did in a drinking club at Oxford, but I'm open to clarification.

It Takes a Nation of Millions... by Public Enemy

Would you listen to it again?
Definitely – first thing in the morning to get me in the mood to leave the house, and with my kids in the car, turned up really loud.

A mark out of 10?
8.

TOKYO

7

The Velvet Underground & Nico by The Velvet Underground

1. Sunday Morning
2. I'm Waiting for the Man
3. Femme Fatale
4. Venus in Furs
5. Run Run Run
6. All Tomorrow's Parties
7. Heroin
8. There She Goes Again
9. I'll Be Your Mirror
10. Black Angel's Death Song
11. European Son

First time listener – Danny Finkelstein

I am an overweight Jew from Pinner. I write columns for *The Times* and sit in the House of Lords.

Danny's top three albums ever?

Revolver – The Beatles
Still Crazy After All These Years – Paul Simon
Pet Sounds – The Beach Boys
I think.

Before we get to Danny, here's what Martin thinks of
The Velvet Underground & Nico

The Velvet Underground, and Nico, finished recording their debut album.

Or at least they thought they had.

Tom Wilson, the producer, listens to it one last time and decides it was missing something – a strong single. To be fair, it was missing any singles. So he asks Lou Reed to write one but, importantly, insists that Nico must be the singer.

It's Nico, after all, who has the more marketable voice and the potential to lead the band to success.

Lou Reed, reluctantly, agrees.

The song he comes up with, 'Sunday Morning', is actually written on a Sunday morning. Reed and his bandmate John Cale were messing about on a piano after a heavy night in Manhattan and the song started to take shape around 6 a.m. They play an early version to their manager, Andy Warhol, who likes it but suggests there should be more paranoia in the lyrics. Reed goes away, adds all that 'watch out, the world's behind you' stuff and it's done.

They're now ready to enter the studio and give the song to Nico to record.

In the corner of the studio is a mini xylophone which John Cale starts to play, just because it's there. The rest of the band, Sterling Morrison on guitar and Moe Tucker on drums, dutifully join in. And then at the last minute it's Lou Reed, not Nico, who steps up to the microphone to sing.

They try and stop him of course – the producer and the management – but he's not interested. He tells them it's his song and he's singing it.

Eventually everyone submits. Lou Reed, not for the first time or the last, gets his own way.

Cale starts on the mini xylophone again, the rest of the band join in again, and Lou Reed sings 'Sunday Morning' – trying his best to sound like a woman.

Nico sits silently in the corner, with nothing to do.

In one small scene you have The Velvet Underground and all its associated parts. Everyone plays their role to perfection – particularly Lou Reed.

By today's standards Reed was your typical all-American teenager – he played sports, loved music, took loads of drugs and was socially awkward. In the late fifties, though, his parents were so concerned about the path he was on that they took him to a psychologist and, incredibly, agreed upon a course of electroshock treatment for their son.

They attached a bunch of electrodes to his head, put something in his mouth so he didn't swallow his tongue, and pressed the switch. He was eighteen years old.

Reed later quipped, 'It was shocking, but that's when I was getting into electricity anyway.'

As soon as he recovered he left home (wouldn't you?) and enrolled at Syracuse University to study journalism, film directing and creative writing – the broadest degree course I've ever heard of.

While he was an excellent student, his time there was not without difficulty. He joins the Reserve Officers Training Corps and gets expelled for holding a gun to a superior's head. He hosts his own radio show on campus and gets sacked for slandering a disabled student on air.

Without anyone around to attach more electrodes to his head he manages to graduate with honours and takes up a job as an in house songwriter at Pickwick Records, a company that specialises in quickie albums and novelty songs – one of the few careers not covered by his degree course.

Straight away he comes up with a song called 'The Ostrich', which has an accompanying dance that Reed described as follows:

'You put your head on the floor and have somebody step on it!'

Despite it sounding like the worst dance ever, particularly if you're playing the role of the head, Pickwick really likes the song and hopes it will create a new craze, a bit like 'The Twist'.

Their next step is to recruit a band that can promote it.

At this stage in the story, Lou Reed was introduced to John Cale – an avant-garde Welshman (the worst kind) who played bass and viola. Cale was in a band of his own that, among other things, were trying to sustain the same note for two hours. Other songs included one where the musicians talked to a piano, and another where they screamed at a plant until it died.

No idea why they didn't make it.

Naturally, John Cale jumped at the chance of working on 'The Ostrich', encouraged to see that Reed had tuned all his guitar strings to one note – exactly the sort of stuff he and his mates were into. They add Sterling Morrison on guitar and a fella called Angus MacLise on drums.

So there you have it – The Velvet Underground were formed. They soon forgot about all that 'Ostrich' nonsense and started performing some of Reed's other compositions around New York – songs like 'Heroin' and 'I'm Waiting for the Man', which didn't have any accompanying dance steps.

Within a small circle they caused a stir. So much so that the music journalist Al Aronowitz went to see them, intrigued by the hype, and Lou Reed's own claim that he was the fastest guitarist around. For company and a second opinion, Aronowitz took Robbie Robertson of The Band along to the show.

Robertson, however, was suitably unimpressed. He turns to Aronowitz and says 'He ain't nothing' before leaving. But the second opinion fell on deaf ears. Aronowitz was hooked and the next day drove to Lou Reed's apartment to make them an offer to be their manager while Brian Jones and Carole King waited in his car downstairs.

'Brian, Carole, I've just got to pull up here and sign The Velvet Underground. Won't be long.'

'OK Al.'

Aronowitz gets them a paid residency at the Cafe Bizarre in New York where he thinks they'll undergo a 'Beatles in Hamburg' transformation and refine their craft. The drummer, MacLise, has other ideas though and quits the band on the grounds that accepting money for art is a sell-out. So enter Moe Tucker, a woman whose approach to drumming involves taking the kit apart, standing the bass drum on its side, and hitting it repeatedly with a mallet. Unlike MacLise, she is more than happy to be paid for that.

The other transformation that occurs as a result of the Cafe Bizarre residency is the band's management. The Velvet Underground had come to the attention of Andy Warhol and his Factory entourage who started to attend the shows and dance on stage with whips. Warhol, spotting an opportunity to dabble in the world of rock 'n' roll, swoops in and catches them in his net.

His first job is to provide a focal point that he believes is lacking, someone who can lead The Velvet Underground from the front. So he agrees to fund an album on one condition – they allow Nico, a European chanteuse (the worst kind) to join the band.

They reluctantly agree, even though they actively don't want her in the band. Warhol represented power, influence and opportunity, and the inclusion of Nico seemed a small price to pay – for now at least.

The bulk of the debut album was recorded in a matter of days, while Warhol just sat back and encouraged the band to be themselves – to capture their live sound, and ignore the fact they're making an album. While the short recording time seems to indicate harmonious efficiency, the truth was very different. Reed and Cale were occasionally at loggerheads over the musical direction of the band and who was in charge. On top of that, everyone constantly shouted at Nico, despite the fact that she'd only been given three songs to sing.

For example, during the recording of 'Femme Fatale', a huge row breaks out over Lou Reed and Sterling Morrison's pronunciation of the word 'Fatale'.

'It should be Fahtale!' screams Nico, 'not Faytale!'

Reed and Morrison just ignore her, no doubt thinking this is rich coming from someone who pronounces 'Clown' as 'Clahn'.

The tension reaches boiling point during the recording of 'I'll be Your Mirror'. If you've always enjoyed her wispy, fragile delivery on that song I'm afraid it was the result of The Velvet Underground shouting at her and criticising her throughout the previous ten takes. Unfortunately, it all got a bit Tippi Hedren in *The Birds* for Nico.

Still, they manage to record an album of songs about S&M and drug-taking, set to music that switched between a lullaby and the sound of a skyscraper collapsing inside your head.

In search of a record company, the band tout the album around town. Firstly, they approach Ahmet Ertegun at Atlantic who turns it down by saying 'no drug songs' – the worst A&R strategy you can imagine in 1966. Next, they take it to Elektra who turn it down by saying 'no violas' – the best A&R strategy you can imagine in any year.

Eventually they give it to Tom Wilson, Bob Dylan's producer, and he brokers a deal with MGM/Verve for the album to be released. Wilson himself re-records three of the songs in LA and oversees the session for 'Sunday Morning' described at the beginning.

After taking forever to create an album sleeve with a banana that you could actually peel, *The Velvet Underground & Nico* is finally released in March 1967. It's brilliant. The guitars are all right hand, the drums effectively repetitive, and 'I'm Waiting for the Man' is probably the best song ever without a chorus. It also provided the soundtrack every time I scored an eighth of cheap eurohash off my mate Dave in the nineties – that's 'legacy' for you.

Upon release, though, it only does OK – nothing more, nothing less. Just as it looks like it might break into the top 100, a dancer from Warhol's entourage notices that his image is on the back of the album and decides to sue MGM/Verve. Rather than paying him off, they halt production and distribution until they can produce a new batch. From a commercial perspective, the album never really recovers.

What usually happens now, in any piece about this album, is a simplification of the past ('it sounded like nothing else around') followed by a dramatic rush to the future ('this album changed everything and influenced *everything* you're listening to today'). Before you know it, you've left 1967, you've left *this* story, and you're suddenly talking about The Jesus and Mary Chain and Sonic Youth. You're saying things like 'everyone that bought it formed a band' even though they obviously didn't.

So the album has been defined by its future – weighed down by broad-brush associations and loose talk of 'influence'.

I get all that, but I'm telling *this* story, with *these* characters, and I've only just started. Let's stay in their shoes for a bit, rather than jumping into ours.

It's March 1967 and *The Velvet Underground & Nico* has just been released to mixed reviews and modest sales. Decisions are there to be made, plans are there to be hatched – the future doesn't just happen. What next for the celebrity manager? What next for Nico, the imported 'star'? And what next for The Velvet Underground?

It was Lou Reed's move, a man literally capable of anything.

So, over to you Danny. Why haven't you listened to it? WHAT'S WRONG WITH YOU?????

In some ways I am very surprised by this myself. I've got thousands of albums and the mid-1960s is a key period for me. Those albums I have that aren't actually made in the mid-1960s have that time as their reference point.

Naturally I possess some Lou Reed and enjoy him enough to have seen him live. And David Bowie's *Hunky Dory*, which bears Reed's imprint, is one of my favourite albums.

In addition, I am a fan of pop art in general and Andy Warhol in particular. While not being so dense that I miss its subversive tone, I think pop art understands that consumer culture is properly to be seen as culture. And also that it enhances life. I deeply approve of that, if I'm allowed to smuggle in a bit of politics.

There's quite a bit about The Velvet Underground in Warhol's memoir, *Popism*, and ever since I read it (maybe twenty-five years ago, perhaps more) I've been meaning to listen to some of their stuff. But I never have. Can't think why.

But all this is a bit dishonest, because deep down I can think why. I really know why.

I always thought it might be a bit, I don't know, difficult. Earnest. Arty. I realise it is supposed to be influential but, well, let's put it this way, I sometimes get up in the morning and feel like something rocky. Sometimes I want music that swings. Or something mellow. Often I want pop that's immediate and familiar. I never get up and think: 'You know what I fancy as I make breakfast? Something influential.'

So every day is a day when I think, gosh, I really ought to listen to that banana album I read about in that book. But every day what I actually do is think that after listening to Jeff Lynne's remakes of ELO, I will put on Billy Joel's *Live at Shea Stadium*. Or Van Morrison's *Moondance*. Or Stevie Wonder's *Songs in the Key of Life*.

Tomorrow I'll do the banana album.

You've now listened to it at least three times, what do you think?

A few years ago *The Times* asked me to do a restaurant review and I worried about the hake. How do you describe what a piece of hake tastes like? I thought I'd probably be able to make the piece work if the hake was horrible or if it was delicious. But what if it wasn't either of those things?

And another thing. What if the hake was actually divine but I couldn't appreciate it because, when it comes down to it, I don't really like hake all that much? How would I know whether it was me or the hake?

Well, in the end, we went to a Thai restaurant and they didn't have hake. So the problem went away. Only to come back now with The Velvet Underground.

I thought the album was... fine. I didn't hate it. I didn't love it. I wondered a lot whether it was me or the album. I had no trouble understanding why no one bought this record at the time, while Sweet had a number one hit with 'Blockbuster'.

One or two songs – 'Sunday Morning', 'Venus in Furs' and 'Waiting for the Man' – were pretty good. One or two – in particular 'European Son' – were terrible. It just went on and on without any tune. Given how many other records do that, perhaps that is why this album is regarded as influential.

I listened with my son and we both separately detected hints of Lovin' Spoonful and The Kinks without either of us feeling the album had their charm or was remotely comparable to, say, *Village Green Preservation Society*.

When I say I can take or leave it, Lou Reed I can take, while Nico I can leave. As my son commented: 'I can see what she was trying to do.' Even Lou Reed is very variable. When I saw him, halfway through his set, my friend whispered in my ear: 'It's Phoebe from *Friends*,' after which every song sounded like 'Smelly Cat'.

I can understand why this album is thought to have launched a thousand bands. When you listen to it, it sounds as if you'd be able to play it without being all that good at your instrument. Although this may be deceptive.

But it was OK. It's just that my instinct was right. I would always rather be listening to *Hotel California* or *Abbey Road*.

Would you listen to it again?
I wouldn't deliberately avoid it, but I bet I won't listen to it much.

A mark out of 10?
6.

8

Marquee Moon by Television

1. See No Evil
2. Venus
3. Friction
4. Marquee Moon
5. Elevation
6. Guiding Light
7. Prove It
8. Torn Curtain

First time listener – Elena Cresci

I'm a social and community editor for the *Guardian*, which means I spend all my time either on the internet or explaining it to people with much better things to do with their day. I tweet too much, am a musical disappointment to my father and will take any opportunity to tell you how Welsh I am.

Elena's top three albums?

Morning View – Incubus
London Calling – The Clash
International Velvet – Catatonia

Before we get to Elena, here's what Martin thinks of *Marquee Moon*

Let's try and get a sense of place.

Because as much as the people you've all read about since, this is actually a story about place, about the why of the where.

New York's Lower East Side was once a thriving hub of factories, tenements and docks. The trade centre of the city and the first port of call, literally, for thousands of immigrants that settled among America's working poor. Africans freed from slavery, Irish, Germans, Italians and Jews fleeing from starvation and oppression. This is where they landed and started again. Chinatown, the Bowery, Little Italy and Alphabet City. A community with a shared experience, where people felt at home.

And then the work dried up.

A process of globalisation and de-industrialisation shut down many of the garment factories and the sweatshops and also reduced the numbers of men on the waterfront. A new subway system then started to move the centre of the city uptown. By the end of the 1960s, it was a shadow of its former self, all empty warehouses and half-empty tenements, with crime, drug use and poverty going through the roof. Next door, Greenwich Village had undergone something of a renaissance in the previous decade as a collection of hipsters and beatniks had descended on it, giving it an allure, an economy and a reason to charge high rents.

But the Lower East Side? It had been forgotten, a no-go area for many people outside its boundaries. An industrial wasteland during the day and empty at night. One part of it, SoHo, acquired a nickname which perfectly summed it up – 'Hell's Hundred Acres'.

So the rents fell.

And this attracted a new type of resident, drawn to the empty lofts and warehouses, not to mention the low rents. That large constituency of people you find in all major cities, people doing dead-end jobs because they want to do something else instead – the artists, writers, singers and musicians. People like Tom Miller and Richard Meyers, who had moved to the area in the late sixties and now, approaching the mid-seventies, decided to shake it up. This is where *they* landed, this is where *they* started again.

It had to happen here.

Miller and Meyers, childhood friends from Delaware, had moved to New York as aspiring poets but quickly turned their attention to music. After a series of aborted projects, they changed their names to Tom Verlaine and Richard Hell, recruited a drop-dead gorgeous guitarist called Richard Lloyd who everyone was having sex with, and a drummer called Billy Ficca. Together they formed Television.

But before the music they needed an image, a point of difference and a break from the past. It was the tail end of glam, the time of the New York Dolls, Bowie and Lou Reed. Androgynous and camp, men dressed as divas from the thirties, adorned with glitter and baubles. And Television threw all that out the window. Instead they cut their hair short and went for a tough fifties street kid look – the Hamburg Beatles in a Nicholas Ray movie. Hell, in particular, looked like he was in the middle of being electrocuted, got bored and decided to form a band instead.

All dressed up, they now needed somewhere to play. Legend has it they were wandering along the Bowery when they saw Hilly Kristal putting up an awning for his new club – CBGB, situated just below a homeless shelter for alcoholics. They asked him what the letters stood for.

'Country, bluegrass and blues,' he replied.

'Great, that's what we play,' they lied.

But they got a gig and promised Kristal they would bring a load of friends who would spend money in his bar. It was just as well that they did, because the first time Kristal heard them in his club he thought they were terrible.

He was persuaded to have them back though. On their third gig, Patti Smith, a local performer and journalist, was in the audience and reviewed the show for the *SoHo Weekly News* where she heavily emphasised the band's sex appeal – 'Confused sexual energy makes young guys so desirable,' she wrote. So desirable that Smith quickly started a relationship with Verlaine and a process of mutual support and influence began. The *SoHo Weekly News* proclaimed them 'the downtown couple of the year'.

Over time, Television start to develop their sound and a loyal following. So much so that Kristal agrees to an unprecedented residency at CBGB in the spring of 1975: Television and Patti Smith, now fronting her own group, played two shows a night, four nights a week, for seven weeks. A total of fifty-six gigs in under two months. An anti-tour in one venue – hunkered down in a no-go part of New York.

And this is where it starts to take off. A following of like-minded kids from the Lower East Side that ventured out to the Bowery to see Television, Patti Smith and the other bands that were starting to migrate from the audience to the stage – The Ramones, Talking Heads and Blondie, to name a few. A community with a shared experience, where people felt at home. And then the subway started to bring the industry downtown – the A&R men, the label executives, the managers. Lou Reed, Malcolm McLaren and David Bowie too. And all this happened, this scene, these bands, within a club that only held 300 people and was supposed to be playing country, bluegrass and blues.

And you know the rest.

Smith gets a head start and releases *Horses*. Meanwhile Richard Hell leaves Television because they've started to grow musically and he doesn't want to. They want him to play this complex ten-minute song called Marquee Moon and he's not able to. He wants to be a punk and jump about a lot. So he's replaced on bass by Fred Smith, briefly of Blondie.

And eventually, in 1977, they release *Marquee Moon*, the album – just eight songs and not very punk at all. There isn't a song under three and a half minutes on the entire album and there are so many guitar solos that they are listed on the album's liner notes alongside who played what. But it's brilliant, the whole thing is brilliant, and the song 'Marquee Moon', the song that Richard Hell struggled to play, is recorded in one take. I'll never get my head around that.

And a word on Richard Lloyd, often lost due to the Hell v Verlaine war that has raged ever since. Not only the best-looking man ever to join a band, not only capable of moments of eccentricity, like eating a raw onion whole or sticking acupuncture needles in his own face while driving, but also a great guitarist without whom this album and this band wouldn't quite be the same.

And you know the rest.

What started there blew up and became the defining genre of its time. All those albums, all that influence – The Ramones, Patti Smith, Talking Heads and Blondie. But it started there, it had to happen there. In a club that held just 300 people.

Because as much as the people you've all read about since, this is actually a story about time and place, about the why of the where. And these are the stories that sometimes get overlooked.

Like the story of how Liverpool got a head start on rock 'n' roll due to a load of American sailors on the docks. How that gave the local kids access to this music before everyone else and they developed their own music as a result. Like the story of how Detroit benefited from the Great Migration of African-Americans to the north. How that created a new black middle class which learned from the production lines in Motor City and then put this into practice in their own businesses – to create their own production lines.

The Beatles and Motown. Stories as much about the time and the place as the people. The why of the where.

If Tom Verlaine and Richard Hell had stayed in Delaware then Television would never have happened, *Marquee Moon* would never have happened. If David Byrne, Debbie Harry, Patti Smith and Joey Ramone had been anywhere else other than New York then all those albums, all that influence, wouldn't have happened either. It had to happen there.

And how those places have changed since.

How the docks in Liverpool and the car industry in Detroit have become decimated. How it's now illegal to start a business from home in Detroit, like Berry Gordy did with Motown in 1959. How the Lower East Side in New York has undergone a period of gentrification that has pushed the rents up and the immigrants and artists out. Those very specific circumstances that helped to create The Beatles, Motown and punk are now all but gone.

But there's always somewhere else – Manchester, Seattle, Brooklyn. There's always somewhere else where it's about to happen. And when it does, I always ask myself why. Why there? And there's always a reason.

Just like there was in 1975, when punk broke on the Lower East Side.

So, over to you Elena. Why haven't you listened to it? WHAT'S WRONG WITH YOU?????

There's one thing you need to know about me before I go on: I am terrible at music.

I am that person who only really gets into a song after they hear it on an advert or if said artist becomes super-mainstream. It's a little odd that I've got into this situation in my mid-twenties, because I was one of those teens creating little mixtapes by running to hit 'record' as soon as the DJ stopped introducing the song on the radio. I had a Beatles phase, I've been to gigs and festivals and stuff. I'm just not very good at keeping on top of it all. There's so much!

I should be better, because my dad is *so* good at music. He is in a band. He had a punk phase. I'm pretty sure he was the first person in our household to get on the digital music bandwagon and he's no millennial. What I'm trying to say is my dad is far, far cooler than I am, most especially in the music department. He tried his best with me. He introduced me to The Clash, Madness… bu-u-ut I'm pretty sure he more or less disowned me when I started my pop band phase.

He hasn't forgotten – in his retirement, between gigging in his pork pie hats, he's finessing the art of getting Facebook likes from my friends by writing on my wall telling me he's just found all my Steps and Hear'Say albums.

There's always been a part of me which feels automatically embarrassed about the music I like. In my first year at Swansea University, I tried to get involved with the student paper's music section. But the music editors were such colossal dicks, making fun of everyone's music tastes and telling me I could only go review a gig if I told the artist how terrible they were. Clearly, they were just pricks, but I didn't have much of a backbone then so I wrote one solitary album review and figured news might be more my forte.

I suppose there came a point where I just stopped trying really. The last band I really truly invested much into was Incubus. Luckily I now *do* have a backbone so if you want to tell me my music taste is shit, I will give you my patented South Walian DEATH GLARE and perhaps send a dragon after you because I think Incubus are the tits.

Nowadays, I'm taking more of an interest – I went to my first *ever* festival last year and discovered all sorts of bands which had totally passed me by. Some of the oldies though, I'm still catching up on. In fact, don't kill me, I hadn't actually properly heard of Television until I was asked to review this album. SORRY.

In short, I guess the reason I haven't listened to it is a mixture of laziness, music snobs being dicks and disappointing my dad thoroughly with my music taste.

You've now listened to it at least three times, what do you think?

For those of you who adore this album, I guess I have good news and bad news. The good news is: I didn't hate it. The bad news is: I didn't fall madly in love with it.

When I looked up the band, I saw something about punk and got hella excited. I love shouty music, me. Then it started, and it wasn't very shouty *at all*. In fact, it was ridiculously chilled. So much so, for a moment, I felt like I was a bit stoned. My initial notes include

'WHERE IS THE SHOUTING' and 'good God this would go well with a spliff'.

The more I listened to it, the more it seemed like a stoner's dream. *Especially* when you get to the song 'Marquee Moon'. There's a bit when you think it's finished and it hasn't actually, then you get a bit spaced out and think oh man how much time has passed, before you realise the song is ten minutes long and that's probably why you're a bit confused. I think if you're going to do a super-long song (shut up, ten minutes is super-long to me), it needs to be a ballbuster, and it's not quite that. Nice enough though, I suppose.

Also, I'm just going to say it: this would be a great album to make out to. You know, the kind you play on like a second or third date, when you're not quite ready to let them in on your real playlist but you also want to seem cool enough to impress. It's perfect! Inoffensive and not too distracting.

I get the impression this is the kind of album people seem to love almost unconditionally. In fact, anyone I spoke to more or less started frothing at the mouth with joy when I said I was listening to it. Except for the one person, who will remain unnamed, who said: 'OH MY GOD IT'S SPELLED MARQUEE MOON? I thought it was Mark E. Moon. Like the older brother of Chuck E. Cheese.'

Anyway, I can see why my more musically literate friends are obsessed with this album. It's full of twinkly guitar bits I imagine musically literate people play super-realistic air guitar to. And that's cool! I'm here for your realistic air guitar. But it didn't quite grab me.

I have a very physical reaction to music I out and out love. If I don't do a happy dance or lip sync for my life to my reflection in the mirror at least once, then it's not quite there for me. I want songs which make me dance so hard I almost pass out. There was no happy dance during *Marquee Moon*. And there was no one to make out with soooo...

Jokes aside. It's OK. But I need something with a bit more punch, a bit more oomph.

Oh, and I texted my dad to ask him what he thinks of it – first off he told me I should have paid more attention to his CDs before admitting it didn't really make an impression on him at the time. SO IT TURNS OUT WE HAVE MORE OR LESS THE SAME OPINION.

Fingers crossed I'm written back into the will…

Would you listen to it again?
I have this huge Spotify playlist of about 700 songs – it's my dumping ground for things I hear out and about and really like, but I don't think anything on here quite makes the guilty pleasures list. But I think I'll probably listen to it again for some easy background music. Or if I match with someone decent on Tinder.

A mark out of 10?
I'm gonna give it a 6. 5 feels too mean and 7 feels too much.

9

Almost Killed Me by The Hold Steady

1. Positive Jam
2. The Swish
3. Barfruit Blues
4. Most People Are DJs
5. Certain Songs
6. Knuckles
7. Hostile, Mass.
8. Sketchy Metal
9. Sweet Payne
10. Killer Parties

First time listener – Jim Waterson

I cover politics for *BuzzFeed*, which is probably the best job in the world for someone who likes the Internet and politics.

Jim's top three albums ever?

Oh I'm not playing that game. I'd go mad trying to decide and anyway, singles are better.

An album to listen to on a long journey: *On Fire* – Galaxie 500

An album to listen to when going out: *Bugged Out Mix* – Erol Alkan

An album to listen to when you just need amazing pop music: *Robyn* – Robyn

Ruth and Martin's Album Club

Before we get to Jim, here's what Martin thinks of *Almost Killed Me*

Our house band – The Hold Steady.

Let me quickly run through the biography.

Craig Finn, future leader of The Hold Steady, was *that* kid in school – neither the first to be picked for the sports team, nor the last. A bespectacled adolescent navigating the school corridors, aware that there's an 'in-crowd' and he's on the outs.

He's the kid in-between – like most of us. Like me.

So what's the plan? How does he get from there to here?

Does he settle or does he aspire?

He does neither. He retreats into a world of books and music and becomes an expert in *his* field. He learns how to play guitar, becomes a fan of local Minneapolis bands like The Replacements and Hüsker Dü, and, even though he's still a kid, he goes to see them at the 'all ages hardcore matinee shows' in town.

Just a quick aside here but 'hardcore matinee shows' sound like the most fun in the world – something to really build a day around and I'd basically vote for any political party that introduced them into the UK.

But back to the story…

In his early twenties, Finn forms a band called Lifter Puller who are simultaneously pretty good but also not quite right. What works, spectacularly, is Finn's lyrics about drugs and the shady characters that surround them, but the 'not quite right' bit is the music – a sort of eighties-inspired synth overdose that, at its worst, sounds like the soundtrack to a Brian De Palma movie and, at its best, sounds like the soundtrack to a Brian De Palma movie.

After a few albums, and a modicum of success, Lifter Puller split up and Finn becomes a financial broker for American Express before moving to New York to work at a digital webcasting company. At this stage in Finn's life it would appear that his brief flirtation with a career in music has ended and he is now on course for a series of jobs in tech and finance. In fact, he doesn't do anything related to music for two whole years. He's just the guy at work, the one who used to be in a band called Lifter Puller.

And then it happens.

Craig Finn is watching Martin Scorsese's *The Last Waltz*, the film of The Band's final concert, and he turns to his friend Tad Kubler and says, 'Dude, why aren't there any bands like this anymore?'

Finn's observation is correct – there are no bands like that anymore and I'm not sure there ever will be. But that's obvious, that's the bit we can all see. Even I've watched *The Last Waltz* and said to my mate Dan (I don't have a mate called Tad, I wish I did) – 'Dude, why aren't there any bands like this anymore?'

No, what I love about this moment is what they did next. Finn and Kubler, there and then, decided to form a band *like* that. They took the completely mad decision in 2003, when everyone was still floored by that Neutral Milk Hotel album and everything it spawned, of creating a band with just guitar, bass and drums.

They called themselves The Hold Steady and there wasn't a singing saw, a zanzithophone or a wandering genie organ in sight.

What started out as an excuse for a bunch of guys in their thirties to hang out, drink, and play the occasional show, then becomes something of a going concern. Finn's lyrics, framed by Kubler's big riffs, created an unlikely breath of fresh air, a sense of celebration. Before long they're signed to Frenchkiss, the best name for a record label ever, and they release their first album – *Almost Killed Me*.

The album, in fact their career, opens with 'Positive Jam', a song that tells the history of twentieth-century America in 171 words. In the background, a lazy guitar struggles to wake up as the events are passed like road signs. It's their first song, on their first album, and after ninety seconds there's been a stock market crash, a world war, and three Kennedys are dead. The lyrical economy is remarkable, the way he deals with each decade precisely and definitively in one sentence.

This is how he nails the fifties:

'We got shiftless in the fifties, holding hands and going steady, twisting into dark parts of the large Midwestern cities.'

No need for the white picket fence trope, no need for Ike or Truman to co-star. Post-war America perfectly reduced to 'holding hands and going steady'. And then the twist tells you the sixties are coming. I got it straight away.

And this is how he nails the seventies:

'We woke up on bloody carpets. Got tangled up in gas lines. I guess that's where it started.'

He rhymed 'carpets' with 'started' and reduced the long-term economic and political effects of the 1973 oil crisis to a line. What's not to like? I can still vividly remember my first listen now – the time, the place, and an album cover of blacked-out faces. It was immediate. I was in.

And I didn't even know then what I know now, that he was providing context – that he was explicitly saying 'we have shared history'. Because at the end of the song, he brings us up to date, the guitar does wake up and the band kicks in. It's then that he tells us that he was bored so he started a band, it's then that he tells us that he wants to start it off with a positive jam.

The first time I heard *Almost Killed Me* I rewound the opening song again and again. I guess the 'positive jam' that the song was trailing was 'The Swish', the second song on the album. But I couldn't get to it, I couldn't get past how good the opener was. I listened to it five times on the spin – by the time I was finished fifteen Kennedys had died.

But then I did get past it. I got to 'The Swish' and my head fell off. Honestly, I stood there laughing, air riffing and dancing, in thrall to my new favourite band after just two songs. The bridge from 'Positive Jam' to 'The Swish' is one of *the* moments in music for me. It simultaneously comes out of nowhere yet evokes a memory. I made it through the rest of the album, breathless and giddy.

I'd never heard anything like it, despite having heard things *like* it.

Does that make sense? That bit really needs to make sense.

You know when *The Sopranos* came out and you thought 'Jesus, not another story about Italian-American gangsters. Surely not *that* again'. But then you watched it and saw that the characters were immersed in that culture as much as the viewer. They existed within their own context and couldn't move without referencing it.

And that was the difference. It was derivative but it was told from an angle so it wasn't head-on.

That's The Hold Steady. That's *Almost Killed Me*.

It would be easy to say it's my favourite album of the twenty-first century if only it didn't have to compete with what they did next – *Separation Sunday, Boys and Girls in America* and, finally, the hangover, *Stay Positive*. Finn had done it. With his friends, he'd made one of the greatest runs of albums ever – an aggregate score of at least 36 out of 40.

At least.

Yes, there were comparisons to things you'd heard before, a familiarity, but for me it was almost entirely different. People screamed Springsteen, people screamed The E Street Band but I never really knew why. These weren't stories about open roads, about making love to the interstate. These were stories about the claustrophobia of community, about the kids in between – confined by drugs and religion. And you know what? Springsteen never swished through the city centre to do a couple of favours for some guys who looked like Tusken Raiders, did he? No he didn't, he was probably driving somewhere.

The Hold Steady wore their influences on their sleeve but they spun them. They humoured them. They said 'tramps like us and we like tramps' and told stories about people who looked like people – people who looked like Rocco Siffredi, Elisabeth Shue, Izzy Stradlin, Alice Cooper, Mickey Mantle, and, of course, Tusken Raiders. They were doing that thing again – they were saying 'We know you know. Because we have shared history.'

But this analysis, my attempt at explanation, is nothing compared to the visceral triumph and joy of a Hold Steady show – the pleasure of watching this band that had been plucked from their own lives and were creating anew. I used to spend hours looking at the bass player. I'd never seen anyone work so hard while standing still – a man who started the night dry and ended it dripping in sweat and smiles.

And then there was Finn – the in-betweener, the most generous of front men. He was always so warm and inclusive to his audience, so glad that they're there with him. Yet he never forgot the rest of the band. Never. And for someone so wordy it's remarkable the gaps he leaves for them – the gaps for them to play and for him to admire. Often he'd be clapping, dancing, and having so much fun in admiration, that I'd worry he'd forget to join in again – that he'd forget that the moment after the gaps were his.

But he never did.

Fast forward to 2014 – to the Holiday Inn, in Brighton, a few hours after a Hold Steady show.

I'd probably had my back to him for about ten minutes, having a nightcap at the hotel bar and thinking about what had come before. But then I turned around and there he was – Craig Finn, sitting alone, a hero rather than a star. I decided to say hello and he gestured for me to sit down. We talked about *The Last Waltz*. I asked him if it was true, whether that's really how it started, and he said it was. We talked about the rest of the film, all those conversations, you know where they go – Joni Mitchell and all her chords; Van Morrison and that ridiculous high kick. And somewhere in the drink and *The Last Waltz* I lost the memory of the night, other than to say he was good company and he paid his way.

And if I met him now?

If I met him now, I'd probably get lost down another rabbit hole – about how we're the same age and how I wasn't picked first for the sports team either. I'd ask him how he feels now, at forty-four, about the start he gave himself at thirty-three – whether that still surprises him, whether it ever did. Whether he knows, *really* knows, that for about four years The Hold Steady were the best band in the world. But more than that I'd tell him about how he influenced, how he inspired, about how Ruth and I always used to say this album club was about spinning familiar stories, about telling them from an angle rather than head on – just like The Hold Steady.

Because that's what we used to say. When we wanted to avoid nostalgia and reheating the past, we used to say it should be 'JUST LIKE THE HOLD STEADY'.

And before I lost another evening, and its fluid memory, I'd like to take the opportunity to thank him for that.

So, over to you Jim. Why haven't you listened to it? WHAT'S WRONG WITH YOU?????

Because I perceived The Hold Steady to be the sort of band that a trendy dad driving a Volvo estate would stick on the car stereo, allowing him to rant about the joys of the open road while sticking to the speed limit on the A64.

At the time it was released, 2004, I was an only child living in a small North Yorkshire village where the idea of entertainment was the annual biggest weed competition at the village fête. Luckily we had a dial-up internet connection and, on the internet, not only can you be a dog but you can also spend every waking minute posting on pre-MySpace music forums under a pseudonym. Which is what I did: it was the last parp of the *NME* era, when they were pushing The Libertines, a scene called 'New Yorkshire', and they could still make the release of a new Art Brut single feel like a world event.

This was a strange crossover period – oooh, a whole eleven years ago – where most music scenes had moved online, making it much easier to get recommendations about new bands and opening up the possibility of talking with people who were into the same stuff. But at that point you still couldn't actually easily get hold of the bloody music online to see whether the tips were good.

Remember what it was like?

People posted in forums based around particular scenes or bands. They'd tip something they'd heard but actually checking out a new band involved waiting forty minutes to download a virus-laden MP3 from Kazaa on dial-up, loading it into Windows Media Player and then feeling sufficiently excited to go into town and spend £10.99 at Track Records on the album. TEN POUNDS NINETY-NINE! Then you'd have to sit on the bus home and read the liner notes before you could hear it. CD singles were considered a legitimate product rather than an overpriced way of getting hold of three minutes of music. MySpace's four song uploads weren't there yet, nor was YouTube available for streaming. This was just a decade ago. I now inject Spotify directly into my bloodstream.

Anyway, I wasn't going to go through all that for a band like The Hold Steady.

Also, in 2004 I was fifteen years old and considered following bands to be a fairly partisan matter. At that point I was a fan of British Sea Power, as much for their worldview as their music. Thanks to lifts around the country from people I met on those forums and blagging guestlists I probably watched British Sea Power play about forty-odd times when I was a teenager. They had a football ultras-style team of regulars and every gig felt like it actually mattered. By comparison I seem to remember some people wearing 'The Hold Steady saved my life' T-shirts but it all seemed too bloody earnest and they were mainly worn by the odd guy with a beer gut.

Soon afterwards I twigged that the way to actually meet the people I liked was to be this thing called 'a journalist' so I set up a badly photocopied fanzine and started turning up to interview bands, managing to get Swedish pop star Robyn to take me out for a steak dinner and eighties oddball Julian Cope to give me a tour of stone circles. But by university I lost interest in guitar music when someone tried to make The Twang into a thing, so going to clubs mixed with Actually Good Pop Music became my thing. Definitely, definitely not some earnest BBC 6 Music-dwelling guitar band from New Jersey.

Almost Killed Me by The Hold Steady

All of which is a very long way of saying: I bloody love music but at every single point of the last eleven years I've quite purposefully avoided The Hold Steady for various reasons centred on my belief that they were earnest bastards playing sub-Springsteen shite for the sort of people who try to recapture lost youth by writing earnest over-long self-indulgent pieces about their teenage connection with music.

Oh.

You've now listened to it at least three times, what do you think?

Don't make me say it. I don't want to say it. Oh OK then: it was perfectly all right. Actually, I quite liked it. Now, as a result of this I'm worried that I'm going through an early mid-life crisis which will end in me moving to Surrey and spending my weekend tending the barbecue at real ale festivals.

There's an awful lot going against this album: there's guitar solos that go on for over a minute for no particular reason, and you've got to have a pretty good excuse to do that. There's earnest 'me-and-my-bottle-of-Budweiser-against-the-world' songs about hard drinking in American bars which always sound a bit bollocks and just make me want to sit down for a quiet pint of Sam Smith's, especially when Guided By Voices do the sozzled guitar thing better. Then there's that goddamn earnestness which I've always hated in American guitar music. I've always got a lingering suspicion that the songwriter writing about their hard-partying life on the edge of society is basically an undercover *Pitchfork* writer doing a feature on what it's really like to get drunk backstage at some fleapit venue.

And have I mentioned that I've always had a largely irrational hatred of Springsteen? And the same for Bob Dylan? These guys really want to be Springsteen and Dylan.

And yet, and yet, and yet, I started listening and The Hold Steady just really go for it. And they don't piss about and they chuck out song after song and sure they all sound a bit the same and sure they're all shouting lyrics about people in bars and sure it's all a bit incomprehensible. But they drive on relentlessly. And there are bits which are basically just Teenage Fanclub with an American accent, which is always going to be all right with me.

I rarely listen to albums properly these days and individual tracks don't really stand out on first listen so it's odd to try and concentrate on a single lump of music for so long. But among the tales of chain-smoking and heavy drinking there's the odd pop song in there. There are still a few too many songs which make me think of blokey men nodding earnestly at the side of gigs while holding a £5 pint of Carlsberg but then I remember I do quite like Bob Mould's Sugar and this sounds a bit like that at points.

At one point they use the lyric 'I've been trying to get people to call me Sunny D, cos I've got the good stuff that kids go for'. This is brazenly awful. They immediately jump in my estimation.

But it's on the fourth listen that their appeal starts to makes sense: they're never going to be my band, this is never going to be an album I truly love, but I can imagine someone getting obsessed with them, getting wrapped up in every story and screaming the lyrics out of the window of their car.

And more than anything I love listening to any band that inspires total devotion in a group of people. It's fandom that makes bands more than just some musicians who chuck out a few songs every few years. It's why One Direction are elevated by their obsessive fanbase and why people still go to see Optimo DJ sets and why the devotion that surrounded smaller indie bands from a decade ago like Forward Russia or The Long Blondes also really, really, really mattered to the relatively small groups of people involved. Fandom is great, music that can inspire fandom and obsession is better than something that's technically all right but worthy and doesn't make you desire more. Fandom is basically the lifeblood of good music and – unlike a lot of bands that make similar music – I can see why someone would get utterly devoted to The Hold Steady.

Almost Killed Me by The Hold Steady

I'm not going to say 'The Hold Steady saved my life.' But I can see why someone might feel that way. And I like them for that.

Would you listen to it again?
Only if I'm driving on the Pan-American Highway with the windows down. Or failing that, heading across the M62 in my mum's Ford Focus.

A mark out of 10?
7.

10

Bringing It All Back Home by Bob Dylan

1. Subterranean Homesick Blues
2. She Belongs to Me
3. Maggie's Farm
4. Love Minus Zero
5. Outlaw Blues
6. On the Road Again
7. Bob Dylan's 115th Dream
8. Mr Tambourine Man
9. Gates of Eden
10. It's Alright, Ma (I'm Only Bleeding)
11. It's All Over Now, Baby Blue

First time listener – Sam West

He's an actor and sometimes a director. He's played Hamlet and Richard II for the Royal Shakespeare Company, Jeffrey Skilling in *Enron* in the West End and the voice of Pongo in Disney's *101 Dalmatians II*. He's also Frank Edwards in all four series of *Mr Selfridge* on ITV.

Sam's top three albums ever?
Impossible, but three I'd hate to be without are:
Superfly – Curtis Mayfield
Another Green World – Brian Eno
English Settlement – XTC

Ruth and Martin's Album Club

Before we get to Sam, here's what Martin thinks of *Bringing It All Back Home*

It's the facts, not the story, that leave you dizzy.

So here we go.

I'm going to skip all that *David Copperfield* stuff because we don't have time. All you need to know is that he begins his life in rural Minnesota – miles away from where he should be. With nothing else to do he idolises Hank Williams, then Little Richard, and, finally, Woody Guthrie. You get the picture. It's the fifties – holding hands and going steady.

Well, that wasn't for him.

In January of 1961 he emphatically decides he's had enough and travels to New York to make his mark. He's changed his name too, signalling his intent in the process. No longer Robert Zimmerman, a name fit for owning hardware stores, he's now Bob Dylan – a name fit for anything. And I love that he did that. That he was nowhere near famous and still thought 'there's no way I'm coming to New York with my silly actual name. They'll get what they're given and I'm giving them Bob Dylan.'

It was the best thing Robert Zimmerman ever did.

On arrival he immerses himself in Greenwich Village – a bohemia of coffee houses and people with roll-necks singing folk songs. An ideal place for a Woody Guthrie fanatic to get involved. And he does, quickly becoming 'the kid' on the scene – a ten-minute support slot here, a lunchtime show there. All the while he's absorbing influence, making contacts and graduating to bigger stages.

Everyone who was around at the time now comments on his uncanny ability to learn a song in one listen. They also tell tales of him stealing records – of him crashing on the floor at night and making off with half their collection in the morning. And finally, his love life explodes too – a series of women smitten by his vagabond charm. Joan Baez would later say 'He could bring out the mothering instinct in a woman who thought her mothering instinct was dead.'

Bringing It All Back Home by Bob Dylan

This is his 'tentative' migration into Greenwich Village then – he basically ransacks the place.

In October 1961 he comes to the attention of John Hammond – the A&R man at Columbia who had signed Billie Holiday. Hammond sees Dylan perform and is immediately taken in. What he sees is in one sense derivative but in another entirely different. It's younger, brighter, spun from the past but with polish and attitude. Hammond, trusting his instincts, signs him to Columbia there and then.

And that's how easy it was. Dylan had come to Greenwich Village in January as a nobody. Just ten months later, he had a record deal.

His first album, brilliantly titled *Bob Dylan*, takes just six hours to record. I know. Six hours – that's not even a full shift at work. He strolled in late and left early. No one records an album in that amount of time. Most people can't even record a song in that amount of time. But, in hindsight, maybe it was too early for him, too rushed. He's still stuck in his Woody Guthrie phase and the album is nothing more than a charming homage – interpretations, like impressions, of the songs he had learnt, alongside just one Dylan original – 'Song to Woody'.

It sells poorly and, for a while, the executives at Columbia have a nickname for their new signing – 'Hammond's Folly'.

Not a great start then.

But look, this is Bob Dylan and he's not about to stand for that. So, smarted by failure, he decides to throw everyone else's songs in the bin and concentrate on writing his own. The time has come for him to trust *his* instincts.

What follows is probably the most prolific and concentrated period of songwriting ever, a time in his life where Bob Dylan literally couldn't stop writing songs. I read an interview with him once where he said that he was even writing songs when he was talking to people. Just imagine that for a second. It's complete madness.

'I caught up with Bob today.'

'How was he?'

'He seemed fine, although he was writing "Masters of War" at the time so it's hard to tell.'

'Right.'

WHO ON EARTH WRITES SONGS WHEN THEY'RE TALKING TO PEOPLE?!

1962 Bob Dylan, that's who.

For his second album, *The Freewheelin' Bob Dylan*, he produces a staggering thirty-seven songs that are so good the only difficulty is deciding what to leave out. One of the songs that doesn't make the cut is 'Tomorrow is a Long Time' – a song so brilliant that, in 2010, it closes the first season of *The Walking Dead*. That's how good his off-cuts are – forty-eight years after he's discarded them they're the perfect song to close a TV series about the zombie apocalypse.

Nothing goes to waste.

But, also, look at the ones that made it – 'Hard Rain', 'Blowing in the Wind', 'Don't Think Twice', 'Oxford Town', 'Masters of War' etc. etc. Just a quick word on 'Hard Rain' because it's so extraordinary. At just under seven minutes, it's a series of opening lines that are majestically put together to create a narrative of impending doom and personal terror. Both Joni Mitchell and Leonard Cohen are on record as saying it's the song that made them want to become songwriters. But what's remarkable is that he was just twenty-one when he wrote it – when the world was on the brink of nuclear war during the Cuban Missile Crisis.

WHO ON EARTH WRITES SONGS DURING THE CUBAN MISS...

Look, you get the idea by now.

The album, helped by the best cover ever, is a success. Dylan's arrived in earnest and people are now covering *his* songs – notably Peter, Paul and Mary who have a huge hit with 'Blowing in the Wind'. With success come the inevitable attempts at ownership and definition from, not just the media, but also his fans. He's quickly labelled as the 'voice of a generation', he's quickly asked to clarify his meaning and his message. All that pressure, all those questions. He's even wheeled out at the historic March on Washington, singing four songs prior to Martin Luther King's 'I Have a Dream' speech – the toughest support slot ever.

Still it's bewildering. Everything's happening so fast and he seems unwilling to rest and take stock.

He follows *Freewheelin'* with *The Times They Are a-Changin'*, another brilliant collection of finger-pointing songs which only serve to increase his popularity. Again, the songs are recorded with the minimum amount of fuss, just a few takes to get them down. Like *Freewheelin'* it's music as still photography, a moment in time from Dylan's life that's captured and recorded for us to enjoy – while he moves on.

And move on he does. It's around this time that he gets less interested in global themes and more interested in Rimbaud and amphetamines. Crucially, he also hears The Beatles' 'I Want to Hold Your Hand' for the first time. Legend has it that he was so excited that he got out of the car, ran around for a bit, and then started to bang his head against the bonnet saying 'It's great!'

Coincidentally, The Beatles were in Paris around the same time and George Harrison returned to their hotel with a copy of *Freewheelin'* (*En Roue Libre* actually) which they played to death.

A mutual appreciation society had begun.

And now Dylan starts the turn.

His next album, *Another Side of Bob Dylan*, is recorded in a single ten-hour session, washed down with a couple of bottles of Beaujolais. Still photography again. And the other side that the title suggests? Well this time it's more personal, its lyrics more poetic. If any fingers are being pointed, they're pointed inwards. But, in places, it's fun too. It's even got a parody of Hitchcock's *Psycho* on it.

The critics hate it. Po-faced and precious, they wonder where *their* Dylan has gone, always in thrall to *their* Dylan and no one else's. They even start to say that he's lost it.

Shortly after it's released, stung by the criticism, he meets The Beatles for the first time in a New York hotel. He turns up looking for his usual drink, cheap wine, but gets offered champagne and pills. He turns them both down and, instead, rolls a massive joint – giving The Beatles their first experience of marijuana. Paul McCartney, out of his head, thinks he's discovered the meaning of life and writes it down on a piece of paper. The next morning he wakes, reaches for the paper and unravels it to see the words – 'THERE ARE SEVEN LEVELS'.

Some joint that, Bob.

But it's worth pausing to wonder what may have gone through Dylan's head as he spent time with them. Could he sense that the sixties were about to take off? And if he did, then he must have realised that these four were his competition – that he would have to change again if he was going to keep up.

He then hears what The Animals have done with 'The House of the Rising Sun', a song from his debut album, and his mind is made up.

He gets to work on his fifth album. Turning again.

In just three days Dylan records *Bringing It All Back Home* – a mixture of acoustic and electric songs that set him up for the rest of his career. I repeat – in just three days. On the last day he recorded the final versions of 'Maggie's Farm', 'On the Road Again', 'It's Alright, Ma', 'Gates of Eden', 'Mr Tambourine Man' and 'It's All Over Now, Baby Blue'. All that, in one day.

It's the facts, not the story, that leave you dizzy.

Musically, it's a riot. Lyrically, it's a dream. And this time it isn't still photography, it's a blur. It's Dylan on the half turn – pulling away and taking his chance.

There's that line on 'Tambourine Man': 'To dance beneath the diamond sky, with one hand waving free, silhouetted by the sea.'

I can only imagine his face when he came up with that. One of his greatest images and, as always with Dylan, it's the detail that does it – the one hand waving free. It makes the song three-dimensional, as if he's stepped outside the verse to acknowledge his own gesture, his own victory.

The album's awash with moments like that.

While a lot has been made of the change in direction that *Bringing It All Back Home* represents, and its subsequent influence, what interests me is what happened to Dylan himself. You can see it most clearly in the promotional video for 'Subterranean Homesick Blues', filmed in an alley behind the Savoy Hotel in London.

An impassive Dylan stands on the side of the screen, tossing aside a shorthand version of the song written on cue cards. He doesn't sing, he doesn't even open his mouth. That's how interested he is in performing for us. But look at him, look how resplendent he is – how lean he is. Look at the change, how he's gone from a Huck Finn character to the coolest person on the planet – to the last person in the world that looks like he needs mothering.

He's taking his chance, grabbing the sixties by the scruff of the neck, and staring us down.

When he gets to the end, there's one last card.

It simply says '*WHAT?*'

It's the only card that doesn't represent a line in the song. He's ad-libbing, but deliberately, looking at his audience and saying '*WHAT?*' And then he throws that on the floor too and walks off without waiting for an answer.

Dylan on the half turn in 1965 – pulling away and taking his chance.

But honestly, you should see what he does next.

So, over to you Sam. Why haven't you listened to it? WHAT'S WRONG WITH YOU?????

Bringing It All Back Home came out in 1965 and so was conceived just before I was. How have I avoided it this long?

WELL. Every teenager has a singer-songwriter-shaped socket in their head. Mine was plugged by Dory Previn, whose records I stole from my da. My aural and political landscape was mostly her; I never reached the whiny male fields beyond.

In the summer of 1980, when my ears were born, I was played three records by a smart looked-up-to friend: *Colossal Youth* by Young Marble Giants, *Closer* by Joy Division and *Propaganda* by Sparks (they'd all still be on my top twenty list). He was also into Dylan, which lent Bob an early cachet. He had the collected lyrics in a book. Why didn't Dylan go onto the turntable then? I wish I knew. Sliding doors.

And why not since? Mystified Bob fans must understand that their mid-sixties man can be intimidating to the uninitiated; the albums are dense, and deserving of respect. Like the late Beethoven quartets, you come to them when you're ready.

Me, I saw *Harold and Maude* (which knocked a serious teen sideways), and so I got into Cat Stevens, a sort of Diet Dylan, and that was enough. I got my anti-establishment noises from punk and ska and Test Dept. US Civil Rights, seen through a Vaselined lens, took on a hazy glow. If I'd had my nose pressed more firmly up against the glass of America, I'd have persevered. But I caught the eighties disease of mistrusting most things American (which wasn't hard at the time, before US culture was quite so everywhere), and Dylan got tarred with that same brush.

So, sorry.

On the other hand, I get to discover him now, so here goes.

You've now listened to it at least three times, what do you think?

I wanted to do this properly, so I bought a nice heavy vinyl copy, stuck it on the turntable and poured myself a whisky. First thoughts: 'Is that a *chaise longue* on the cover? Not very rock 'n' roll. Who's that scarlet woman on it? Looks like Jessica Raine. I know it's not Joan Baez (did they have a thing?). Is she a muse, or a silent companion, like on the Mastermind box?'

Bringing It All Back Home by Bob Dylan

The First Pass: Meeting It All Head On. (Whisky: Ardbeg ten-year-old.)

Brief impressions: deceptively simple 8-bar blues of the sort I struggle through on the piano. Four-bar blues. Five-and-a-half-bar blues? Wit, wit, wit. Half rhymes! Punchlines! Bob's got problems. He's trapped. But in what? Simple recording, the man himself quite central. A tight band that rocks. Sticky tunes so good that the first time you hear them, you think you've heard them before.

Impossible to separate form and content. Does Dylan sing like that because he writes like that? Consistently arriving at each word just before the beat, giving the lines a terrible power. Listening on LP emphasises how much this is an album of two halves – the first electric, the second mostly acoustic. I knew there was a big row about Bob making music with stuff that had to be plugged into the mains. Couldn't see the problem myself. But the division is obvious, and the order of the tracks unarguably right. The whole inspired but not limited by Kerouac. Whassit all about, Bob? We don't know. He won't say.

Child comes in, knocks whisky over. Decide that the second pass two days later should be For the Words (Whisky: Caol Ila twelve-year-old.)

Is it cheating to look up lyrics online? I tried following a few songs like that, but oddly found I wasn't listening as carefully (which Bob maybe knew when he left out a lyric sheet) so I put down the iPad, went back and started again.

Could 'Subterranean Homesick Blues' really be by George Formby, as *The Day Today* once suggested? I remembered a jolly version from *The Young Ones* but nothing prepares you for the original two-minute-seventeen-second Dylan torrent. Taut, pushy, it's the song version of the glasses that allow you to see the world as it is in Carpenter's *They Live*.

Didn't the Weathermen, a US revolutionary collective, take their name from the line 'Don't need a weatherman to know which way the wind blows'? Blimey. Imagine having that sort of penetration – a danceable manifesto giving its name to a radical Communist movement. The times they have a-changed.

'SHB' is followed by its own B-side, 'She Belongs to Me'. She obviously doesn't. A portmanteau of Dylan girlfriends, their power anatomised in squirm-inducing detail; he later wished he hadn't written it. 'She can take the dark out of nighttime, and paint the daytime black... But you will wind up peeking through her keyhole down on your knees.' Yup, been there.

Who is this Maggie, who we met in track one? She's back and she's got a farm. Dylan couldn't know that Steve Bell would use 'Maggie's Farm' as the title of his *City Limits* cartoon strip, so maybe her farm isn't the military industrial complex by another name. I knew this was the track Dylan opened with at the Newport Folk Festival, in a very punchy electric version with the Butterfield Blues Band; they famously became the Butterfield Booed Band as soon as it ended. Bad manners, I think. Even if you think 'going electric' is 'going commercial', you have to allow an artist to do their thing. One of my favourite poets, the Palestinian Mahmoud Darwish, had the same struggle: activists wanted useful slogans they could chalk on buildings, he sometimes just wanted to write. Perhaps 'Maggie's Farm' is Bob bringing his electric chickens back home to roost. This idea became more important as I went along.

The last three tracks of side one, 'Outlaw Blues', 'On the Road Again' and 'Bob Dylan's 115th Dream' seemed to form a set, which I called The Funny Ones. They start off mocking the 'Woke up this morning/Had all the symptoms of typhoid' school of sixties blues. But despite the Gilliam silliness of 'Dream' with its giggling false start, they quickly turn from funny ha ha to funny peculiar, from on the run through the oddness of in-laws to nightmare surreality. The tale of Captain Arab and the Pope of Eruke (Irooq? Iraq?), listened to only a week after Trump's anti-Muslim nonsense, now had a prophetic flavour. Around the high harmonica scream that begins 'On the Road Again', it feels like 'where are we going?' becomes 'I have to get out of this place'. To which end, Bob Dylan, titling himself in the third person, flips a coin to decide whether to return to a ship and escape, or go back to jail (and perhaps help his imprisoned protest movement friends):

> It came up tails
> It rhymed with sails
> So I made it back to the ship

Can't help noticing that 'tails' is much closer to 'jail' than 'ship', Bob. You got the wrong flip, but you contrived to escape anyway. So ends the electric side. Dylan flips, and so do I.

Side Two was all recorded on 15 January 1965, which makes it possibly the greatest day's work ever. Except it starts with the only stain on this Parthenon of an album, 'Mr Tambourine Man'. Having spent side one saying 'I can go where I like', why go here? At first I found it foursquare and clumpy. The internal rhymes grated, Bruce Langhorne's bell-like electric lead guitar seemed over-present in the mix and Dylan's new Pied Piper muse was an annoyingly jangly little fucker, too close to *The Fast Show*'s Bob Fleming and the Bavarian excesses of Morris dancing for comfort. And it starts with a chorus, which is ODD.

The irony of the acoustic/electric row is that the electric band setting holds two purely acoustic jewels. Arriving at 'Gates of Eden', I thought, 'This is more like it.' First solo song on the album, a relentless nine verses. Listen to the way he sings 'No sound ever comes from the Gates of Eden' – nothing's getting in the way of that. Unapologetically ugly at times, bitten and savage, Dylan's 'Evidently Chickentown'. I took the lyrics as I found them, with no attempts to shovel the glimpse into the ditch of what each one means.

'Eden' softened me up for the knockout blow of 'It's Alright Ma (I'm Only Bleeding)', which is surely one of the most powerful noises ever committed to vinyl. The fancy guitar-picking sounded new, forensic and particular. It promised insight, and delivered. Dense, fast, depressed and depressing. And so elegantly concise. Very hard to choose one fridge-magnet line, but 'He not busy being born is busy dying' is worth the album price on its own. The tender need to hold and be held by Mother reminded me of Linton Kwesi Johnson's 'Sonny's Lettah'. That first harmonica sigh, a breath-made music, feels like air snatched above the rising sludge. The uneven length of the verses is vicious – each will go on just as long as it needs to, thanks. It's so boldly based around one note that, like 'Tomorrow Never Knows', all movement away from the tonic feels like only temporary relief. It's life and life only – a sentence that ends with death.

Then 'It's All Over Now, Baby Blue', the last song of last songs. A friendly walking bass giving a very false sense of security. Dylan's yelled, sweetly tired high notes are left undubbed. 'That's yer lot,' he seems to be saying. 'Get out there and live.'

At some point before the Third Pass (whisky: Lagavulin sixteen-year-old), having to listen to *BIABH* became wanting to listen to *BIABH*. A good sign.

Maybe it was the Lagavulin, but Dylan's voice had never sounded warmer than on 'Love Minus Zero', the whiny insistence of 'Maggie's Farm' and her skiffle friends delighted me, even the annoying tambourine chappy, protected by a harmonica break I hadn't really heard before, revealed himself in the last verse to be a gorgeous enchanter, and the weird guitar rush of 'Let me forget about today until tomorrow', where the Pro Plus kicks in and the disciple realises his safety dance can't last, made Bob sound touchingly human.

The easy, rolling accompaniment of the band now seemed like a velvet glove. The words punched hard, their stream-of-consciousness indulgence alarm silenced. I trusted Dylan the poet now. Again and again, as I examined the luggage of some freighted phrase, it unpacked itself and refused to go back in the box.

In the end, the reason I'd never heard this album before turned out to be the reason I enjoyed hearing it so much. It's *hard*.

Bringing It All Back Home by Bob Dylan

Would you listen to it again?

I already have.

A mark out of 10?

Reader, I loved it. I'm so glad you made me listen. I can't do the whole 'this is the best Dylan album, or the third best' thing, because I don't know many of the others either, but I did get a big fat kick from it.

So, because nothing is perfect, a very solid 9/10.

11

Meat Is Murder by The Smiths

1. The Headmaster Ritual
2. Rusholme Ruffians
3. I Want the One I Can't Have
4. What She Said
5. That Joke Isn't Funny Anymore
6. Nowhere Fast
7. Well I Wonder
8. Barbarism Begins at Home
9. Meat Is Murder

First time listener – Brian Koppelman

I'm a co-creator/executive producer/showrunner of the television series *Billions*. Before that I worked on a bunch of films like *Ocean's Thirteen*, *Solitary Man*, *Rounders*, *Runaway Jury*, *The Illusionist* and *I Smile Back*.

Before all that, I was executive producer of Tracy Chapman's first album.

Brian's top three albums

I could list three Bob Dylan albums, and I wouldn't be lying.
I could list three R.E.M. albums, and I wouldn't be lying.
I could list three Lou Reed albums, and I wouldn't be lying if one of them could be a Velvet Underground album.

Before we get to Brian, here's what Martin thinks of *Meat Is Murder*

My favourite origin story. I can't believe it's taken me this long to tell it.

Anyway.

An eighteen-year-old Johnny Marr is in need of a singer. Despite his young age, he's already been in a succession of failed bands. The usual story of the usual lads meeting up and giving it a go – giving it a go until it falls apart.

So he decides to turn it on its head.

He decides the rest of the band can wait. The bass, the drums, he'll get to them in due course. They're the easy bit. Before that, he needs a singer, a singer who can also write the songs and front the band.

And he's heard of someone.

Someone that he met briefly at a Patti Smith gig three years before but has never come across since. A slightly odd, enigmatic character who is unemployed, has few close friends and spends most of his time in his bedroom. Somehow Marr thinks this might be his man and, in either an act of desperation or the most inspired piece of recruitment ever, decides to just turn up, uninvited, at his house.

Taking a mate along for moral support, he boards the number 263 bus in Manchester, resplendent in his best clothes to try and make a good impression – vintage Levi's, biker boots and a US-style men's flying cap that sits back from a tinted quiff. Yes, a tinted quiff. Imagine seeing that on a bus in Manchester in 1982.

'Where's he off to then? With his tinted quiff.'

'Dunno, probably going to form some band called The Smiths who will go on to become the most influential group of their time and inspire a religious devotion among their legion of fans. Give it a couple of years, this bus will be full of tinted quiffs. Mark my words.'

'Oh.'

Anyway, Marr and his mate get off the bus, head to 384 Kings

Road and knock on the door. And nothing happens. They knock again. And nothing happens. Then, just as they're about to leave, they hear the footsteps of someone slowly coming down the stairs and eventually the door opens. And there he is, with a cardigan and a quiff of his own – the twenty-two-year-old Morrissey.

Now as much as I love this story, we have to leave it for a moment so I can just give you more of an idea of who it was that came down those stairs that day.

So here's the potted biography.

Like virtually all the pupils in his primary school, Morrissey failed his 11+ and was sent to a secondary modern school that specialised in preparing teenagers for the factory floor while simultaneously physically abusing them via an endless, and at times random, regime of corporal punishment. Basically that school in the film *Kes*. To save time, assume he went there.

While other pupils were seemingly hardened by the experience (there were accounts of some pupils fighting back and hitting the teachers) this definitely wasn't the case for our hero, delicate flower that he is. He hated it, every minute of it. One his classmates has since eloquently said:

'He was too clever for us. We were all fucking dur duro from the council estate fighting each other and robbing each other. He shouldn't have been in that school.'

Another classmate has said that the young Morrissey avoided the bullishness of the playground and, during breaks, just wandered around the school's corridors on his own, 'looking at things intently'.

Any attempt he made at social inclusion outside of school backfired too. He once went to watch Manchester United play and fainted because he thought George Best was beautiful. He once went to a fairground too, but someone head-butted him for no reason.

So, naturally, he withdrew into his shell and provided his own curriculum. And it's all the things we know and love about him – Oscar Wilde, British New Wave cinema, James Dean, Sandie Shaw, more Oscar Wilde, Republicanism, sixties girl groups, Feminism, The New York Dolls and Oscar Wilde. As a result, he leaves school with barely a qualification to his name but an exhaustive knowledge of the aforementioned subjects.

It's worth noting here how much Morrissey is a product of the education system of his time. Had he been born in the nineties it's reasonable to assume that he would have avoided the brutality and misery of a secondary modern and become one of the 40 per cent that now end up at university, where he could mix with like-minded souls and develop his interests further. No doubt he'd have done a degree in English literature and, instead of being the lead singer in The Smiths, he would now be working at *BuzzFeed* creating listicles of hamsters that resemble Lord Byron.

But he never goes to university. Instead, he goes from dead-end job to dead-end job, punctuated by large periods of unemployment. All the while his lifelines were music and writing. He becomes the scourge of the music press, dispatching missives from his bedroom about all the things that they're getting wrong, constantly writing letters to them and submitting his own reviews whether they want them or not – generally being an incorrigible pest. He also has a string of pen pals, relationships with people around the country, where he displays early evidence of the narcissism that his detractors are all too happy to accuse him of. He opens one of his letters with:

'So pleased that you enjoyed my last letter. Why don't you just admit that every word I write fascinates you?'

So here he is in 1982, a Lee Harvey Oswald character, a legend in his own mind if not quite in reality. A lonely, depressed, obsessive writer with an overdeveloped sense of his own destiny.

I'm not even joking with that comparison by the way. Look at these lines from Oswald's diary:

'Watch my life whirl away. I think to myself, "how easy to die" and a sweet death, (to violins).'

See what I mean?

If only a great guitarist had knocked on Oswald's door in November 1963, the course of history might have been different. Maybe they did, maybe he wasn't in.

Morrissey was in though. Of course he was. As he's said since with customary drama, 'I was just there, dying, and he rescued me.'

So here we are, back on the doorstep, and now you have more of an idea who came down the stairs that day.

Morrissey invites Marr in and they go up to his bedroom where he sees a life-size cutout of James Dean, a bookshelf full of Wilde, Delaney and Sillitoe, and a load of seven-inches from Cilla Black to The Fall. It's like Johnny Marr has walked into the bedroom of the biggest Morrissey fan in the world – which, in some respects, he has.

Marr picks out the B-side of a Smokey Robinson single, puts it on, and about an hour later they decide to form a band. Simple as that. The next time they meet, about a week later, they write 'The Hand That Rocks the Cradle' and 'Suffer Little Children'. Simple as that. They sit down and write two songs that will appear on the first album. Within a year of them meeting they've been signed by Rough Trade and their first single, 'Hand in Glove', is released.

It's incredible really, the extent to which there is no trial and error and nothing is discarded. They rush out of the blocks, two finished articles meeting each other and just getting straight down to it. Morrissey's lyrics and Marr's guitar – developed in isolation but coming together and working straight away. To put this into context, Lennon and McCartney met in 1957 and it took them five years to write *Love Me Do*. And, let's face it, Lennon and McCartney were not known for wasting their time.

Morrissey and Marr then audition a load of drummers who fail to impress until Mike Joyce turns up, powered by magic mushrooms, and wins them over with his 'energy'. Andy Rourke follows suit on bass shortly afterwards and there you have it – The Smiths. Marr got to them in due course, they were the easy bit.

Over the next five years, the time it took Lennon and McCartney to release one single, The Smiths release 108 songs, four studio albums, three compilation albums and a live album. A phenomenal level of output made all the more remarkable by how brilliant it is. In fact it's so good, so consistent, that the ten worst Smiths songs are better than any other band's ten worst songs – a bizarre award category that I acknowledge I've just made up to demonstrate EXACTLY how great they were.

On top of this recorded output they left a cultural mark too, which, ironically, took hold among the students of the colleges and universities that Morrissey himself missed out on. While their devotion was tribal, The Smiths were anything but. From the commonality of their name, the mundanity of their dress, all the way to their pure pop sound, they were entirely inclusive. Neither goth, nor punk, nor new wave – they defined 'indie' before it was even a term. They allowed people like me to dance with a cardigan stretched over my hands, with a fringe that covered a multitude of sins, with a load of other kids that were *different*, different just like me. Those halcyon days of the UK indie disco before 'Give It Away' by The Red Hot Chili Peppers brought along a load of kids wearing shorts, who mostly danced with their hair and generally ruined the whole thing because we were too soft and shy to do anything about it. The bastards.

But Morrissey. Our hero.

My dad absolutely hated him. Physically repulsed by a topless Morrissey, he once turned off *Top of the Pops*, complaining that he was trying to eat. But I loved him. Not in the religious, devotional way that Smiths fans are often accused of. I'm not vegetarian or celibate, and I've got huge issues with the film *Saturday Night Sunday Morning*. No, it wasn't any of the baggage. It was him, just him.

He was one of the greatest front men I've ever seen, having way more fun than all the other eighties pop stars. While his lyrics may have reflected a time when he was 'dying', the success and adulation that followed very much brought him to life. Ripping his shirt open and proposing, doing a pirouette with a load of flowers in his back pocket – Simon Le Bon wasn't doing any of that, was he?

No, of course he wasn't.

But Morrissey was. A teenage casualty that opened the door to a great guitarist and grasped his opportunity as if his life depended it. As if his very life depended on it.

And who even knows, maybe it did.

So over to Brian, why haven't you listened to it? WHAT'S WRONG WITH YOU??????

There's no way for me to talk about The Smiths without talking about R.E.M. first. Because R.E.M. saved my life.

Overly dramatic? Maybe. But as we are talking about The Smiths, I think overly dramatic is fine. Called-for, even.

And anyway, that's how it felt, nineteen years old, driving around freezing cold Boston, Massachusetts in a Jeep CJ-7 with broken windows, the music of Michael Stipe, Peter Buck, Bill Berry and Mike Mills the only thing keeping me from turning the damn thing right into the Charles River.

I had come to their records a bit late; *Fables of the Reconstruction* had just been released. Before, in high school, I was a heavy metal fan – Van Halen, Iron Maiden, AC/DC – and a fan of American rock and rollers like Bruce, John Cougar and Pat Benatar. But then, college, a bad breakup, driving through the snow in the busted-up Jeep, and a friend handing me *Murmur* with the following instructions: 'Put it on while you are doing something else, cleaning, studying, reading, and just let it kind of seep in. They'll become your favourite band.' (And no, it wasn't you, Martin, though it sure as fuck sounds as if it could have been.)

I did as ordered, the album did as promised, and R.E.M. and I were, forevermore, bound together.

From there, I dived headlong into The Replacements, The Cure, Hüsker Dü, and back into The Clash and Wire and The Velvet Underground and Lou and every other band of that lineage. Every other band, that is, except The Smiths. I avoided The Smiths with the same focused determination I used to avoid the girl who had put me in a perilous state of mind in the first place.

Here's why: I didn't think you were allowed to like both Morrissey and Michael Stipe. Somehow, I had got it into my head that they were rivals, that Morrissey, with his British intellect, witty literary references and arch demeanour, was staking a claim for voice of his generation, our generation, when I had already made the decision that Mr Stipe was that man.

This belief was reinforced when I'd come across an interview with Morrissey and look at pictures, or when I'd be at some concert and a guy with a God Save the Queen shirt would be standing next to me, posing as he smoked clove cigarettes, and acting as superior as I believed Morrissey would act were he standing there with us. I mean, sure, I was posing too, in my black jeans, black T-shirt, black boots way, but I knew deep down that I meant it. And he was just pretending.

As the years went on, my generalised antipathy for The Smiths dissipated. I'd see a picture of Stipe with Morrissey and think, 'huh'. When I'd hear The Smiths spun at a party or on the radio, I'd recognise Johnny Marr's brilliant playing, and when I'd catch a lyric, I'd smile, sometimes, and admit to myself that Morrissey was, in fact, every bit as clever as he thought he was.

But something in me, some vestigial unasked-for loyalty, prevented me from ever buying or streaming a Smiths album. Prevented me from ever really giving them a chance.

Until now.

You've now listened to it at least three times, what do you think?

The First Listen

I want to like this. That's the thought running through my brain as I slide the iPhone into its speaker cradle and hit play.

Then the music starts. Jaunty and emotional at the same time.

Meat Is Murder by The Smiths

I'm lying in bed, lights are off, it's late at night, and my plan is to allow the music to seep in as I drift off to sleep. I do this every night. Usually with my favourite bands playing. I start earlier than usual this time, because I am meant to actually listen to the entire thing before sleep. I succeed. But also fail. Which is to say that I do make it through every single song. But I also cannot make myself like it.

The voice, the affect, the whole thing grates on me. I can hear that it is a sturdy record. That the guitar playing is excellent, that the melodies are catchy, that the thing has a unified tone and is, distinctly, a work of art.

It just doesn't appear to be a work of art I like. Yet.

This is, after all, just the first listen.

The Second Listen

On a bicycle, riding downtown on the path adjacent to New York City's West Side Highway, the Hudson River and New Jersey to my right, all of Manhattan to my left.

Earbuds in, nothing to distract me from the music, nothing but Morrissey and me gliding along together.

This time, The Smiths sound like The Smithereens, only without the raucous urgency. And I realise that there is no garage rock influence on the band at all. The music I love often feels like it might come apart at the seams. This doesn't. It feels thought-out, planned, executed at a very high level. Boring. Even the folk music I love has a recklessness about it. It's missing here.

I ride on to my destination, starting to understand that it might not just be my atavistic dislike of Morrissey. I might just not like what The Smiths do.

The Third Listen

At home. On the couch. This time, with lyric sheet in front of me.

And it turns out that Morrissey, the lyricist, is my favourite part of the band. He is, without a doubt, every bit the wordsmith he thinks he is. Important subjects, deeply considered, personally revelatory and universally significant. I understand the lineage from which he comes, the poets from the past with whom he is engaging, the way it must have hit like-minded kids of the era.

I respect the fucking hell out of it. But I still don't actually enjoy it.

Would you listen to it again?
Nope.

But I wouldn't turn it off if you put it on.

A mark out of 10?
It is a record of high quality and purpose. And so an objective mark would be 8.

12

Pet Sounds by The Beach Boys

1. Wouldn't It Be Nice
2. You Still Believe in Me
3. That's Not Me
4. Don't Talk (Put Your Head on My Shoulder)
5. I'm Waiting for the Day
6. Let's Go Away for A While
7. Sloop John B
8. God Only Knows
9. I Know There's an Answer
10. Here Today
11. I Just Wasn't Made for These Times
12. Pet Sounds
13. Caroline, No

First time listener – Bonnie Greer

I was born on the South Side of Chicago, the eldest of seven children. My late dad was a young GI here in Britain for the D-Day offensive, a life-changing experience for a guy born in segregated Mississippi. I was raised a Roman Catholic kid and attended Catholic school – with a brief two-year hiatus in high-school until I got my undergrad degree from university.

I was active politically in high school and university – the first #blacklivesmatter generation. I was a Motown teen largely, and when *Pet Sounds* came out in 1966, I wouldn't have been there to greet it.

135

Ruth and Martin's Album Club

Bonnie's top three albums ever?

I have a lot of favourite albums, but if these three were played on my deathbed (they say hearing is the last sense to go) I'd be absolutely happy. They are:

Here Comes the Sun – Nina Simone

Nevermind – Nirvana

Sketches of Spain – Miles Davis

Before we get to Bonnie, here's what Martin thinks of
Pet Sounds

Welcome to the alternative history of The Beach Boys.

It begins with three brothers in California.

First up, there's Brian Wilson.

Brian was the oldest and liked nothing more than sitting in his room listening to music – despite being deaf in one ear. In particular, he was a huge fan of a harmony group called The Four Freshmen, and the first album he ever bought was brilliantly called *Four Freshmen and 5 Trombones*.

The Five Trombones weren't another band – there were just five trombones on the album.

Next in line, there's Dennis Wilson.

Dennis was smart, rebellious, and everyone fancied him because he was bloody gorgeous.

He also played drums and occasionally went surfing – the only one of the brothers that did. Remember that, it's sort of important.

Finally, bringing up the rear, there's Carl Wilson.

Carl, the youngest of the three, was basically ignored by everyone else on account of him being quiet and chubby. So, left to his own devices, he learned how to play guitar. In a strange quirk of fate, he was taught guitar by a local kid called John Maus who would go on to become the fella in The Walker Brothers who wasn't Scott Walker.

So there we have it, the three Wilson brothers.

Add an ambitious cousin called Mike Love, a friend called

Al Jardine, and a band started to take shape. It's probably worth mentioning here that Jardine, the only one who wasn't part of the family, was given his chance because Brian Wilson broke Al's leg once when playing football and felt like he owed him one.

In fact, you could say he got his big break after his… oh forget it.

The band initially started singing clean-cut doo-wop under a variety of silly names like The Pendletones and Carl and the Passions. However, they were just another group of kids that could sing, the type that make it to the house on *The X Factor* but then get booted off before the live shows. A local record label was on the verge of showing them the door for the last time, satisfied they had exhausted every angle, when suddenly Dennis piped up with a suggestion.

'How about surfing?' he said.

They looked up to see an excitable, and gorgeous, Dennis Wilson regaling them with stories of the local surfing scene. He buzzed about how it was the next big thing and all these local teenagers were listening to the surf report on the radio before planning their day around the size and location of the waves.

One minute they're saying goodbye to another failed prospect and then, out of the blue, he's got his foot in the door and starts banging on about surfing. And it wasn't just the label that were taken aback. The rest of the band were equally surprised at Dennis's last-ditch attempt to save the group.

Once he'd caught his breath, he said:

'Brian already has a song called "Surfin'". We could practise it for you and come back?'

Dennis had, remarkably, found the angle.

The label nodded their consent, seeing a ready-made audience in the scene that Wilson had described, and the band scurried off. It didn't matter that Dennis was the only one with any experience of surfing or that the other four, judging by their shirts, looked like they'd be more at home with an ironing board than a surf board. They sensed an opportunity and they weren't going to let small details get in the way.

The band rehearsed the song all weekend and went back to the label, who recorded it straight away. It was then released as a single and, without even consulting them, the label decided on a new name for the band – The Beach Boys.

It really is worth pausing here to take in what's just happened.

A fella has saved his band by suggesting they write a song about a relatively niche pastime – surfing. In fact, it's so niche that 80 per cent of the band have never done it before. Even though it sounds like the worst idea ever, *everyone* thinks it's the best idea ever, and the band are called The Beach Boys for the *rest of their career*!

I guess the equivalent would be a band that had never played Dungeons & Dragons but exclusively wrote songs about thirty-six-sided dice, dexterity scores, and how to keep your chainmail in good nick. And for good measure, they called themselves The Games Workshop.

They wouldn't stand a chance.

The Beach Boys, on the other hand, were on their way.

'Surfin'' was followed by 'Surfin' Safari' which was then followed by 'Surfin' USA'. By sticking to a winning formula (basically making sure the first word of every song is surfin') they became the biggest band in America before you could say 'bushy bushy blonde hairdo'. And they did it with joy and harmony – epitomising a way of life that was in tune with the elements and promising triple fun for everyone that joined them.

Such was the success of their sound, and their spirit, that they even had the nerve to start singing songs that had nothing to do with surfing at all. There were introspective ballads like 'In My Room' and, of course, there were the best Beach Boys songs of all – the car songs.

It's the sheer joy and excitement that cuts through. This is not about *the road*, that endless American obsession with an arduous journey to a mythical destination. No, these are kids who understand that the car itself *is* the destination and the thrill is just sitting still and admiring where they are – taking in the rubber, leather and chrome.

The message is simple and effective – 'I'M IN A CAR AND IT'S THE BEST THING THAT'S EVER HAPPENED TO ME'.

They're the only songs that make me want to learn how to drive.

It's probably also worth mentioning here that during this time in their career, The Beach Boys were responsible for some of the best opening lines ever. Here, in a quick detour from the story, are my top three:

3) 'Surfin' USA'

'If everybody had an ocean across the USA, then everybody'd be surfin', like Californi-a.'

I'm giving them top marks for managing to make California rhyme with USA there.

'Can we get away with that? Just separating the A so that it rhymes?'

'It's the least of our worries mate, none of us even surf.'

The only issue I have with the line is that there are 320 million people in America and if everyone really did have their own ocean it would be a bit like that *Waterworld* film starring Kevin Costner – i.e. terrible.

2) 'Little Deuce Coupe'

'I'm not bragging babe so don't put me down, but I've got the fastest set of wheels in town.'

Hmmm. Sounds like a massive brag to me, mate.

1) 'Help me Rhonda'

'Well since she put me down, I've been out doing in my head.'

Hands down, the best opening line to any song ever.

But back to the story…

As the early sixties inevitably turned into the mid-sixties, the band were influenced by a new wave of sounds. First, The Beatles came over and the entire country watched them on *The Ed Sullivan Show* singing songs that weren't about cars or surfing. Then Bob Dylan started to release a series of albums that were so good that Brian Wilson actually wondered whether he was out to destroy music with his genius.

And, if that wasn't enough, there was Phil Spector.

Spector had harnessed the power of the studio and started producing songs with layers upon layers of orchestration – mini symphonies that turned pop songs into epic dramas. When Brian Wilson first heard 'Be My Baby' by The Ronettes he sat with his face pressed against the speakers so he could feel the sound and the vibrations – a huge grin on his face as he let the immense sound wash over him.

In fact, he was so taken by what he had heard that he decided to quit touring and stay at home so he could play in the studio instead.

He informed the other Beach Boys of his decision, whereupon Al Jardine started to have stomach cramps and Dennis threatened to hit someone with an ashtray. Still, they quickly got over it and brought in a bloke called Bruce Johnston who looked a bit like Brian Wilson. Most people couldn't even tell the difference.

Free from the rigours of touring, Brian Wilson started to work on a new sound that relied on a vast array of session musicians and innovative studio techniques. You can first start to hear it around the time of 'California Girls'. Gone was Carl Wilson's simple Chuck Berry guitar and in its place were fourteen musicians playing all sorts of weird instruments. One of them was called a Vibraphone, which, if I'm being honest, conjures all sorts of unpleasant images.

Buoyed by his successes, and free from interference, Brian Wilson told his wife that he was going to make the best album ever. He recruited a lyricist called Tony Asher and they began to sketch a series of new songs, each one starting with a conversation – something to set a mood to write within. Wilson discussed a series of topics with his new partner – his childhood sweetheart, Carole Mountain; the temptation he had for his wife's sister; the optimism of young love versus, in his view, its pessimistic conclusion.

It's some shift, only a year before they were singing songs like this:

Tried Peggy Sue
Tried Betty Lou

Pet Sounds by The Beach Boys

Tried Mary Lou
But I knew she wouldn't do
Barbara Ann, Barbara Ann

Still, this was a new mood and the songs came thick and fast – 'God Only Knows' taking just twenty minutes, which is obviously the best use of twenty minutes by anyone ever.

Once the songs were complete they went to the studio and, with the help of over sixty musicians, they weaved the magic that you can hear today. Wilson was in charge throughout, meticulously conducting the disparate parts to realise his vision. There were so many people that even the most up-to-date release contains, at best, a guess as to who contributed what. My favourite entries from the liner notes, which are illustrative of the sheer weight of numbers on show, are as follows:

Ron Swallow – Tambourine (uncertain).
'Tony' – Sleigh bell.

The use of inverted commas around Tony has been making me laugh for about thirty-two years now.

Meanwhile, back in 1966, the rest of the band returned from Japan to overdub their vocal parts.

'Japan was great Brian, what have you been up to then?'

'I've just made *Pet Sounds*, lads.'

Carl Wilson then sang 'God Only Knows' at the age of nineteen and the rest of the group chipped in with their harmonies, despite some of them raising various objections about the change of direction. Mike Love said 'it sure don't sound like the old stuff', and, you know what, he was absolutely right about that.

Pet Sounds was released to moderate sales and only a distant fanfare. Lennon and McCartney heard it and went straight home and wrote 'Here, There, and Everywhere'. Andrew Loog Oldham took out a full-page ad in the *NME* and declared it the greatest album ever made.

Brian Wilson, meanwhile, took it home and played it in bed.

He was twenty-four years old and was overwhelmed by what he'd managed to produce.

As he listened to it, he cried his eyes out all the way through.

Which is where we bring the story to an end – Brian Wilson lying in bed with *his* sound washing over him.

For me, it's a joyous conclusion, one that celebrates the veneer and refuses to dig deeper – that tells a different truth to the other truths that are out there. It could just be me, but sometimes the journey doesn't have to be so arduous – it doesn't *always* have to be about the destination.

Sometimes you can just sit still and admire where you are.

Thanks for reading my alternative history of The Beach Boys.

So, over to you Bonnie. Why haven't you listened to it? WHAT'S WRONG WITH YOU?????

When I was a very young child, at the end of the fifties, we lived in a neighbourhood in the notorious Lawndale community on the city's West Side. It was gang-riddled and you had to watch your back. But in the midst of all that, in those days, there were doo-wop groups on every street corner. There were impromptu doo-wop contests, so I heard lots of falsetto, exquisite falsetto. Plus our local Roman Catholic Church had a superb Irish tenor who sang Low Mass every day before we went to class – Bach mostly.

Then, as a teen, it was Little Anthony and the Imperials; then Curtis Mayfield, Jerry Butler and The Impressions; the entire Motown stable; Mahalia Jackson in Gospel; Muddy Waters and Koko Taylor, the blues; my dad had Frank Sinatra albums; Johnny Mathis. There was Sam Cooke and Jackie Wilson; Dinah Washington, Miriam Makeba. Throw in the entire Civil Rights Movement – a big part of my growing up – and why would a kid like me listen to some California surfing dudes?

Plus… they just didn't look like they would know anything about me and my life. The Beach Boys were what was known as 'white bread' – clean-cut; nice lives. What would they know about segregation or gangs, or having to endure getting your hair chemically straightened every month?

If you watched TV – and I did a lot then – they were kind of all over it. I mean their ethos. They seemed to me to be that all-American dad, coming through the front door after a day at the office yelling: 'Honey, I'm home!', and mom emerging from the kitchen in a lovely dress, heels and pearls and the perfect meal ready.

'Surfin' USA' was their theme, not mine.

If my friends and I were going to the beach in those days, it was to de-segregate it.

That's the truth.

You've now listened to it at least three times, what do you think?

Let me start by saying that I'm a synaesthete. Synaesthesia is a cross-wiring in the brain in which several senses come together. Until about a decade ago, I thought that everyone heard music the way I do: I see images… whole movies even, sometimes in colour and sometimes with their own smell. So needless to say, listening to any music is not a simple experience for me. Which is why I have instinctively avoided *Pet Sounds*.

And was quite right to do so!

Let me take you into my world. I'll start at the bottom and take you to the top:

1. The barking dogs almost made me want to commit homicide. I'm still shaking. I get it, but it's so jarring, so thrown-in. The train. It really jarred me because Wilson felt to me like he was tripping. I read later that he was experimenting, and it's all over some of these instrumental sections. I can understand why it didn't chart well in America at the time because those bits seem careless, and a loss of control compared to everything else. Horrid.

2. The instrumental segments… made me wonder if Burt Bacharach had listened to them and created his Broadway show *Promises,*

Promises out of them. I'm saying this as a compliment. If Wilson had gone on to write for Broadway, just with those bits he would have been a zillionaire. I don't know where they come from, or how they came to be. They're just there – out of the blue and quite, quite amazing. It still blows my mind hours after hearing it. Very skilful, and throw away all at the same time.

3. Now to the masterpieces:

   a) The minor one: 'Sloop John B'
      Frankly, if you ever want to know what the folks who flock around Donald Trump have playing in their brains – it's this. This is Middle America (I almost said 'the whole shooting match'!), the thing-that-they-are. Wilson nailed it and that's why everybody in America at the time was singing it. Even me at times. Real sing-along 'God Bless America' stuff with those gorgeous harmonies.

   b) 'Caroline, No'
      Exquisite. It's about being a guy on the edge of manhood. In love with a girl. This is the stuff sixteen-year-old guys feel and you know it as a sixteen-year-old girl, and you also know that you have the upper hand. It's really naked; keening. Perfect.

   c) 'God Only Knows'
      In Sonnet 43 Shakespeare writes:

      When most I wink, then do mine eyes best see,
      For all the day they view things unrespected;
      But when I sleep, in dreams they look on thee …

      The pop version of that sonnet is 'God Only Knows'. For me, this was a piece of cinema, so I don't have the space to talk about it. But it's a singer's K2 of emotion; control; picture painting; mood-setting. Out-there and beyond. It's about a human being trying to save their life and it pulls no punches. Really surprised that my idols: Nina; Miles; and Kurt never covered it. Would have been great to hear what they would have done with it.

Would you listen to it again?
Not soon. No. It's too much for my brain, really.

A mark out of 10?
If you can take it: a 9.

13

Ram by Paul McCartney

1. Too Many People
2. 3 Legs
3. Ram On
4. Dear Boy
5. Uncle Albert/Admiral Halsey
6. Smile Away
7. Heart of the Country
8. Monkberry Moon Delight
9. Eat at Home
10. Long Haired Lady
11. Ram On
12. The Back Seat of My Car

First time listener – Martin Carr

Daydreamer, ex of The Boo Radleys. Writes songs but has still to write a really good one, tick tock tick tock.

Martin's top three albums ever?

Liquid Swords – GZA
Johnny in the Echo Chamber – The Aggrovators
Violent Femmes – Violent Femmes

Before we get to Martin, here's what Martin thinks of *Ram*

It's September 1969 and McCartney tries to cajole The Beatles into one last hurrah.

He suggests a tour of small clubs, their first live dates since 1966, in the hope they'll rediscover their confidence and reignite their spark. He even floats the idea of a pseudonym, that they could turn up unannounced and play under the worst name ever – Rikki and The Redstreaks.

It's unclear who was down to play the part of Rikki.

Lennon looks at him like he's mad.

'I think you're daft,' he says, 'I'm leaving the group. I want a divorce.'

And that was that – the beginning of the end for The Beatles.

They'd played over 800 hours in Hamburg, 292 times at the Cavern, and recorded thirteen albums in seven years – the majority of which took place in just one room that saw the recording of virtually everything from *Please Please Me* to *Abbey Road*, with barely a pause in between.

But now it was over. Lennon had his own Plastic Ono Band to get on with and McCartney had been spat out of the whirlwind. Remarkably, he was only twenty-seven when it happened – The Beatles done and dusted and he's not even technically in his late twenties yet.

It's worth noting that for all the documentation and analysis of this part of McCartney's life, his perspective is entirely different – completely unique. He was the other side of the lens, living the life that was being captured and all the bits in between that weren't. By all accounts his memory of these years is sketchy, his knowledge lacking compared to the fans that have pored over the record since – his own recollection different to the snapshots, or lost in the living.

I once read an interview with him where he was asked about meeting Muhammad Ali and the famous photo where Ali appears to knock out The Beatles. McCartney couldn't even remember it and the interviewer had to show him the photo as evidence that it happened.

As I said, a whirlwind life up to this point – so much so that he kind of forgot the time he had a bit of a laugh with Muhammad Ali.

But back to 1969. The Beatles have run their course but decide to keep it a secret until *Let it Be* is released further down the line.

For the first time in years – a pause in the action.

McCartney, in a state of depression and anxiety, takes his wife and children to High Park Farm – a rundown farmhouse on a hill, in the middle of a misty Scottish nowhere. With the rarity of nothing to do, he hits the bottle, the drugs, and ends up playing rhythm gardener to Linda's lead. And, in time, it's Linda that starts to pull her husband together – taking his mind off The Beatles' split and occupying him with household chores and projects of renovation.

For Christmas Linda buys Paul a tractor, which must have been the hardest present in the world to wrap.

For Christmas Paul buys Linda twelve pheasants, which must have been the hardest pheasants in the world to wrap.

Still, they grow into their countryside selves and put their troubles behind them. Paul makes use of his tractor to plough a vegetable patch where he grows runner beans, turnips, potatoes and spinach. He also builds a basic four-track studio in the farmhouse which he names The Rude Studio and starts writing songs again. Imagine an early episode of *Grand Designs* but the subject has a drink problem and has just left the biggest band in the world.

However, just as everything is starting to go well, stories appear in the press that Paul McCartney is actually dead.

A rumour that had started in a student paper in Iowa has, bizarrely, taken hold among people that are enjoying the sixties too much. According to the 'legend', McCartney had stormed off from a Beatles session in November 1966 and crashed his Aston Martin – decapitating himself in the process. Rather than just admitting that McCartney had died, the surviving Beatles apparently staged a secret Paul McCartney lookalike contest which was subsequently won by a Scottish fella called William Campbell. He then underwent some plastic surgery, because it turned out he didn't look that much like Paul McCartney after all, and joined the band.

Now, as luck would have it, Campbell turns out to be something of a genius and writes most of *Sgt. Pepper*, comes up with the idea for *Magical Mystery Tour*, and more than shares the load on *The White Album*, *Let It Be* and *Abbey Road*. An unbelievable result for everyone involved, not least Campbell, who thought he was just entering a lookalike contest. In fact the whole enterprise is so successful, The Beatles so improved by Campbell's introduction, that it makes you wonder why they didn't stage a Ringo lookalike competition straight away.

Maybe they did.

In short, the 'Paul is dead' stuff is the worst/best conspiracy theory ever. The worst because it's obviously total nonsense and none of the supposed 'clues' are clues at all; the best because I read about a bloke once who studied McCartney's bass playing after November 1966 and he convinced himself, and me for ten minutes, that it wasn't the same man who was playing bass before November 1966.

Notwithstanding the obvious flaws in the theory, though, it is prevalent enough in late 1969 for *Life* magazine to dispatch one of their reporters to the Scottish Highlands to see if McCartney is dead after all. They find him, somewhat dishevelled and surprised, strolling across the land with his family, his stepdaughter Heather looking like she is about to attack anyone that comes near them.

McCartney agrees to an interview, whereupon he declares the 'Beatle thing is over', a huge scoop that somehow gets lost in among the bigger news – i.e. that he isn't actually dead. It's one of the strangest aspects of the whole Beatles story – the first public announcement that they've split up doesn't even make the front page.

Feeling recuperated, almost back to his old self, McCartney decides to travel back to his home in London to start recording his first solo album, with a four-track the size of a fridge that he wheels to his house from Abbey Road. The resulting album, brilliantly titled *McCartney*, is scheduled to be released in April 1970 via Apple.

And that's when his problems with the rest of The Beatles go from bad to worse.

Ram by Paul McCartney

Lennon and Harrison write a letter and make Ringo hand deliver it to McCartney. The letter states that Apple won't be releasing *McCartney* in April because they want to release *Let It Be* first, and there's also a Ringo Starr solo album to consider.

The letter ends with – 'We're sorry it turned out like this – it's nothing personal. Love, John and George'.

For McCartney, though, it's the final straw and he mentally breaks with the rest of The Beatles for good, telling Ringo Starr to fuck off out of his house in the process. He also stands his ground on the release date, ensuring that *McCartney* is released in April 1970 as planned. It's *Let It Be*, The Beatles' final album, which actually gets pushed back. With the release of *McCartney* comes an accompanying press release in the form of a Q&A where he again reiterates that The Beatles are over and he has no interest with working with Lennon again.

And this time the story catches on. Front pages everywhere – 'Paul quits The Beatles'.

Despite Lennon quitting nearly a year before, despite Harrison and Starr having previously walked out on the group on separate occasions, it is McCartney who is set in stone as the villain of the piece – as the man responsible for the breakup of The Beatles.

Haunted by his part in the drama, McCartney then starts to have weird dreams about Allen Klein, the new Machiavellian Beatles manager and actual villain of the piece. In the dreams, Klein is a demented dentist chasing McCartney around with a massive hypodermic needle – trying to 'put him out' for good. And when he isn't dreaming about Klein and big needles, he's reading interviews with the rest of The Beatles where they tear into him and his new album.

Lennon, in an interview with *Rolling Stone*, said McCartney led The Beatles round in circles after Epstein's death, that his new solo album was rubbish, and that his former partner was all form and no substance.

Ever since, an image has been formed of McCartney as a sly control freak who took his ball because he couldn't get his own way.

History gets re-written, battle lines are drawn. Lennon was the true 'genius' and McCartney the teacher's pet with an unhealthy obsession with vaudeville and classical middle eights. Most bizarre of all, though, a man who literally had more sex, drugs and rock 'n' roll than almost anyone somehow gets painted as a square – the very opposite of that most tiresome of clichés.

McCartney had left The Beatles and, in the eyes of many, had suddenly become a dark version of Rodney Bewes out of *The Likely Lads*.

So he goes all in.

He files a lawsuit to dissolve The Beatles partnership once and for all and flies to New York to start work on *Ram*, his second album – with a bunch of musicians hired in secret by Linda. The resulting album again gets slaughtered by critics and ex-Beatles alike. Lennon admits that he likes bits of 'Uncle Albert/Admiral Halsey' but the rest of the album is awful. Even Ringo weighs in, giving the following review:

'I don't think there's one tune on *Ram*. I just feel he's wasted his time. He seems to be going strange.'

Worth noting here that this is the same Ringo Starr who had just released an album called *Beaucoups of Blues*.

But never mind, as I said battle lines had been drawn and McCartney couldn't get a break. It's tragic really. The ganging up, the accusations, that awful scene in Lennon's *Imagine* when the rest of The Beatles get together and sing 'How Do You Sleep?' about their former bandmate. It would have been hard enough following The Beatles with a fair wind, but under these circumstances?

He didn't stand a chance.

Everyone reviewed the context and a genuinely great album was ignored, an album of total joy and optimism – a joyride of drunken newlyweds on the run. It stretches and it yawns, it springs into life and takes you everywhere but ultimately nowhere. For all its flights of fancy it remains rooted – pinned down by the familiarity of its sheer 'McCartney-ness'. Because that's what *Ram* is, the

Ram by Paul McCartney

triumphant sum of its one individual part – the glorious result of pure, uncut McCartney.

He seems happy here. He seems at his very best.

After *Ram* is released he returns to England and wins the first battle in court to formally end The Beatles. The day after the verdict Lennon, Harrison and Starr drive round to McCartney's London home in a white Rolls Royce and throw bricks through his window.

It had come to this. The greatest story ever told had reached the grubbiest of ends. The 800 hours in Hamburg, the 292 gigs at The Cavern, and the thirteen albums in seven years that were mostly recorded in one room.

All that was over and the only one who seemed free, if only for forty-three minutes, was Paul.

So, over to you Martin. Why haven't you listened to it? WHAT'S WRONG WITH YOU?????

It came out when I was two and a half. I was living in Thurso and everybody was more interested in the new lifeboat. I do have a memory of being in a big old pram outside my nan's house in Manchester and 'Hey Jude' being on the radio and my Uncle Christopher's voice saying 'Beltin' song, is this.' I might have made that up but, if I did, I made it up when I was very small so it's the same thing.

Anyway...

At the age of twelve, me and my friend Sice were Beatles daft. It wasn't cool but who needs cool when you're in love? His next-door neighbours were a young couple with a baby and sometimes we would watch the baby while they popped out and did fuck knows what. They had a record player and records and one of those records was the first Paul McCartney album, the enigmatically titled *McCartney*. On it went, we didn't like it and the baby cried. Once the neighbours had returned from doing fuck knows what we went back to Sice's and I decided there and then that I wasn't interested in the solo careers of John, Paul, George or Ringo. My mum bought me *Tug of War* for

Christmas a year later, I had really liked 'Take It Away' and I played the album to death, not because I loved it but because it's what you did then. I haven't listened to it since then but I can remember all of it. 'Here Today' is the best track, but you know that. Somebody played me *McCartney II* once, didn't like it much.

'But what about "Temporary Secretary"?'

What about it?

Never liked Wings, Sice used to play *Band on the Run* a lot on the tour bus. I would go to my bunk and listen to something else. I love The Mull though, The Mull rules. Confused? Me too.

My Uncle Chris had the Lennon comp *Shaved Fish* and I would listen to that when I was at my nan's house. It's pretty good, I've got his first two albums and they have their moments but I've never made it through any of his others. There's something missing. I don't listen to George Harrison's *All Things Must Pass*, it's too long, most of the songs aren't that great and I hate the way it's mixed. Also, there's something missing. One day my dad brought home his 1979 album, the enigmatically titled *George Harrison*. It's awful, I didn't play it to death. I've never listened to a Ringo album, I like 'It Don't Come Easy' but who doesn't?

What is missing on those albums are the other three. It took four men to make that magical and spiritualistic brew, Mouth of John, Eye of Paul, etc. On their own, they have no hold over me. I will always love them for the pleasure they bring me, even now, but I can't be bothered to listen to their albums. A friend of mine took me to see McCartney a couple of years ago (I don't like gigs at the best of times, I like records) at the O2, the tenth circle of hell. I was charged twelve grand for a large whiskey and had to sit next to Kasabian. Then Paul McCartney came on and systematically and with malice aforethought brutalised his best songs, right there in front of me, on my bloody birthday. 'WHAT THE FUCK ARE YOU DOING?' I screamed.*
He took those dreams, those precious jewels and turned them into meat 'n' two veg clogalongs. 'THEY'RE NOT ROCK SONGS, YOU

Ram by Paul McCartney

IDIOT' I yelled.* I hated it, all sixteen hours of it. The next day a few of my friends texted to say they'd seen me on the big screens looking really miserable while everyone else sang and clapped.

Kasabian loved it.

So, the short answer is I haven't listened to it because I don't think I'll like it. Because it'll probably be full of rubbish like 'Teddy Boy' and 'Mrs Vandebilt'. Because life's too short and if it was any good I'd have heard it by now.

*later, into my pillow

You've now listened to it at least three times, what do you think?

I was going to listen to it while I tidied my studio, it's a proper tip. But I spent most of the album looking through a box of old photographs that once belonged to my grandfather, Jim. I don't listen to records the first time I play them, I put them on and do something else. I let them breathe. I introduce them to the room and the room to them, see how they get on. I was calm, sober and straight. It seemed to go on a bit but nothing stood out as being particularly unpleasant, I remained calm and happy with my photographs and the room was pulsing good vibes. I recognised 'Dear Boy' from Simon Love's (excellent) album, *It Seemed Like a Good Idea at the Time* and the single 'Uncle Albert/Admiral Halsey' but, to my surprise, nothing else. 'Uncle Albert' is a song that has always annoyed me, I love the beginning and the arrangement but it goes somewhere else and kills the mood. In my twenties I used to take acid and listen to *Bitches Brew* but in my late forties I'm getting a powerful kick out of listening to 'Uncle Albert' while looking at faded photographs of long-dead members of my family.

I listened properly the next morning. I sat in front of it and played it loud. My God, what a fool I've been, what a joy this record is. There's hardly any of the twelve-bar I was expecting and there isn't a twee moment to be found. I adore the first bars of 'Too Many People', his beautiful tramp voice over those fab four chords into *Pet Sounds* snare hits. Honey to my bee. Lyrically he sounds like he's kicking some demons around, eating apples, settling scores and having a ball doing it. *Ram* sounds like it was recorded at 9:12 a.m. amid a sea of sunflowers under a hazy sun. It's high as monkeys, full of itself and oh my, what a fool I've been. 'Ram On' sounds like the whole of the Department of Eagles album *In Ear Park* (which I love) and 'Uncle Albert' is fine as it is, all of it. I'm not that bothered about 'Eat at Home'. 'The Back Seat of My Car' is like a track off the Beach Boys album *Friends* except better, much better. It's one of his best songs and I've never heard it.

Third time, I take it downstairs. I light candles. I dress smart and bring gifts. I'm in love and oh what a fool I've been. I'm uplifted, uploaded and upended. His singing is great, the musicians are right on the money and the sound is perfect (it is a truth that all records made in the early 1970s sound fantastic). I buy an original German pressing off eBay, I wrestle the cat to the ground by the ears and get one of the kids to take a photo. I grow a beard and wheel around the room. I wonder about all the other old records I've never listened to, the treasures I've denied myself. 'Monkberry Moon Delight' is a screamer, is it about weed? I buy some, just in case. There's not as much Linda as I thought but I like everything she does. There's so much going on I still can't take it all in. It's the kind of record I should have been playing to death in my teens when the days stretched out and things-to-do were for other people. It's a fist-clenched cry of emancipation, an epic blast. He's unapologetic, free to be himself without anybody sneering or asking why. He's confident, swaggering, unbowed. I love him. *Ram* is so far up my alley, he could reach into my mouth and sign the sleeve.

What a fool I've been.

Would you listen to it again?
Nah.

Ram by Paul McCartney

A mark out of 10?

Knock a couple of tracks off and it's a 10, so 9, but I don't know which tracks I'd knock off so let's call it 9 and a bit.

14

Harvest by Neil Young

1. Out on the Weekend
2. Harvest
3. A Man Needs a Maid
4. Heart of Gold
5. Are You Ready for the Country
6. Old Man
7. There's a World
8. Alabama
9. The Needle and the Damage Done
10. Words (Between the Lines of Age)

First time listener – Brian Bilston

I write poetry but I (and others) would hesitate to call myself a poet. I write about the stuff of everyday life, with a particular emphasis on buses and bin days. My first collection of poetry, *You Caught the Last Bus Home*, is now available.

Brian's top three albums ever?

Hatful of Hollow – The Smiths
Different Class – Pulp
Doolittle – Pixies

Before we get to Brian, here's what Martin thinks of *Harvest*.

So much happens here, until the very best part – when nothing happens at all.

Let's begin with a whistle-stop tour of Neil Young's childhood.

1) He was born in Toronto in 1945 and, by all accounts, was a bit chubby and grinned a lot.

2) He then contracted polio at the age of five and it looked like he might die. I know, that escalated quickly didn't it?

3) Fortunately he survived and, at the age of ten, decided he wanted to be a farmer and raise chickens. He even saved up his pocket money and bought a coop.

4) He swapped the coop for a guitar when he heard Elvis Presley and Chuck Berry on a local radio station called CHUM.

5) CHUM is the best name for a radio station ever and, while not integral to the story, I thought it was worth mentioning and dedicating a whole point to.

6) His family were constantly travelling and he ended up going to something like eleven or twelve schools as a result. That's basically a school every year, which is a bit mental. Eventually he dropped out in the eleventh grade, having decided that school wasn't really for him. He would know, to be fair – he tried loads of them.

And this is where we pick him up.

He's sixteen years old and walking at six-foot-three with an air of detachment befitting someone whose chicken-farming days are behind him.

So he gets busy.

After a short-lived spell in an instrumental band called The Squires, Young hits the road as a solo artist under the influence of Bob Dylan. What follows is a series of impromptu performances at Canadian folk clubs and coffee houses. He's a fleeting figure with a guitar strapped to his back and sideburns that had taken on a life of their own. Along the way he meets Stephen Stills and Joni Mitchell for the first time and on his nineteenth birthday he writes 'Sugar Mountain' – a song he must have known was a bit special.

His own image of himself at the time is of someone walking around in the middle of the night in the snow, wondering where to go next – always with another destination in mind. On the one hand he's thrilled at the troubadour life he's living, while on the other he naturally worries where it will all lead to as each year passes without any sign of breaking through.

Enter an admirer to give him a hand.

A bass player called Bruce Palmer was so taken by the sight of Neil Young just walking down the street that he introduces himself and suggests a jamming session.

Simple as that – 'That tall fella looks dead cool, I wonder if he wants to come back to mine and be in a band with me?'

It worked though. Young went back to Palmer's house and, before long, they formed a band called The Mynah Birds, with a young black singer called Rick James. In keeping with the breakneck pace of this story they somehow got signed to Motown just three weeks after their first gig and were on their way to Detroit to record their first album.

But then disaster struck, which is why you're not reading a piece about The Mynah Birds' classic debut album.

Firstly, their manager overdoses on heroin. Secondly, their singer is arrested and jailed after it was discovered that he was a deserter from the Navy. Neil Young returns to Canada a dejected figure and, in what must have been his lowest ebb, he is then beaten up while hitchhiking and left unconscious in a ditch. When he eventually comes round, he decides to hit the road again.

He sells everything he owns, buys a hearse and drives to LA to seek out an old friend – Stephen Stills.

It's here that his next band, Buffalo Springfield, are formed. Despite being named after a particular type of steamroller they quickly cause a stir within the LA garage rock scene and are soon playing alongside contemporaries like Love and The Doors. They even have a huge hit, the Stephen Stills-penned 'For What it's Worth', which was quickly adopted as *the* anti-war anthem of its time.

Success, but it's far from perfect.

Stephen Stills is very much the boss and, to make matters worse, he often wore a cowboy hat. Young naturally rebels and feels that the band are not the best outlet for his vision – despite the fact that he was turning out brilliant songs of his own like 'Burned' and 'Mr Soul'. It's also at this point that he experienced his first epileptic seizure and was put on medication that made him even more moody and withdrawn than he was anyway. After a couple of albums, multiple arguments with Stills and a seizure live on stage, Young decided to quit Buffalo Springfield for good in May 1968.

You'd think he'd relax for a bit now, be a bit more Neil Young and take it easy. But no, he's on the move again.

Over the next eighteen months he releases two solo albums, forms a new backing band with a bunch of tough guys called Crazy Horse, and starts hanging around with the singer-songwriter and would-be serial killer Charles Manson. At one point he even tries to convince Warners to sign Manson in what would have been the worst decision by a record company since Motown decided to sign The Mynah Birds.

Inexplicably, he also decides working with Stephen Stills again is a good idea and joins the board of the worst firm ever – Crosby, Stills and Nash. Why he thought this was a good idea is anyone's guess and the inevitable happened straight away. Not only was he clashing with Stills, but now he had to put up with Crosby as well – the pair of them taking so much cocaine that they once considered calling the band The Frozen Noses.

Can you think of anything worse?

OK – Crosby, Stills, Nash, Young and Manson would be worse, but you get my point.

After one album that took over 800 studio hours to complete, the band descended into a predictable haze of drugs and competing egos. When Nash ran off with a woman that Stephen Stills fancied the band thankfully broke up for good – but not before Neil Young had wasted a load of time on them and some more great songs like 'Helpless' and 'Ohio'.

He momentarily returns to Crazy Horse, but after seeing them beset with drug problems of their own he finally decides it would be best for everyone if he stopped messing about with a load of dysfunctional bands and just became Neil Young Solo instead.

He's starting to slow down. He's getting there.

In September 1970, he releases the brilliant *After the Gold Rush* and celebrates by moving to a big isolated ranch in LA. And finally, it's here that it happens – the pivot from which the whole story revolves.

While moving some slabs of polished walnut, Neil Young does his back in and spends the next few months in bed.

At last, we now have him where we want him.

After a lifetime of perpetual motion and bad company he finally takes shelter in solitude and inactivity – it's the part where nothing happens, where he takes time out and just reflects. He doesn't even have the strength to lift his electric guitar so he has to play an acoustic instead. And the songs start pouring out of him – songs about the old man that lived on the ranch, the friends he'd seen ravaged by drugs and, best of all, a song about a lonely boy who just packed it all in and went down to LA. Gone was his clawhammer style, his wild abandon, and, in their place, was a sparse finesse that suited the material perfectly.

It's the sound of someone recuperating – not just from his present ailment but from everything that had come before.

He now just needs an opportunity to do the songs justice in the studio and, again, a happy accident provides the solution.

In February 1971, Young travels to Nashville to appear on *The Johnny Cash Show* and, while in town, has dinner on the Saturday night with a producer called Elliot Mazer. Throughout the dinner Mazer tries to convince Young to record his next album in his studio. After the meal Young effectively says, 'OK, ready when you are.'

Mazer probably thought that meant they were going to schedule a slot in the studio for some future date but Young actually meant he was *ready*, i.e. let's do it now. Mazer makes a few calls to see who was about and rounds up a bunch of local session musicians including Kenny Buttrey, who had played drums on *Blonde on Blonde*. The bass player was found because he just happened to be walking down the street at the time – a great example of why you should never stay in on a Saturday night. They went to the studio and started recording *Harvest* – THAT EVENING!

How mad is that? One minute you're having dinner and the next minute, completely unplanned, you're recording one of the best albums ever.

'Oh but hang on, who can we get to play drums?'

'Will the fella who played on *Blonde on Blonde* do?'

'Of course he will!'

But look, the whole thing gloriously comes together. Young is in charge like never before, working with a bunch of musicians who are content to play from the sides. Everyone does as they are told and they do it *really* quickly – most songs being completed in just a couple of takes. Any attempts at virtuosity and showmanship are outlawed in favour of a sound that is simple yet beautifully effective. On the song 'Harvest', for instance, Buttrey plays the whole thing with one hand, yet it's some of the best drumming you'll ever hear.

After the sessions in Nashville, Young enlists the help of the London Symphony Orchestra while on a visit to the UK and records a couple of songs with electric guitars in a massive barn on his ranch. Unbelievably, he invites Crosby, Stills and Nash along to provide some backing vocals.

Once the album is finished Mazer sets up a huge outdoor stereo system with one stack of speakers in the barn and another in Young's house. He then plays it to Neil Young while he's rowing in a nearby lake.

Young, from his boat, shouted, 'More barn!'

It's the image that sums the whole thing up for me – Neil Young having a massive laugh while listening to his new album on a lake.

While some critics have accused *Harvest* of being compromised, I prefer to see it as pure – as the work of a man who was forced to slow down and enjoy the sound of his own company. Glistening and still, it represents a noble ambition: that doing nothing can be productive, and being busy can get you nowhere.

Harvest by Neil Young

That's the album in a nutshell, the luxury it affords – the imposition of time and space, from the artist to the listener.

And it's why I love it so much. Because, whatever I'm doing when I hear it, it always slows me down.

So, over to you, Brian. Why haven't you listened to it? WHAT'S WRONG WITH YOU?????

My life is a litany
of things unachieved,
unbegun tasks, unfinished deeds;

the unwritten novels
and untaken goals,
unfulfilled words, unfilled holes,

jobs unhad
and places unbeen,
unchosen paths, unfollowed dreams,

unseen films, plays, artists,
and all that unlistening to
Neil Young's *Harvest*.

But why? Such reasons
are long since lost
to the passing of the seasons.

Maybe I saw him wearing a hat.
I never like it
when musicians do that.

Or did I think it rather
the sort of thing
liked by my father,

some kind of AOR accident,
a middle of the road spill
on the Highway to Grownupville.

For I have never held
much stock
by either country or rock,

it said nothing to me
about my life
and besides, I was busy

in my unachieving prime.
I had *so much* not to do
and so little time.

You've now listened to it at least three times, what do you think?

Out on a weekday, earplugs in,
iPod synced in to my plod,
preparing for the worst.

The opening bars plod along, too,
catch up with me and, together,
we head into the verse.

His tenor comes to greet me
with the resignation
of the condemned

Harvest by Neil Young

and I listen in close
to the words he's penned
See the lonely boy out on the weekend

and it's then that I know
I have a new friend.

You made me feel, Neil Young.
You made me feel as though spring had *not* sprung.
You made me feel when your songs were sung.

And although I thought
I would never be ready for the country,
I became a harvester,

went out into the fields,
reaped, gathered, stored.
A few crops left me bored

but I brought them in anyway,
and grew to love them over the days.
Because a man needs some maize.

But others rippled proudly
in golden fields
and those I played loudly

until pins and needles begun
to tickle my ears,
and the damage was done.

I carried these songs inside,
having chopped them down
with my scythe,

and though I wonder
what my young self
might have thought,

I've been in my mind,
it's such a fine line
that keeps me searching

for a heart of gold
and now that I'm getting old,
I think I'm getting Young.

Would you listen to it again?

I'm all out of poems now, thankfully.

Yes, absolutely. I found it something of a ragbag of an album but, almost in spite of itself, it somehow seems to hang together. The highs when they come are glorious and I can see myself returning to this many times.

A mark out of 10?

8.

15

Setting Sons by The Jam

1. Girl on the Phone
2. Thick as Thieves
3. Private Hell
4. Little Boy Soldiers
5. Wasteland
6. Burning Sky
7. Smithers-Jones
8. Saturday's Kids
9. The Eton Rifles
10. Heatwave

First time listener – Shabana Mahmood

Labour MP for Birmingham Ladywood; born and bred Brummie, practising Muslim, cooker of Kashmiri cuisine, weight-training addict, recovering Netflix-holic and lover of all things Marvel.

Shabana's top three albums ever?

Oh the pressure of a list with the words Top and Ever. After (too) much deliberation, a fair amount of stress, and feelings of guilt and disloyalty that are totally unbecoming for a thirty-five-year-old adult, I finally settled on:

A Northern Soul – The Verve
50 Greatest Hits – Nusrat Fateh Ali Khan
Everything Must Go – Manic Street Preachers

Before we get to Shabana, here's what Martin thinks of
Setting Sons

'Hello Richard.'

'Oh, hiya Martin, you all right?'

'Yeah, great thanks. What you up to?'

'I've just got a new job haven't I.'

'I don't know, have you?'

'Yeah, I'm working on that Large Hadron Collider aren't I.'

'I don't know, are you?'

'Yeah, I start on Monday.'

'Oh aye, what's all that about then?'

'Well, basically we fire a load of particles together.'

'What for?'

'So we can try and understand more about the basic laws governing the interactions and forces among the elementary objects, the deep structure of space and time, and in particular the interrelation between quantum mechanics and relativity.'

'Bloody hell.'

'Anyway, what you up to?'

'I'm writing an article that will try and reclaim Paul Weller from his haircut and convince people that he used to be really cool.'

'Fucking hell mate, good luck with that.'

Here's my 11 reasons why The Jam are one of the best bands ever.

1) Accidents will happen

In the mid-seventies, The Jam were a terrible band that wore black shirts, black and white brogues and huge white kipper ties. Basically, imagine a version of *Bugsy Malone* that's set in Woking and everyone sings Small Faces songs instead of that one about wanting to be a boxer.

This is how they originally lined up:

Steve Brookes – Guitar

Bruce Foxton – Guitar

Rick Buckler – Drums

And playing a Hofner bass, just like his hero, was a seventeen-year-old Paul McCartney fanatic called John Weller. In fact, he idolised McCartney so much that he called himself Paul.

Anyway, one day there was a big fight in the back of the van and Bruce Foxton sat on Weller's bass and snapped the neck in two. Weller responded by saying 'Right, you can play bass now, I'm on guitar.'

Shortly after, he bought a Rickenbacker 330, a copy of The Who's *My Generation*, and off they went.

That's right everyone. Paul Weller's entire career comes down to a fight in the back of a van because someone sat on his bass.

As pivotal moments in rock history go, it's definitely up there.

Oh yeah, they got rid of that Steve Brookes fella too and, crucially, stopped wearing kipper ties.

2) Off they went

After gatecrashing the London punk scene, The Jam released their first album, *In the City*, in May 1977.

Over the next four years and ten months, the band released six studio albums, of which three are brilliant (*All Mod Cons*, *Setting Sons*, *Sound Affects*), two are very good (*In the City* and *The Gift*) and one is just good (*This is the Modern World*).

To make this even more impressive, they also released nineteen hit singles nine of which they couldn't even be bothered to put on the albums.

So yeah, the complete discography takes place in less than five years and sees them dabble with punk, mod, new wave and soul in the process.

The secret to this?

Well, other than an incredibly pushy record company, they treated the band as if it was a job – they worked ten to six in the studio so Weller could get home to watch *Coronation Street*, and they even had a Christmas party every year.

The Jam – what a great place to work.

3) When you're young

Paul Weller was only twenty-three when The Jam recorded their final album. If you really think about it, about everything The Jam did, it's mad to have all that ticked off at such a young age.

The only other band I can think of that broke up at such a young age were Bros and they don't count because they wrote the following lyric:

'I read Karl Marx and taught myself to dance.'

4) A forensic analysis of 'Down in the Tube Station at Midnight'

I'll be honest, this is one of the most ridiculous songs I've ever heard and it actually keeps me up at night.

The story is basically this – Paul Weller is in a tube station at midnight when a couple of dodgy fellas approach him and ask him if he has any money.

Weller replies:

'I've a little money and a takeaway curry, I'm on my way home to the wife. She'll be lining up the cutlery, you know she's expecting me, polishing the glasses and pulling out the cork.'

First, if someone approaches you late at night and asks if you have any money, the answer is always, 'No mate.'

Second, what's going on in the Weller household?

Why does the poor Mrs Weller have to stay up till past midnight before she can have her meal? It's not really fair, and if I'm being honest, I've spent the best part of thirty-seven years feeling sorry for her and hoping that she finds someone else – someone who lets her eat her tea earlier in the evening.

And why is she opening a bottle of wine? And setting the table? For a curry?

I could understand all of this if the song was called 'Down in the Tube Station at about 7 p.m.' but it isn't.

Anyway, back to the story.

Setting Sons by The Jam

The two fellas proceed to mug the witless Weller before leaving him beaten on the floor. As he lies there, no doubt regretting his entire approach to this incident, he says:

'I'm down in the tube station at midnight. The wine will be flat and the curry's gone cold.'

Paul, I hate to break this to you mate, but wine IS flat!

Before anyone makes a case that Mrs Weller might have opened a bottle of Babycham, or any other fizzy wine, let me point you to a lyric in The Jam's 'Saturday's Kids':

'Saturday's girls work in Tescos and Woolworths, wear cheap perfume 'cause it's all they can afford, go to discos, they drink BABYCHAM . . .'

There you go, Paul Weller is quite capable of specifying Babycham if he wants to.

Notwithstanding all of this, 'Tube Station' is a brilliant song, and it gave their career a kick-start after they'd been written off as punk has-beens.

What's really remarkable, though, is that it nearly didn't happen.

By all accounts Weller had thrown the handwritten lyrics in the bin where they were found by their producer – Vic Coppersmith-Heaven. It was Coppersmith-Heaven who then convinced the band to record it.

'But Vic, it doesn't make any sense. The whole wife thing, it's crazy. And the time contradiction too. Basically, I've set a scene in the house that's definitely early evening but the scene in the tube station is at midnight. Oh, and it IS Babycham that she's opened. Me and the wife, we love a bit of Babycham with our curry, but I couldn't get the lyrics to scan because it has too many syllables. So I used "wine" instead, even though I know wine is obviously flat. That's why the song doesn't really work and I threw it in the bin.'

'Don't worry Paul, no one will pick up on that.'

'Ok, let's record it tomorrow. *Coronation Street* starts in an hour.'

5) I'm so bored of the USA

In 1980 The Jam were on tour in America when their label phoned them with the news that 'Going Underground' had entered the charts at number one.

They immediately cancelled the rest of the tour, flew back to England and appeared on *Top of the Pops* where Paul Weller wore an apron.

I don't know what other evidence you'd need to convince you that, along with Robert De Niro and Björn Borg, Paul Weller was the coolest man on the planet between 1980 and 1982.

6) Rick Buckler's autobiography

I'd always assumed that Rick Buckler, the drummer in The Jam, was a no-nonsense sort of fella – a bit like Terry in *Minder*.

Then I read his autobiography and discovered that he's actually more like Alan Bennett.

Consider this paragraph about his dad's life as a postman:

'My dad, along with a lot of others from his generation, smoked cigarettes. Smoking was the norm and he would get into trouble when he lit up in the sorting office. Postmen weren't allowed to do that in case they set fire to the mail, but he was always sneaking a fag here and there though. Players Number Six was his brand of choice and they came with coupons that could be saved up and eventually swapped for something like a new teapot.'

I didn't think anything could happen that could increase my love for The Jam, but imagining Rick Buckler as a frustrated Alan Bennett made me like them even more.

I also imagined Alan Bennett trying to play the drums on 'Funeral Pyre' but, to be honest, that didn't really work.

7) I don't even like mods

That's an understatement actually, I hate mods. There's no excuse for that haircut and anyone that does their top button up without wearing a tie is obviously mad. I wish they'd all just have a day off, by which I *don't* mean have a day off and go to the seaside with your other mod mates and do mod stuff. I literally mean – have a day off.

Every time I see a mod in the twenty-first century I think about a TV show that I haven't written yet called *Brit Pops*.

'So what's the idea behind *Brit Pops* then?'

'Well, it's about those mods who persist with that haircut while struggling with the responsibility of fatherhood. In the first episode, two of the dads meet at the school gates to discuss how many mirrors on a scooter constitutes too many mirrors. They're so absorbed in their conversation that their children get kidnapped and the dads end up having to sell their original pressing of *Ogdens' Nut Gone Flake* to pay the ransom.'

'Is it a comedy?'

'Not really.'

Look, I get it, every generation watches *Quadrophenia* and thinks it might be a good idea to be a mod. And don't get me wrong, I love *Quadrophenia* – I used to have it on VHS and watch it all the time.

But I also loved *The Blues Brothers* and you don't see me driving around in an old police car ordering four fried chickens and a Coke every five minutes do you?

No, you don't.

So, look, it's testament to how brilliant The Jam are that I can get past the mod thing.

8) Guitar hero

Bruce Foxton wrote an average song called 'News of the World' and then Paul Weller decided to make it brilliant by adding a great solo.

Off the top of my head, the only other solo that he does in The Jam is the one on 'Start'. I imagine his thought process there was:

'Everyone's going to say I took the chords from "Taxman", so just to shut them up, I'm going to show Paul McCartney how he should have done the solo.'

Paul Weller's guitar style then – helping out his mates and starting fights with The Beatles.

What a great bloke.

9) Bonus endings

Most bands adopt the following song structure:

Verse, Chorus, Verse, Chorus, Middle Eight, Chorus.

The Jam, though, sometimes did this:

Verse, Chorus, Verse, Chorus, Middle Eight, Chorus, Bonus Ending.

Often these 'bonus endings' were entirely different from the rest of the song but always brilliant. See 'Smithers Jones', 'Strange Town', 'When You're Young' and, best of all, 'Little Boy Soldiers'.

Paul Weller has continued the 'bonus ending' theme in his solo career too, but with a slight variation – i.e. it's a bonus when any of his songs end.

Fair play to him.

10) The video for 'The Bitterest Pill'

Possibly the strangest four minutes of film I've ever seen. From what I can work out, Paul Weller has broken up with his partner and she decides to go out with the other two members of the band – probably because they'll let her eat before midnight.

At one point, Paul Weller looks through a window and sees his lost love having a great time in front of the fire with Bruce Foxton and Rick Buckler.

You can see why The Jam broke up shortly afterwards.

11) The breakup

The second-best decision Paul Weller ever made was to break up The Jam at their absolute peak. Their last single, 'Beat Surrender', had entered at number one and, having sold out five nights at Wembley Arena, they had to plead with the promoter to stop adding any more.

And his reasons were impeccable – he didn't want to damage the legacy, to drag it out and become a middle-aged man singing songs that were written by an angry young man. He wanted to create a time capsule, a body of work that was preserved forever and would never fade.

The best decision he ever made, the one he makes every single day, is to never reform The Jam and ruin that.

Bonus ending:

'Hello Richard.'

'Oh hiya Martin, you all right?'

'Yeah, good thanks. How's that job at the Large Hadron Collider going?'

'It's mad you know. Sometimes I have to marvel at the scope of what we're trying to achieve, y'know, trying to recreate the circumstances of the Big Bang and all that.'

'It does sound mad.'

'One of the fellas there has this theory that we're all in a Large Hadron Collider.'

'You what?'

'Yeah, he reckons that we're living out a previous experiment where some other scientists had created the big bang and our whole world is being monitored in another Large Hadron Collider somewhere else.'

'Bloody hell. I don't think I can cope with this, Richard. My head's starting to hurt.'

'That's quantum physics for you, Martin. Anyway, how did that Paul Weller article go?'

'All right. I did this whole bit about "Down in the Tube Station at Midnight".'

'I LOVE that song. It was mine and Julie's first dance when we got married.'

'Your first dance was "Down in the Tube Station at Midnight"?'

'Yeah. We met in Tottenham Court Road tube station, at around midnight, and there aren't many songs that cover that. It just seemed appropriate and we both really love the song. We listen to it all the time and it reminds us of when we first met and, of course, our wedding.'

'Oh.'

'Anyway, what did you say about it?'

'Not much. I just pointed out the internal contradiction within the heart of the song – namely the time inconsistency between the two places, the issue with the wine, and the fact that it makes no sense whatsoever. But then you probably knew all that anyway.

Richard? You knew all that, right?

Richard?'

So, over to you Shabana. Why haven't you listened to it? WHAT'S WRONG WITH YOU?????

Well I really wish I could lay claim to some irrational prejudice against The Jam in order to answer your question but I don't have one. I had definitely heard of them, because there seemed to be a time (during my peak Oasis obsession) where you couldn't read a Noel Gallagher interview without him talking about how much he loves Paul Weller.

I wonder if he still does that?

I definitely remember being reliably informed, I believe by *Heat* magazine, that the whole mod thing was a thing. But me actually listen to their music? It just never happened.

And the reasons for that? Well it's a bit complicated.

'English' or 'Western' music did not feature much in my house when I was growing up. Both my parents are first-generation immigrants who came to this country from Pakistan – my dad in the sixties and my mum in the late seventies. The soundtrack to my early childhood therefore has a very deep 'sub-continent' flavour; qawwali, naats and ghazals. Lots of Nusrat Fateh Ali Khan (hence his inclusion in my top three ever list). I absolutely loved this music even though most of the time I hadn't a clue what was actually being said because

a) I am appalling with music lyrics, which I often get wrong, and b) I didn't learn Urdu or Punjabi until my very late teens.

So for a long time I just didn't have other music on my radar. But part way through secondary school, when I was about thirteen, I knew this had to change. My 'major swot' status, which I secretly revelled in, already made me massively uncool. Retaining 'total music loser' on my charge sheet didn't seem very smart as it was something I could actually change. And so it came to pass that my first proper and concerted foray into non-Asian music, at the tender age of about thirteen, was East 17.

I fully realise this probably puts me firmly back into the 'total music loser' box, perhaps forever, but in my defence it was what my friends were into, and though this is a very low bar, they were much cooler than me. And my deeply religious, strict parents definitely didn't approve. And I, their deeply religious, strict daughter also didn't entirely approve, so that had to be a win, right? And East 17 were way better than the pretty boys of Take That. Even I knew that.

After that, most of the music I got into was through my friends, and all the staples of the nineties and noughties featured – Oasis, Radiohead, Nirvana, Manics, Kings of Leon, The White Stripes, Eminem (even Coldplay, for mention of which I sincerely apologise), interspersed with the pop music which we all publicly derided but secretly loved (Britney, Sugababes, Backstreet Boys, Kylie).

There were some random obsessions along the way too which I seemed to have conjured up all by myself, for which I blame MTV (does MTV still exist?) – Linkin Park and Staind to name but two. I have no idea how these happened and they are not things I actually admitted to at the time. But my abiding obsession is the first proper band I discovered for myself and not through someone else – The Verve.

Being a tech-know-nothing I seem to have bypassed most of the turning points in the way in which music is consumed. I have gone from cassettes to CDs straight to injecting Spotify directly into my bloodstream with nothing in between. The only constant is Heart FM, which basically means I have spent twenty years listening to 'Careless Whisper' on repeat.

So in a nutshell I haven't listened to The Jam before (not just *Setting Sons*, but no Jam at all, ever) because I got into non-Asian music quite late (it's my parents' fault), none of my friends ever suggested them to me (it's all their fault), I didn't discover them for myself in that haphazard and random way in which people like me come across new/old music, Heart FM never seem to have them on, the Spotify algorithm obviously doesn't think I would like them and they're not The Verve.

And lastly, because this album was released in 1979 and I was born in 1980. I'm just not that good with music from before my time. Even the stuff I have heard of and listened to I usually don't like or get. I am afraid this includes some biggies like The Beatles. And The Rolling Stones.

So I approach this task with some trepidation, especially given the fervour with which fans of The Jam have been filling up my Twitter timeline, and cause these days I am a politician and seeking approval is a *thing*, indeed a *professional requirement* in this line of work...

You've now listened to it at least three times, what do you think?

It's a bit complicated.

The first listen was awful. I barely understood most of the lyrics. I told you I am appalling with music lyrics. And before anyone wisecracks about me needing to refer myself to one of David Cameron's English classes for Muslim women, let me assure you English is my first and only fluently spoken language. And there really isn't anything wrong with my hearing, I've had it checked. I'm just bad with music lyrics. So partway through the first listen I barely understood it and started feeling all defensive. But without getting all of the words, the music on its own was not enough to hold my attention, which wandered straight to 'why do people think this is A Classic?', 'what degree of music loser does this make me?' and a fervent prayer that none of The Jam fans reading this live in my constituency.

And the brutal truth, dear reader, is this: if I wasn't listening to this album for the purposes of this blog, I would have gone straight back to my current Spotify list of Florence + The Machine and the soundtrack to *Rocky IV*.

But the listen to it three times rule is a good one. So for my second listen I armed myself with the lyrics and gave it another go. The slight downside of this though was that knowing I had to listen to the music, read the flipping lyrics *and* write this, meant that by this time the whole experience felt like my weekly essay crisis at uni minus the 2 a.m. trip to Hassan's kebab van to buy chips.

So, still not enjoyable.

It took me another five listens before I had enough familiarity to start to work out what I think. And I still don't understand why it's A Classic. It's too confusing to be A Classic surely?? 'Girl on the Phone' and 'Heatwave' are both incongruous and feel out of place. That they are placed at the beginning and end of the album just messed with my head. I know every song doesn't have to 'fit' for an album to make sense and hang together but these two songs feel out of step in a way that doesn't sound like it's deliberate. Or if it is I'm afraid I just don't get it. And 'Girl on the Phone' is a stalker song, which might have been OK in 1979 but feels a bit creepy in 2016.

I thought the songs about friendship ('Thick as Thieves', 'Burning Sky') were OK, sort of sad but not memorable.

The bit of the album that reflects on ordinary lives ('Private Hell', 'Wasteland', 'Smithers-Jones', 'Saturday's Kids') was good, with its critique of society, and honesty about boredom, but in my world that's what the Manics are for. I realise that middle-aged men and women who love The Jam reading this will be thinking something along the lines of 'bloody kids these days know nothing' but there you have it. If I'm looking for leftist politics and culture in my music it's James Dean Bradfield not Paul Weller for me.

But I did love 'The Eton Rifles'. I thought it was powerful, I got it straight away. There was no need to check the lyrics, not because I could make them all out (I couldn't, but he definitely mumbles some of them I'm sure) but because I didn't need to in order to get the song. It was just ace, A Classic even. I sincerely hope I don't now discover that this is the one song on this album considered Not A Classic.

But on its own is it enough to carry the whole album? As good as I think it is, the answer is no.

Would you listen to it again?
I'd listen to 'The Eton Rifles', but probably not the rest of it.

A mark out of 10?
The Eton Rifles – 10/10.
The album as a whole – 4/10.

16

Good Kid, M.A.A.D. City by Kendrick Lamar

1. Sherane a.k.a Master Splinter's Daughter
2. Bitch, Don't Kill My Vibe
3. Backseat Freestyle
4. The Art of Peer Pressure
5. Money Trees
6. Poetic Justice
7. Good Kid
8. M.A.A.D. City
9. Swimming Pools (Drank)
10. Sing About Me, I'm Dying of Thirst
11. Real
12. Compton

First time listener – Geoff Lloyd

I host a radio show with my friend Annabel Port at 6 p.m. weekdays on Absolute Radio. I never know how to describe it, but the *Radio Times* once called it 'near hip'. Annabel and I witter on with ourselves, and there are interviews with comedians, writers, musicians, scientists and so on. It's a podcast, too.

I also host *Beatles Brunch* on Absolute Radio 60s – two hours of Beatles music, Sunday mornings from 10 a.m.

Geoff's top three albums ever?

(With the caveat that this top three is non-binding)

Ruth and Martin's Album Club

Abbey Road – The Beatles
High Land, Hard Rain – Aztec Camera
Workers Playtime – Billy Bragg

Before we get to Geoff, here's what Martin thinks of *Good Kid M.A.A.D. City*

When we booked Geoff Lloyd as a guest, we'd just come off the back of editions about Led Zeppelin, Neil Young and The Beach Boys. Knowing that we also had Meatloaf and Genesis to come, I was worried that we might start to get a reputation and people would start knocking on our door and want to have Curved Air listening parties.

With awkward incidents like this on my mind, I decided to limit Geoff's choice to some of my favourite albums that have been released since 2012. This is what we offered him, along with some potential ideas that I had for the intro:

Killer Mike – *R.A.P. Music*

There's a song on this album called 'Reagan' which is probably my favourite protest song from the last ten years. The best bit is a sample of one of Reagan's speeches on the Iran-Contra affair where he actually says the following:

'A few months ago I told the American people I did not trade arms for hostages. My heart and my best intentions still tell me that's true, but the facts and the evidence tell me that it's not.'

That sentence is easily the maddest thing an American president has ever said and I could have spent at least 70 per cent of my intro talking about that.

Cloud Nothings – *Here and Nowhere Else*

I'm a huge fan of their drummer and, when I listen to this album, I often think he would win that Omelette Challenge on *Saturday Kitchen*.

For those of you unfamiliar with the concept, the Omelette

Challenge is a thing where professional chefs race each other at making an omelette. It includes lots of vigorous stirring, hence being ideally suited to a drummer with incredibly fast hands.

This led me to think of an Omelette Challenge that exclusively involved musicians and I concluded that, without a shadow of a doubt, Leonard Cohen would come last.

This could have been my best intro yet.

Father John Misty – *I Love You, Honeybear*
This album really reminds me of early Elton John and I *love* early Elton John.

The repeat chorus in 'Rocket Man' is amazing, 'Bennie and the Jets' is the best name for a band ever, and wouldn't it have been amazing if he actually sang 'Crocodile Rock' at Diana's funeral instead of that dreary re-write of 'Candle in the Wind'. Imagine that – funny glasses, outlandish costume, and a full band joining in:

I remember when rock was young,
Me and Susie had so much fun.

That would have got the assorted dignitaries dancing and, let's be honest, it's what she would have wanted.

It then occurred to me that I should probably just get someone to do an Elton John album one day so I could expand on this.

Sufjan Stevens – *Carrie & Lowell*
No idea why I included this. It's about the death of Sufjan Stevens' mother and, as such, there are literally no jokes. I was pretty delighted when Geoff didn't pick it to be honest.

Kendrick Lamar – *Good Kid, M.A.A.D. City*
And here we are – the album that Geoff went for.

So, let's begin.

1) The good kid

Kendrick Lamar was born and raised in Compton.

Once asked about his childhood, he said, 'I'm six years old, seein' my uncles playing with shotguns, sellin' dope in front of the apartment. My moms and pops never said nothing, 'cause they were young and living wild too.'

When he was nine years old it got even worse – after finishing his cereal one morning he ventured out to the streets of Compton only to see someone get their head blown off.

I know, maybe Sufjan Stevens wouldn't have been so bad after all.

Fortunately, for the sake of this story as much as anything, something happens that doesn't involve anyone getting shot – his father took him to the Compton Swap Meet to watch Dr Dre and Tupac film the video for 'California Love'.

Hundreds of people turned out to watch the homecoming of the two heroes and a star-struck crowd greeted them accordingly. The young Kendrick Lamar witnessed the whole thing, perched on his dad's shoulders, and later said:

'I knew then, consciously or subconsciously, that this is what I wanted.'

It's also around this time that Lamar began a process of meditation. Every morning, for ten minutes, he would stare at himself in the mirror to try and discover his true self.

When I read about this, I thought I would try it myself.

So I went into the bathroom and started to look at myself in the mirror. At first it just seemed weird but then after a while I could feel something happening, that I was being taken off somewhere and losing all sense of my surroundings. Then after about six minutes my partner knocked on the door because she needed a shit.

It sort of ruined the whole thing to be honest.

2) The mad city

As a teenager, Lamar gravitated towards the Compton street life and became involved in gangs, drugs and shootings. Like any teenager, he tried his best to fit in with his peer group – it's just that they were either in gangs or in jail.

What set Lamar apart, though, and sent him on a different path, were two parents who encouraged him to do better, who relentlessly warned him against repeating their mistakes. He worked hard in school, becoming a straight 'A' student, and, when he wasn't studying, he devoted himself to music – perfecting his lyrics and performing in a series of rap battles in the neighbourhood.

Everyone rated him, they knew he had something special straight away, and when he recorded his first mixtape, he knew it too.

'The first time I heard my voice play through the speakers I was addicted. That was it.'

I love that. Most people recoil when they hear themselves for the first time. Not Kendrick Lamar, though – he literally loved the sound of his own voice.

3) The education

At the age of sixteen, Kendrick Lamar is signed by Top Dawg – an independent record label working out of Compton.

What follows though is one of the longest apprenticeships ever. He spends the next seven years working in studios and learning the art of production. Seven years! And all he really has to show for it is a hook here, a guest verse there, and six mix tapes that he releases under the name of K-Dot.

Still, all the time he's learning – figuring out his sound and delivery.

His problem, which he ultimately recognises, is that he's too susceptible – he's too influenced by the legends of gangsta rap and swayed by everyone's advice on how he should sound. Tired of it all, and bored of going nowhere, he does something brilliant – he changes his name from K-Dot back to Kendrick Lamar and decides to do it *his* way.

4) What a great bloke

He releases his first EP and it has seventeen songs on it!

People in the industry were confused by such an obvious breach of convention that they question what he's doing.

He doesn't care though.

'I don't give a fuck,' he said. 'Play it and call it whatever.'

See, I told you he didn't care.

He was beginning to gain confidence in his own identity and stand out from the crowd. You can see the transformation in any of the videos filmed around Compton at this time. While his friends are pranking and excitable, fluttering all over the place, he's perfectly still and assured.

He quickly followed his seventeen-song EP with his first official album – *Section 80*. It would go on to sell 100,000 copies in the first few months, a decent performance for an independent artist, and it earned recognition from the wider hip hop community. In 2011, he's invited to perform at a concert with Dr Dre, Snoop Dogg and The Game, where they anoint him as 'The New King of West Coast Hip Hop.'

He broke down in tears on stage and would later say, 'That's the moment I realised I made it.'

Under Dr Dre's wing, Lamar starts work on his second album in 2012 – *Good Kid, M.A.A.D. City*.

What he does is remarkable: he reverts back to an album that he's had in his head for years. The cover, the idea, the story – it was all premeditated and a long time coming. It was the prequel to everything that's happened since – the story of his own life, told through a series of events that take place over a single day in 2004.

Everything's there – the family, the neighbourhood, the peer pressure to succumb when, instead, you want to achieve. It's a story that, on the one hand, is resolutely set on the streets of Compton but, on the other, is told from a new perspective – the good kid that wants the permanent happy ending rather than the short-lived honour.

Good Kid, M.A.A.D. City by Kendrick Lamar

That's what I love most about Kendrick Lamar – he went backwards to tell his own story and, in the process, gave himself a future. Rather than being anchored within his environment, and the traditions of gangsta rap, he created something that transcended both.

He gave himself the freedom to move, and the opportunity to become a superstar.

What a great bloke.

So, over to you Geoff. Why haven't you listened to it? WHAT'S WRONG WITH YOU?????

I'm at pains to point out it's not because I'm anti hip hop.

If that sounds overly defensive, it's because I've spent the best part of two decades working at a radio station which has occasionally embarrassed itself by claiming to play only 'real music' (defined as The Stereophonics, Razorlight and everything in between). At one particularly low point, they made jingles that said 'All rap is crap' and featured a sound effect of Ms Dynamite exploding. I don't subscribe to this: I'm always delighted when a rapper headlines Glastonbury – not out of any particular desire to buy a ticket, but because of how much it enrages a certain type of narrow-minded, *Shine* compilation indie music fan.

All that being said, I can't remember the last time I listened to a hip hop album. It's a very under-represented genre in my collection, and most of what I have is almost thirty years old – *3 Feet High and Rising*, *It Takes a Nation of Millions*, *Paid in Full*, etc. Clearly, I stalled at some stage. A similar thing happened to me with swimming – after a few weeks of lessons, I got a perforated eardrum and wasn't allowed in the water for months. I only ever mastered the breaststroke, but I keep telling myself I'll get back to learning one day, possibly in retirement. I've resigned myself to the same policy on hip hop.

By the mid-nineties, I was already falling behind. My go-to type of music is fey, jangly pop, and it was a boom time for that subset of music fans who also enjoy bookshops, stationery and cardigans.

My head was full of Belle and Sebastian, Pulp, Saint Etienne, Divine Comedy, etc. My friend Chris would stick hip hop stuff he thought I'd like under my nose, but I was losing even a vague grasp of what was around. I finally admitted defeat around the time of that Jay-Z song which sampled 'A Hard Knock Life' from the *Annie* soundtrack. I was done for: I couldn't reconcile the worlds of musical theatre and rap – those weren't things that belonged together. People went nuts for it, and I didn't understand. I couldn't keep up. I decided to set hip hop aside, to be revisited at a later date.

I've been fairly resolute since then. A few things have trickled through – Outkast, M.I.A., Scroobius Pip – but even the biggest of names have passed me by. A young person once mocked me for calling 50 Cent '50 Cents'. I know who Kanye West is married to, and that he enjoys his anus being interfered with, but I've never knowingly heard one of his records. My most frequent exposure to modern hip hop is seeing it performed by mostly white, middle-class people at karaoke, and nothing about that makes me want to dip back in.

And so to Kendrick Lamar: I'd heard the name, but I genuinely thought he was a former *Fame Academy* contestant, and it would be R&B. I'm not joking. Since I've now learned he's one of the biggest and most critically acclaimed stars of his generation, I'm deeply ashamed of this. I can offer little by way of a defence; I rarely listen to music radio, save for a bit of BBC 6 Music here and there, and Radio 2 while I'm performing my ablutions. Most of the new music I hear is through recommendations from friends and social media, so I must be mixing with the wrong kind of people.

You've now listened to it at least three times, what do you think?

I didn't get along with it on my first go. I listened on headphones while distracted – popping to the post office, taking the bus, buying some light bulbs. The music was the soundtrack to my errands, but I was only dipping in and out of the lyrics; I wasn't really hearing them in the context of the songs, let alone the whole album. I felt terribly self-conscious with 'bitch' this, and 'pussy' that ringing in my ears as I pottered around my neighbourhood. I've always struggled to circle the square of misogyny in hip hop: I know that it's a reflection of a culture, but I'm squeamish when it's so blatant. Objectification of women tends to be insidious in most of the music/film/TV I consume, so I don't actually have to confront it.

The only thing I liked on my initial listen was the track where he says that, like Martin Luther King, he has a dream. He then goes on to explain that his dream is that his penis will grow to the size of the Eiffel Tower, so he can fuck the world for seventy-two hours. It suggested a sense of humour I wasn't expecting. By and large, though, I was pretty nonplussed the first time around. I tried to write down some positives, and scribbled 'great production!' which boded poorly: if you've got nothing nice to say, say something about the production.

I gave it another go a couple of days later, this time at home. On the previous listen, I'd found it on Spotify and immediately shoved my phone back into my pocket. This time I looked at the artwork, and saw it was subtitled 'A Short Film by Kendrick Lamar'. Embarrassingly, only then did I realise there was a narrative arc to the album, and it probably deserved more careful attention. This terrified me – I associate album-as-story with stuff like Jeff Wayne's *War of the Worlds*, or the work of Meatloaf.

I read some background on the album to give me context, and I'm so pleased that I did. I'm the sort of person who doesn't even like to read the labels in art galleries – I've convinced myself it's because I want to have a pure emotional reaction to the paintings, but it's probably more to do with laziness. Doing a bit of homework on Kendrick was one of two things that unlocked the album for me. The other was reading along with the lyrics while I listened. My friend Annabel has started watching all television with subtitles, to stop her mind from drifting. I applied the same technique to *Good Kid, M.A.A.D. City*, and I was gripped.

I preferred the tracks that adhered to the story structure. I could live without 'Bitch, Don't Kill My Vibe' (although it has become my new catchphrase around the house), and as much as I enjoyed the Eiffel Tower/penis dream in 'Backseat Freestyle', it didn't do much to drive the plot forward. I really liked almost all of the rest of the album, though. I loved the way the opening track ('Sherane a.k.a. Master Splinter's Daughter') left me itching to know what happened next, like finishing a TV box set episode and immediately having to watch the next one. Another early-ish track I liked was 'The Art of Peer Pressure' – I particularly enjoyed the line 'hotboxing like George Foreman, grilling the masses'.

My favourite was 'Sing About Me, I'm Dying of Thirst' – it's brilliant, character-led storytelling. In fact, that's true of pretty much the whole LP; it does an incredible job of applying the classic get-your-protagonist-up-a-tree/throw-rocks-at-him/get-him-down-again formula to an album, which is a trick I've never heard pulled off before. It's properly filmic, and although on first listen, I really didn't like the inclusion of answerphone messages and clips of dialogue, finding it to be a handbrake, I've done a complete volte-face, and now think it's a very smart structural device.

It's a shame about the last track, 'Compton'. It's awfully cheesy compared with the preceding three-quarters of an hour. I was especially disappointed, because it featured Dr Dre, and I've heard him. It's like a big ensemble number at the end of a stage musical. And I enjoy musical theatre, but as I established earlier, I strongly feel it's something that should be kept away from hip hop.

I think I really enjoyed this album. I think I'm excited to listen to the follow-up, *To Pimp a Butterfly*. However, a tiny part of me wonders if I forced myself to like it, to prove I'm still open-minded about hip hop. There's an episode of *The Larry Sanders Show* where Hank tries to demonstrate he's still hip and relevant by telling the Wu Tang Clan how much he enjoys their latest album. He (of course) humiliates himself. I hope I haven't just done the same.

Good Kid, M.A.A.D. City by Kendrick Lamar

Would you listen to it again?
I intend to, but I'll probably keep putting it off.

A mark out of 10?
8.

17

Slanted and Enchanted by Pavement

1. Summer Babe (Winter Version)
2. Trigger Cut/Wounded Kite at :17
3. No Life Singed Her
4. In the Mouth a Desert
5. Conduit for Sale!
6. Zurich Is Stained
7. Chelsey's Little Wrists
8. Loretta's Scars
9. Here
10. Two States
11. Perfume-V
12. Fame Throwa
13. Jackals, False Grails: The Lonesome Era
14. Our Singer

First time listener – Hadley Freeman

Hadley Freeman is a journalist and is mainly to be found in the *Guardian*. She's also written a couple of books; the most recent one, *Life Moves Pretty Fast*, is a slightly obsessive fan letter to eighties movies. She was born in New York and now lives in London with a sportswriter from Somerset, their seven-month-old twins and a five-year-old Norfolk terrier named Arthur.

Hadley's top three albums ever?

Like a Prayer – Madonna
Paul's Boutique – Beastie Boys
Disintegration – The Cure

Before we get to Hadley, here's what Martin thinks of *Slanted and Enchanted*

I've got so much to say here that we're launching right into it – I don't even have enough time for one of those imaginary conversations that I like to do.

'Oh go on.'

'No.'

Here's my story of Pavement in ten parts.

1) Our hero

A fella called Joseph Campbell once wrote a book called *The Hero with a Thousand Faces*. In it, he argues that all heroes follow the same journey, which is essentially this: an innocent youth meets an older 'guide' and they embark on an arduous quest before a decisive victory is won.

He uses various ancient myths and legends to support his case – from Jesus to that Athenian bloke who killed a Minotaur in a maze – and it's been argued that his work has inspired contemporary stories such as *Star Wars*, *Harry Potter* and *The Lion King*.

Anyway, here's Pavement's Stephen Malkmus talking about his childhood:

'I was a playful kid, you know, like good champagne. I wore little Lacoste jumpsuits and went to the beach with my grandma, who loved me. I had a good tan.'

So there you have it, the repetition of a theme – a child being mentored by an elder.

But unlike Luke Skywalker, Harry Potter or Simba, Stephen Malkmus was dressed in Lacoste and had a great tan.

What a great start.

2) Stars of track and field

While Malkmus was at school in Stockton, California, he thought American sports were a complete waste of time and decided to play soccer instead.

This fact alone automatically makes him cooler than virtually all other Americans.

It's also led to me having a series of incredibly pleasant daydreams about Stephen Malkmus playing football. I'd imagine him as an American version of Alan Hansen – elegant and graceful, a last line of defence wearing a plaid shirt.

To satisfy my curiosity, I asked him on Twitter what position he played.

Unbelievably, he replied:

'The guy at the edge of the wall who ducks when the free kick comes.'

I should have known.

It was on the football pitch, though, that Malkmus would meet another cool kid – Scott Kannberg.

3) The ridiculously easy first EP

In 1989, fourteen years after they first met on a football pitch, Malkmus and Kannberg form a band and borrow enough money to record a single. Naturally, they decide the best place to do this is at a local studio run by an alcoholic hippy called Gary Young.

Young describes their music as 'weird guitar noise' and asks if he can join in on drums. Malkmus and Kannberg agree, the three of them making the whole thing up as they go along, and four hours later they've recorded their first EP – *Slay Tracks*.

Upon hearing the finished product Young said of our hero, 'this Malkmus idiot is a complete songwriting genius.'

A thousand copies of the EP are produced and, before the inevitable happens, I want you to consider one thing – imagine if Gary Young couldn't play drums.

4) Big in Austria

As *Slay Tracks* is due to be released, Malkmus decides it might be a good idea to go travelling around the world.

In a record shop in Austria, he hears the EP playing on the stereo and is so shocked that he asks whether he can see it. After confirming that it is indeed the single he recorded with his mate and some weird hippy fella, he tells the shop assistant that Pavement are his band.

The shop assistant replies:

'That's a good name, somebody had to use it.'

Malkmus phones Kannberg back in the States and tells him that he's just heard the single being played in Austria. Kannberg, who doesn't remember sending any copies to Austria, wonders what on earth is going on.

The Austrian shop assistant was correct in his assessment by the way – Pavement is a brilliant name and, according to the National Word Association of America, it's one of the twenty most pleasant-sounding words in the English language.

'Serendipity' is also on that list though, and I just want to make it clear that I would set fire to any band that had the nerve to call themselves that.

5) Bigger in Leeds

After Austria, the *Slay Tracks* EP then fell into the hands of The Wedding Present – a sort of indie-pop prequel to *Last of the Summer Wine*.

They liked the EP so much that they covered one of the songs, 'Box Elder', and this led to generous airplay on John Peel's radio show. Before long, people wanted to know more about Pavement.

Who were they? Why have they got such a brilliant name?

The Wedding Present didn't even know, they'd never met them or even asked their permission to cover the song. It was a mystery. The only information available was on the liner notes to the Wedding Present EP:

'Box Elder, written by Pavement from Stockton, California.'

Again, word reaches Kannberg of the news – this time that indie legends in the UK have covered one of their songs. He goes mad.

'Who do they think they are? How dare they cover our songs without asking us?'

He then realises that the exposure might be good for the band and calms down.

And how does Malkmus react?

No one knows because he's still on his holidays.

6) The best story ever

Malkmus finally decides to return home.

Pavement release another couple of EPs, again with Gary Young on drums, and then Malkmus decides on another brilliant career move – he goes to New York to become a security guard.

While in New York he moves into an apartment with Bob Nastanovich and David Berman where they form a side project called Silver Jews. Then this, the best story ever, actually happens:

Somehow they manage to get the home phone number for Thurston Moore and Kim Gordon from Sonic Youth. Once or twice a week, they get drunk, phone the number and record a jam on their answering machine!

Imagine that. Thurston Moore and Kim Gordon come home from a gruelling tour, listen to their messages only to find that some experimental art band have been playing songs down their phone for a laugh.

Again, I reached out to Twitter to satisfy my curiosity.

This time I asked Bob Nastanovich whether Sonic Youth ever discovered the identity of the band who left all those songs on their answering machine.

Unbelievably, he replied:

'I honestly don't know. Seems like Malkmus would have told Kim. They're good friends.'

Bob Nastanovich would later go on to join Pavement and become a massive fan of horse racing.

Wanna hear a great fact about him?

He's the only known American to have visited all sixty racecourses in the UK. Weird that, isn't it? If someone had told you that only one American had achieved such a feat, I'm guessing the last person you'd think of was a fella who used to be in Pavement.

I have two more things to say in this section.

Firstly, the former members of Pavement give great customer service on Twitter. I've asked two of them questions now and they've both got back to me within an hour. East Midlands Trains could really learn a lot from this.

Secondly, I've already written a letter to the BBC to try and get funding for my new sitcom – *Stephen Malkmus, Security Guard*.

7) *Slanted and Enchanted*

During the Christmas of 1990, Malkmus stops bothering Sonic Youth via their answering machine and returns home to Stockton, California.

It's here that Pavement record their first album – *Slanted and Enchanted*.

The process, if you can call it that, was just as shambolic as the process of recording their first EP. Malkmus and Kannberg would turn up at Gary Young's home studio at around noon and eat chicken and vegetables that had been cooked in the fireplace. They would then work on barely rehearsed songs, often making lyrics up on the spot, and jam until about 10 p.m.

When they felt they had something they could commit to tape, Young would go into the laundry room, start the tape, and then run barefoot back into the studio to play drums. After the song was finished, he then ran back into the laundry room to stop the tape. As you can imagine, this became exhausting after a while so they eventually decided to settle on the earlier takes of each song.

Ten days later Pavement have finished their first album. Two kids who met playing football, messing about with an alcoholic who just happened to be a brilliant drummer.

It's one of the best albums of the nineties.

8) A real band

Pavement now recruit two new members – the aforementioned Bob Nastanovich and Mark Ibold.

Mark Ibold played bass and smiled a lot, and Bob Nastanovich was brought in as 'Assistant Time Keeper' – essentially to keep the brilliant, but erratic, Young in check.

In fact, they're the only band I know of where one of the members is an assistant to another one.

Yet, off they go.

The initial live shows are reminiscent of a debauched frat party and Young, in particular, is quite the character. He couldn't understand why bands would hang out backstage before the gigs so, instead, he would greet the fans at the door as if they were coming round his house.

Often he would say things to them like 'May I ask you what brings you here this evening?'

Most people just thought he was mad and ignored him, and virtually no one believed he was in the band until they saw him on stage.

On another occasion, he made toast for the entire audience.

'I could sit there and play drums,' he said, 'but where's the fun in that? Don't you think it's more fun to give out cinnamon toast? I sat there for forty-five minutes at London University with a toaster and four loaves of bread and a tub of butter and some cinnamon and I made cinnamon toast for the audience.'

At a gig in Berlin, he greeted fans at the door and gave them a cabbage.

Like me, you're probably reading these snippets of Young's behaviour and thinking he sounds brilliant. Pavement, on the other hand, had to live with it on a daily basis and the antics, and his alcoholism, soon wore thin.

As a result, Young and Pavement parted company.

The new drummer was a fella called Steve West. He probably wasn't as good a musician as Young but, on the plus side, he didn't greet you at the door with a vegetable.

9) The rest of their career in 190 words

They release five more albums and become one of the best bands of the nineties – providing much-needed relief from Britpop and that drummer from M People who was absolutely everywhere.

In 'Range Life', Malkmus improvised some lyrics that took the piss out of The Smashing Pumpkins and The Stone Temple Pilots.

In 'Unseen Power of the Picket Fence', he wrote an entire song dedicated to how brilliant early R.E.M. were.

There's this lyric by The Hold Steady:

'It's a funny bit of chemistry, how a cool car makes a guy seem that much cooler.'

I can't drive and I hate cars so, to me, that lyric is about Pavement. Let me explain.

Take the most uncool person you can think of – for example the Conversative MP Chris Grayling. Now imagine that you've just read an interview with him where he says his favourite band are Pavement.

See, suddenly Chris Grayling is much cooler.

That's Pavement in a nutshell – they were brilliant and, whether by accident or design, they were the coolest band around.

But even more importantly, they weren't Weezer.

10) Everything's ending here

Stephen Malkmus once said Pavement didn't have any real plans because they weren't a real band.

Yet, that's exactly what they became. And in 1999, he decided he didn't want that anymore.

Their final show was at Brixton Academy and Malkmus played the whole gig with a pair of handcuffs attached to his microphone. During the gig, he told the audience that the handcuffs symbolised what it was like being in a band for all these years.

They ended the show, beautifully, with 'Here' from *Slanted and Enchanted*, and then their record label put out the following statement:

Pavement are retiring for the foreseeable future in order to:
1) Start Families!
2) Sail around the world!
3) Get into the computer industry!
4) Dance!
5) Get some attention!

The bit they left out, and it's crucial, is that a decisive victory had been won.

So, over to you Hadley. Why haven't you listened to it? WHAT'S WRONG WITH YOU?????

There is a two-word answer to why I have never listened to this album by Pavement or, indeed, any album by Pavement: Jamie Macintosh.

Jamie Macintosh was the cool boy at my school, or, at least, he seemed like the cool boy to me: he was a bit of a skater and he smoked weed. To a sheltered teenager from Manhattan's Upper East Side that is pretty much the bleeding cutting edge. In fact, he was a lot like Travis in *Clueless*, who I still maintain is the real heartthrob in that film (sorry Paul Rudd). He was also – and this is possibly not entirely relevant to today's discussion, but what the hell – cute as a button, with sad eyes and curly hair and a long lanky body. Obviously, I knew he had no idea who I was, but I knew everything about him, such as that he was a big Pavement fan, and I didn't need to be Sherlock Holmes to work that out because he wore a Pavement T-shirt to school pretty much every other day.

Now, some girls might spot a boy they fancy, figure out what band that boy likes and then obsessively listen to that band so as to have something to discuss with him. I, however, am a girl who didn't even kiss a boy until she was almost twenty, so obviously my flirting technique as a teenager was somewhat lacking. No, my conclusion upon learning Jamie's musical taste was that I should never listen to Pavement because it was obviously cool music and therefore I'd hate it.

I was not a cool teenager.

When people say that now they mean they were a cool geek, in a sort of Michael Cera or Jesse Eisenberg way. Let me reiterate this point: I was not a cool teenager. I was not a cool geek teenager. I was just a big dork. Or at least, that's how I saw myself, so I had this idea that anything cool people liked would be utterly alien to me, whether that was smoking, music festivals or Pavement.

When I was in my twenties and mildly less self-loathing than I was in my teens, I tried out two of those things and it turned out that I was right about smoking (disgusting) and wrong about music festivals (fun, sometimes). But I never bothered to investigate Pavement, mainly because it continued to be the band all boys I fancied liked, and, even in my twenties, I found that weirdly off-putting.

Maybe I found these boys so weirdly incomprehensible anyway that I avoided any further evidence of their difference from me. I remember one boy telling me when he was twenty-five that he once house-sat for Stephen Malkmus. I knew enough at this point to pretend to be impressed, but I also suspected that this guy was lying. That tableau – of him lying about Stephen Malkmus to impress me and me pretending to be impressed to impress him – pretty much captures all my memories of dating in my twenties.

There was another issue: I was not really into a lot of nineties music. Nineties music to me seemed to be divided into four categories: R'n'B, dance, grunge and Britpop. Of those four, only R'n'B and some dance music were acceptable – everything else was depressing and pretty much unlistenable, and I strongly suspected Pavement would fall into the 'tedious miserable grunge' category.

So there you have it, that's why I never listened to Pavement: because I was a total dork who was too busy listening to Boyz II Men.

You've now listened to it at least three times, what do you think?

The first time I listened to it I was basically BaaadDad from *The Adam and Joe Show* in the episode when he reviewed The Prodigy: what *is* this? It's just NOISE! I hate this! O cruel world!

The second time I didn't hate it: I was mainly amused at how it seemed like a sonic encapsulation of the nineties, with Malkmus sounding slightly bored but then also CARING VERY INTENTLY; the guitar feedback; the song titles that make absolutely no sense. All that was lacking was someone encouraging me to wear a Kookai floral dress over a pair of French Connection black trousers (classic look). For a moment I wondered if I'd once made out with a boy to 'In the Mouth a Desert', but then I realised it just sounded like the kind of song I thought I'd make out to in the nineties (in fact, the first time I made out with some guy to music it was to The Verve, and I bloody hated The Verve).

The third time I actually listened to it and thought it was... fine. I thought it was fine. I could do without the ones where Malkmus is screaming into the mic ('No Life Singed Her', 'Conduit for Sale!'), and the strummy ones ('Zurich is Stained', 'Trigger Cut/Wounded Kite at :17') bored me, but others – like 'Summer Babe' and 'In the Mouth a Desert' – were rather lovely. I also liked how obvious it was that Damon Albarn had been listening to 'Here' on loop before he wrote 'Tender', and I see why: it's a good song to listen to if the love of your life has just left you.

So of course I can see the appeal in the album – I'm a dork but I'm not deaf – but it just isn't for me. If an album isn't going to make me want to dance (Madonna) or rap in front of my mirror (Beastie Boys), then it has to have moments of transcendent beauty (The Cure), and *Slanted and Enchanted* just didn't have that for me. And I guess I knew all along that's how it would be for me and Pavement.

So here's a funny story about Jamie Macintosh, because I'm sure you're all dying to hear how that turned out. So I left the school I went to with Jamie after my GCSEs to go to boarding school for my A-levels, and it was about two weeks after I started my new school that something incredible happened: Jamie called me. Three times! In one month! Can you imagine how shocked I was? Can you fathom what it would take to make a sixteen-year-old boy call up a boarding school just to speak to some random girl he'd hardly ever spoken to before? Can you grasp just how badly I misread the whole situation the year before?

And then something even weirder happened: I did not encourage his phone calls. What I mean is, I never asked him to call again, let alone visit, and I never called him, and eventually he stopped bothering – and who can blame him? At the time, I put my handling of the situation down to me being a giant dork with no social skills. But in retrospect, I think the truth was that I liked to look at him, but I knew we actually had nothing in common, so I left it at that. Just like Pavement, really: I can see the appeal, but not for me. And you know what? I think I'm fine with that.

Would you listen to it again?
Probably not deliberately, no. But I wouldn't leave the room if it came on. How's that for high praise?

A mark out of 10?
7.

18

Murmur by R.E.M.

1. Radio Free Europe
2. Pilgrimage
3. Laughing
4. Talk About the Passion
5. Moral Kiosk
6. Perfect Circle
7. Catapult
8. Sitting Still
9. 9-9
10. Shaking Through
11. We Walk
12. West of the Fields

First time listener – Eddie Argos

I am Eddie Argos, I am the singer in a band called Art Brut and a few other bands, I'm a lo-fi punk rock motherfucker and I also write and paint a bit.

Eddie's top three albums ever?

Just like everybody else says, this changes on an almost hourly basis. At 22:59 p.m. on Tuesday 3 May 2016 it is:

Shiney on the Inside – David Devant and His Spirit Wife
Sexy World – The Yummy Fur
The Kids Are All Square – Thee Headcoats

Before we get to Eddie, here's what Martin thinks of *Murmur*

Here, without any ado at all, is the story of R.E.M.

1) Buck meets Stipe

The young Peter Buck was the sort of fella who listened to so much music that, had we existed at the time, he would have thought that even Ruth and Martin's Album Club couldn't find a blind spot.

'I've heard everything,' he'd say. 'I got heavily, and I mean *heavily*, into *Exile on Main Street* by The Rolling Stones when I was fifteen. After that I bought as many albums as I could. At last count, I had 25,000.'

'That's what they all say,' I'd reply, 'but I always find something.'

Back in 1979, Peter Buck does the two most obvious things that all fellas like him end up doing – he learns how to play guitar and gets a job in a record shop so he can listen to even more music.

One of the regular customers catches his eye – another teenager who was always surrounded by beautiful girls and buying *exactly* the same records as him. They get talking and discover they both bought *Horses* by Patti Smith on the day it came out.

For this reason, as much as any other, Peter Buck and Michael Stipe decide to form a band and move into a disused church in Athens, Georgia.

2) Berry meets Mills

Bill Berry was a juvenile delinquent and a bully.

Mike Mills was a smart bespectacled kid who all the grown-ups liked. He looked a bit like Richie Cunningham in *Happy Days*.

'We hated each other,' Berry would later say. 'He was the class nerd, straight As, and I was just getting into drugs and stuff.'

All right Bill, calm down mate.

'He was everything I despised: great student, got along with teachers, didn't smoke cigarettes or smoke pot.'

All right Bill, you've made your point.

During tenth grade, one of Bill Berry's mates asks if he would like to play drums on a boogie-woogie jamming session. Berry agrees and drives across town to the house where the rehearsal is due to take place. Once he arrives, he carries his kit down a load of stairs to the basement.

Shortly after, the bass player arrives – Mike Mills.

Berry has since said that if he was playing any other instrument, i.e. something more portable, he'd have stormed off there and then. However, because he can't be bothered to move his drums again, he decides to stay put and make peace with his nemesis.

'This is ridiculous,' Berry said to Mills.

'Yeah,' Mills replied.

With that, they shook hands.

The mad part of this story isn't that they've been best friends ever since, or even that they became the rhythm section in one of the biggest bands in the world.

No, the mad part is that anyone other than Jools Holland would agree to take part in a boogie-woogie jamming session.

3) Everyone meets everyone

At the start of 1980, the two halves of R.E.M. were still unknown to each other – Peter Buck and Michael Stipe were trying to get something going in a disused church, whereas Bill Berry and Mike Mills were in a series of bands that went nowhere.

A mutual friend was needed and she came in the shape of Kathleen O'Brien. Kathleen lived in the church, and also had a huge crush on Bill Berry. So, knowing that her two church-mates needed a rhythm section, she brought everyone together.

This is it.

It's *the* pivotal moment in alternative American music and Bill Berry sums up the meeting perfectly with the only thing he can remember about it:

'It was cold out and we were all wearing coats.'

Thanks Bill.

Stipe, on the other hand, remembers meeting a really drunk Mike Mills who could barely stand up.

'No way! NO WAY!' said Stipe, 'I'm not going to be in a band with this guy, there's no way on earth!'

Berry eventually talked him round and the four of them set a date to rehearse at the church. When the day arrived, though, somebody didn't turn up so they decided to knock the whole thing on the head.

A couple of weeks later Peter Buck bumped into Berry, purely by chance, and said, 'Let's give it one more try.'

4) Kathleen's birthday

Having brought the band together, Kathleen decided that their first gig should be at her birthday party, held in the church.

I have to say that I'm a big fan of this Kathleen. I think she's the first person I've come across that has formed a band and then made them play their first gig in her honour.

I mean she's pushy, but I like her.

Exactly 125 people were invited to the party but something like 600 turned up – ready to witness the first performance of a band that, at this stage, were called The Twisted Kites.

Despite the fact that they were playing a gig in their own house they were, in Bill Berry's words, 'scared shitless'. They proceeded to get drunk and staggered through as many covers as they could remember – including 'God Save the Queen' by The Sex Pistols and a fifteen-minute version of 'Roadrunner' by Jonathan Richman.

However, towards the end of the gig, members of the audience had to take over on vocals as Michael Stipe had badly burned himself with a cigarette.

And that was supposed to be that. A one-off gig for a friend's birthday.

5) A second gig

An unexpected downside of the debut gig was that the brilliant Kathleen was now in debt – largely because everyone had drunk a load of booze that she only paid a $200 deposit for. In order to help her out, the band decided to put on a fundraising gig at the 11:11 Koffee Club.

'I really didn't want to play there,' says Bill, 'but we had to get some money for Kathleen.'

This story really would be awful without Kathleen, you know.

The band also decided they didn't want to be called Twisted Kites anymore so they held a meeting at the church where everyone got drunk and wrote a load of names on the wall.

They awoke the next morning and whittled it down to the following choices:

Negro Eyes

Slut Bank

Cans of Piss

R.E.M.

I know, they picked the worst one.

To make matters worse, the gig at the Koffee Club was a disaster. The police were called and shut it down after a couple of songs because the club didn't have a licence for alcohol. Everyone had their names taken and the establishment was subsequently closed for good.

It's probably worth a quick recap of where we are.

A woman called Kathleen has formed a band made up of two kids that met in a record store and another two kids who used to hate each other. During their first gig the singer nearly set fire to himself, and their second gig resulted in a local venue going out of business.

What a great start.

6) Their first EP

In 1983, R.E.M. started work on their first EP – *Chronic Town*.

Michael Stipe was so nervous about his voice that it was mixed as low as possible. Then, just to make sure, he sang all five songs with a rubbish bin on his head. You could barely hear him, and you had no idea what he was singing. Still, the EP was so good that when a record label called I.R.S. heard it they offered them a deal.

'But our singer sings with a rubbish bin on his head.'

'Don't worry, it'll be fine.'

7) *Murmur*

They start the sessions by putting two dinosaur mascots on the speakers for good luck.

Despite these, Stipe is still so nervous that he records his vocals lying down in the dark on top of a staircase outside the main studio. Bill Berry has to play alongside a click-track in order to keep in time, and Peter Buck plays an acoustic guitar for the first time in his life.

When they record 'Talk about the Passion' it's the first time they've ever played it the whole way through – it was supposed to be a rehearsal take. It's brilliant though and the producer tells them they needn't bother playing it again.

That's the final version you hear on the album.

It's not only one of the best debuts ever, it's one of the best albums ever. For all the jokes, the haphazard approach, they come out of the blocks as the most assured band in America.

They keep the dinosaurs and bring them along for all future albums.

8) **Their first TV performance**

In 1983, R.E.M. appear on Letterman and perform 'Radio Free Europe'.

While the rest of the band throw themselves at the occasion in the spirit of a dream come true, Stipe looks absolutely terrified. He spends the whole performance motionless, hiding behind his long hair and clinging to the microphone for dear life.

After the performance, Letterman walks over and Stipe exits the stage so he can watch the host interview the rest of the band. Stipe then comes back on and sings 'So. Central Rain' – again nervously attached to the microphone the whole time.

Stipe is so absent from the 'performance' that the Musicians' Union assumes Peter Buck is the band leader and pays him twice as much money as everyone else.

9) *The Tube* in 1985

It's now two years later and R.E.M. appear on *The Tube* to perform 'Can't Get There From Here' from *Fables of the Reconstruction*.

The band are still as energetic as before, they look virtually identical, but Stipe is a changed man. He's dyed his hair with mustard, he's found his feet, and proceeds to show us his moves.

For the next three minutes and twenty-nine seconds he doesn't touch the microphone once.

To this day, it's my favourite TV performance from any band ever.

10) Stipe, Buck, Mills, Berry, me

Stipe would go on to become one of the great frontmen. By 1989 he was topless on *Top of the Pops* and singing 'Orange Crush' through a loudspeaker.

Peter Buck started out as the weakest musician in R.E.M. – a guitar band where the guitarist wasn't that good – but he got much better. He also got so drunk on a plane once that he tried to insert a CD into the drinks trolley because he thought it was a CD player. What a great bloke.

Mike Mills sang the best backing vocals of all time on 'It's the End of the World as We Know It (And I Feel Fine)' and is the member of R.E.M. I'd most trust to look after a cat.

Bill Berry was so good, so important to the band, that they were never quite the same when he left in 1996. He also wrote 'Perfect Circle', which may be the best song ever written by a drummer.

Being a fan in the eighties was the nearest thing I've ever had to being a member of a secret society. It warranted its own handshake

– a sign that you could give to others that you were also into this band with unintelligible lyrics that once lived in a church in the Deep South.

And it never wore off. Even when the lyrics made sense and the mystique had faded, they were always capable of being brilliant.

Put simply, the ten albums from *Murmur* to *New Adventures in Hi-Fi* are probably the best run of ten albums that anyone has ever produced.

Kathleen should be really proud.

So, over to you Eddie. Why haven't you listened to it? WHAT'S WRONG WITH YOU?????

It's not just *Murmur*, I haven't listened to any R.E.M. albums. I mean what's the point? I've heard enough R.E.M. songs on the radio to know what R.E.M. sound like. They warrant about as much investigating of their back catalogue as Coldplay do.

I suppose the problem is that *Murmur* came out when I was three years old. By the time I was old enough to start getting excited about music, R.E.M. were already defined by their MASSIVE HITS.

I know what I like about music. I like it to be experimental, to be about empowerment or reinvention, to contain heart-on-the-sleeve sincerity. I like songs to be about something and to have a bit of personality. I can only really get passionate about bands that do interesting things or have some kind of punk or independent outsider spirit to them. R.E.M. as defined by their MASSIVE HITS contain none of these qualities.

Perhaps if R.E.M. had been less ubiquitous in my formative years I would have had an inclination to go back and find out more about them.

But they were everywhere.

My least favourite song by R.E.M. is 'Everybody Hurts'. I find that song to be an annoying litany of patronising greeting card-style platitudes, cynically designed to sell mawkish sentimentality to anguished angsty teens and middle-aged people who should definitely know better. I hate it. The first time I heard it I knew I never wanted to hear it again. It is a completely empty song devoid of any actual real feeling. It is the song equivalent of someone not really listening, but just nodding along and making sympathetic noises to you as you tell them your problems. It is an insincere bastard of a song.

Despite the fact I have actively avoided 'Everybody Hurts', I could definitely sing – well maybe not sing but certainly speak – all of it to you right now, just from the sheer number of times I've had to endure it by being close to a radio I've not been in charge of. The very fact I have a least favourite song by a band I have no real interest in shows you just how inescapable R.E.M. are.

I suppose the short answer to why I have never heard *Murmur* before is that R.E.M. get played a sufficient amount everywhere I go without my permission, so I've never really felt the need to play them at home.

You've now listened to it at least three times, what do you think?

I just want to say, before I begin, that even though I have just ranted about R.E.M., I really was genuinely excited to give this album a try. I'm a big fan of The Replacements and when I'm sneaking around on the internet reading about The Replacements on forums and Facebook groups and whatnot, I see a lot of their fans also like early R.E.M. This has always made me feel that perhaps I'm missing out on something, that maybe R.E.M. were amazing in their early days, before their massive career-defining hits, and I just arrived too late to the party. Being asked to listen to *Murmur* seemed like a great opportunity to find out.

I never normally listen to music in the shower, but because I was excited about hearing *Murmur* for the first time, and because I didn't have a lot of time, I made an exception. I brought my iPad into the bathroom, turned the water on and put the album on as loud as I could – so it was possible to hear it over the top of the running water.

Murmur begins with some strange noises and in the shower it sounded a lot like somebody hitting the underneath of a car with a spanner. That was unexpected, I thought, and quite exciting. Fuck! I think I might actually really enjoy this record.

Then 'Radio Free Europe' began and it sounded a lot like 'Roadrunner' by Jonathan Richman. I believe that 'Roadrunner' by Jonathan Richman is mankind's greatest achievement, and always have a lot of time for any song that bears even a passing resemblance to it. My curiosity was piqued. I turned the shower off, sat in the bath and started to give *Murmur* my full attention.

I could hear the R.E.M. that I know in 'Radio Free Europe' for sure, but to my ears, on this first listen, it was a more provocative R.E.M. than the one I know from their HITS. R.E.M. songs often have very similar choruses, and this one definitely followed the same format, but on this occasion it caught me completely off guard. I loved it. It sounded like it had been flown in from a different song, and flawlessly fitted on to this 'Roadrunner' pastiche. In a good way. All of a sudden the song was new and vibrant and exciting; it made me think of how exhilarating it must have been for R.E.M. to record *this*, the first song on their debut album. They weren't fully moulded yet, not really, they were still playing with style and form and I imagined how they might have even surprised themselves with how great 'Radio Free Europe' had come out. I thought of all the amazing potential this debut album must have coursing through it, to have made everybody listen to it at the time, helping R.E.M. become one of the biggest bands of all time. This album was a big deal, it is a lot of people I respect's favourite album. All my cynicism went, I even had goosebumps thinking of the treat that lay in store for me.

Then with a feeling of dread I suddenly realised:

'Oh shit, I'm totally going to massively enjoy this album and have to write that I had an epiphany about how amazing R.E.M. are while I was sitting in an empty bath. I've become the sort of person I despise.'

Then 'Pilgrimage' began. It used the same 'weird noises before the song starts' trick as 'Radio Free Europe' but then the most amazing bass guitar part came in, and again I thought:

'FUCK! I really am going to have to write about having some kind of transformative experience with R.E.M. while lying naked in an empty bath.' (Sorry for putting that image in your head.)

Thankfully though, once the singing started the song turned out to be totally shit, an unbelievably boring dirge. I waited for the next song, just in case this is the exception, but it turned out to be the rule. The next song is called 'Laughing' and again, despite a promising intro, it turned into what sounds like a discarded Tom Petty demo.

I stand up and turn the water back on. While I'm thankful I don't have to write about having an epiphany in an empty bathtub, I am still hopeful that something will grab my attention and make me sit down and turn off the water again, totally enthralled. Nothing does.

The second time I listen to the album is later the same day. I'm not in such a rush this time and so give it my full attention. I lie down on my bed with my headphones on and promise to myself that I will give it a fair trial.

There is no water running this time, so I hear that what I thought was a spanner hitting the bottom of a car at the beginning of 'Radio Free Europe' is actually just some kind of synthesiser noise, or a sound the studio made and they just decided to leave it on the recording. Not as interesting as I thought. I don't enjoy 'Radio Free Europe' this time as much as I did in the shower, mainly because now I know it's not the beginning of an exciting odyssey into a band I'd been denying myself, but just an OK song at the beginning of quite a slog of an album. I brace myself for what is to come.

That intro to 'Pilgrimage' sounds great still, as does the intro to 'Laughing' and '9-9', but this now feels like a cruel trick as I know what the songs that follow those intros sound like, and it is a sudden and very steep drop in quality.

On this second listen through *Murmur*, I can kind of hear in places why some Replacement fans also like early R.E.M. I can definitely hear shades of that life-changing incredible band on songs like 'Laughing' and 'Catapult'. I manage to convince myself I would actually like 'Catapult' if Paul Westerberg from The Replacements had been involved in some way, it has a nice tune. Unfortunately, Michael Stipe has none of the wit, charisma, talent, intelligence, passion, humour or presence of that immense front man. In fact, by the time I've reached 'Catapult' on my second listen through the album, I start to doubt that Michael Stipe exists at all. Perhaps he is also just a strange studio noise 'accidentally on purpose' left on the recording.

I persevere. I finish the album. I was ambivalent after the first listen but as I cross the finish line this time I have decided that I hate this record and anybody who likes it. This makes me a little bit sad. I'm definitely the type of man that enjoys having a strong opinion, but I also love having my expectations confounded, and I really was secretly hoping this would happen with *Murmur*.

To celebrate making it through *Murmur* without falling asleep I have a chocolate biscuit and start toying with the idea of only pretending to listen to it a third time.

But I am a man of my word, Martin from Ruth and Martin's Album Club seems like a good guy and I did promise him I'd listen three times, so reluctantly I give *Murmur* one last seemingly never-ending run around the block.

I hate 'Radio Free Europe' now. It is still by quite a large margin my favourite song on the album, but the false promise it gave me on that first listen has made me despise it. I feel conned.

However, by this point it is the only song on the record that can conjure up any emotion from me whatsoever, so I savour the hate I feel for it and prepare myself for the beige blank page that is the rest of the album.

I find it very hard to concentrate. I really don't understand the point of this record. It is a nothingness. I've been listening to it using my girlfriend's Spotify account. Yvonne has a premium account and I'm beginning to sort of wish she didn't as some shouty adverts might break up the tedium of *Murmur*. Anything with a bit of personality would be welcome at this point.

Murmur could easily be radio static. My mind starts to drift, I start to think about my favourite conspiracy theory – that the CIA funded the Abstract Expressionism art movement because they wanted to give prominence to an art form that you can't put any kind of message or meaning into. I start to think that perhaps the CIA also funded R.E.M.'s rise to prominence, because, just like Abstract Expressionism, it is also impossible to put messages or meaning into R.E.M. songs.

Murmur drifts onwards. I start to think that if I hadn't had to write down my feelings about it, I might have forgotten it exists at all. Are these three playthroughs really the first time I've heard it? Perhaps it is just the first time I've managed to recall listening to it. Mediocre music, no personality, weird for weird's sake, laughable lyrics that are understandably buried deep in the swampy mix; there is nothing here to hold onto and certainly very little to enjoy.

On the upside, like the R.E.M. songs that I know, at least these ones will be gone by the morning.

I look forward to forgetting *Murmur* again.

Would you listen to it again?
No.

A mark out of 10?
I'm really sorry as I know a lot of people love this album, but I give it nothing out of 10. It is not for me.

Epilogue
Remember I told you how much I loved Kathleen?

Well, I wasn't the only one.

A regular reader called Dani Lawrence was so taken by her story that she made it her mission to find her and sent a series of emails to tourist information in Athens, Georgia. All she had to go on was her name, the fact that she lived there in 1981 and was somehow involved in the formation of R.E.M.

Remarkably, after much effort, she was found in Decatur, Georgia, where Dani sent her an email along the lines of 'I'm not sure if you know about this but someone has written a piece about R.E.M. but it's actually all about you!'

Kathleen then contacted me, told me how much she enjoyed the piece, and we've been in touch ever since.

It's a bit like that film *You've Got Mail*, if *You've Got Mail* was a film about two people discussing the early days of R.E.M.

19

I Can Hear the Heart Beating as One by Yo La Tengo

1. Return to Hot Chicken
2. Moby Octopad
3. Sugarcube
4. Damage
5. Deeper into Movies
6. Shadows
7. Stockholm Syndrome
8. Autumn Sweater
9. Little Honda
10. Green Arrow
11. One PM Again
12. The Lie and How We Told It
13. Center of Gravity
14. Spec Bebop
15. We're an American Band
16. My Little Corner of the World

First time listener – Iain Lee

Iain Lee hosts a late-night radio phone-in show on talkRADIO – weeknights from 10 p.m. He recently got canned from the BBC for calling a someone a 'bigot'. He also got in trouble online for suggesting that maybe Beach Boy Mike Love is 'an all right guy'.

You may remember him as the bloke from *The 11 O'Clock Show* or *Big Brother's Bit on the Side*.

Ruth and Martin's Album Club

Iain's top three albums ever?
Instant Replay – The Monkees
Revolver – The Beatles
Sunflower – The Beach Boys

Before we get to Iain, here's what Martin thinks of *I Can Hear the Heart Beating as One*
Here's the story of Yo La Tengo – my favourite band.

1) Ira Kaplan's conversation with Ray Davies

Ira Kaplan grew up in Hoboken, New Jersey, and was obsessed with music from an early age. In particular, he was a huge fan of The Kinks and saw them play approximately thirty times when he was growing up.

In 1975, he went to see them three nights in a row.

On the first night, during a break in songs, he shouted for 'Autumn Almanac'.

Ray Davies responded with, 'Oh, that's a terrible song.'

On the second night, he shouted for 'Dead End Street' – Davies heard him once more and responded with, 'Oh, that's a good song. We'll do that one tomorrow.'

On the third and final night, The Kinks played 'Dead End Street' and the young Ira Kaplan went crazy.

We're only 121 words into our Yo La Tengo edition and if you don't already think Ira Kaplan is the coolest bloke ever then, frankly, you may as well not bother with the rest.

Not only is he dictating The Kinks' set list from the audience, not only is he right about 'Autumn Almanac' when Ray Davies is wrong, but he's also about to become the indie rock star that sounds most like a protagonist in a Philip Roth novel.

Note: I'm not even going to mention the fact that Kaplan also loved The Monkees and once wrote, individually, to all four of them asking a load of fanboy questions.

That would obviously be unfair to Iain.

2) Ira the music journalist

Ira continued being an A+ music nerd and became a regular at CBGB – catching early performances from the likes of Television, Patti Smith, Talking Heads and Blondie.

Desperate to join the conversation, he began to write articles and reviews for the *SoHo Weekly News* where he also launched the brilliantly named 'Swinging Singles' review column. From there, he would go on to work at the *New York Rocker* and the *Village Voice*, becoming one of the most respected music journalists around.

For example, he was one of the first writers in New York to pick up on an act from Georgia who he described as possessing 'wistful minor chords and jangling Byrds' guitars'.

He finished the article by saying – 'By all means, check out R.E.M. live.'

In short, he was a far better music journalist than I'll ever be, and if he had registered the domain name swingingsingles.com he would have made an absolute fortune.

3) Ira the promoter

After a terrible time interviewing Kiss, Ira decided he didn't want to be a music journalist anymore so became a promoter instead, working out of Folk City in Greenwich Village. His remit was to put on a night of new music every Wednesday which he called 'Music for Dozens' – his optimistic projection of how many people would turn up.

He did two brilliant things though.

Firstly, he operated a strict 'no guest list' policy which, trust me, is the best guest list policy.

Secondly, he booked Sonic Youth and is the first promoter in New York to put on The Replacements, Hüsker Dü and The Minutemen.

He's now in his late twenties and so far he's been a brilliant fan, writer and promoter. It's probably about time he stopped mucking about and found someone to form a band with.

4) A partner

Like Ira Kaplan, Georgia Hubley was a total music geek who lived in Hoboken, New Jersey.

She saw The Who's *The Kids Are Alright* and thought that Keith Moon was having so much fun that she decided to become a drummer – the entirely correct response for anyone watching that film.

Having seen each other in record shops around town, Ira and Georgia finally met at a Feelies gig. They were both immediately taken by the similarities they saw in each other – a certain degree of shyness they hoped to overcome, a love of baseball and, of course, a shared obsession with music.

Ira and Georgia decided to form a band and get married – the entirely correct response to meeting anyone of the opposite sex at a Feelies gig.

5) The advert

With Ira on guitar and Georgia on drums, they placed an advert in the *Village Voice* looking for others. It read: *Guitarist and bassist wanted for band that may or may not sound like The Soft Boys, Mission of Burma, and Love.*

A huge part of me thinks this advert is a work of art, in the way that it simultaneously encourages and discourages people from applying. I mean, do you apply if you're a massive fan of Love or not? It's like an unsolvable puzzle – intriguing yet utterly confusing.

The other part of me thinks it probably explains why they went through fourteen different bass players before they settled on James McNew.

Of the previous thirteen candidates, my absolute favourite is a fella from Switzerland called Stephan who was so tall that he couldn't fit in their rehearsal space. As if being an actual giant wasn't bad enough, he barely spoke either – a friend of the band once described him as 'literally the quietest person with the known capacity for speech I'd ever met'.

One day he asked the rest of the band the following question:
'What is a puddle?'
This is what happens if you place cryptic adverts in the music press.

6) Yo La Tengo

Regular readers of the blog will know that I'm childishly obsessed with band names and the story behind them. So, it's with great fanfare that I'll tell you how Yo La Tengo acquired theirs.

In 1962, the New York Mets had one of the worst seasons in the history of baseball, losing 120 out of 160 games. Despite the multitude of problems that contributed to this failing, i.e. being terrible at baseball, there was one particular issue they looked to resolve.

Every time a ball went up for a catch, a fella called Richie Ashburn kept colliding with another fella called Elio Chacón.

Ashburn would track the ball in the air, shouting 'I've got it! I've got it!' Meanwhile Chacón, who only spoke Spanish, would also track the ball and eventually run into him. Rather than doing the obvious thing and teaching Chacón the one English phrase that would solve the problem, they did the opposite – they taught the rest of the squad the Spanish for 'I've got it! I've got it!'

They even had a meeting, an actual meeting, where all the players were told to shout the new phrase when the ball was in the air.

During the next game, the ball went up in the air and Ashburn tracked it, this time shouting 'Yo la tengo! Yo la tengo!' – Spanish for 'I've got it! I've got it!' Chacón understood this time and backed off, leaving Ashburn clear to make the catch.

Unfortunately, there was one player who didn't attend the meeting – a left fielder called Frank Thomas, who ran straight into Ashburn. As the pair got up, and dusted themselves down, Thomas said:

'What's a yellow tango?'

Ira and Georgia were huge fans of the Mets and decided to take their name from this mad anecdote. It's obviously one of the best names ever and, if you don't believe me, just ask Iain Lee.

In 2016, I sent him a list of about thirty albums to choose from and he picked Yo La Tengo because a) he thought they had a cool name and b) he couldn't stand the prospect of listening to Roxy Music.

7) The career

Yo La Tengo begin with all the professionalism and confidence you would expect from a bohemian couple with a revolving door of comedy bass players. During their first gig, Ira is paralysed by fear and can barely sing. He also forgets the importance of taking a backup guitar with him, so every time he breaks a string (basically every night) he has to sit at the side of the stage and take ages re-stringing his guitar.

'Georgia, maybe tell the audience how we got our name while I sort this out.'

'Sure thing, Ira.'

When they eventually enter the studio to record their first album, Georgia is so nervous about singing that they have to build a screen for her to sit behind. Notwithstanding this, or because of it, the first album is a charm and includes the best liner note ever:

'Ira Kaplan – Naive Guitar.'

Over the next ten years, while contemporaries like R.E.M. and Sonic Youth rise and fall, Yo La Tengo plough their own unique furrow – never becoming *the* band of any moment or nailing their sound to any particular genre. They become, if anything, the sound of their own eclectic taste – happy to follow a ten-minute thrash with a three-minute bossa nova.

They also manage to avoid the darker clichés of rock, the moods and the drugs, and present an image that's often undervalued – they're nice people. They sit around and watch game shows like *Wheel of Fortune*, they play charades, they make homemade granola, and when they've done all that, they'll go on stage and burst your eardrums.

An indication of the level of confidence and independence they achieve is best illustrated by an incident in 1992.

Their record label ask them to come up with a hit – something that can be played on the radio. Yo La Tengo present the label with a twenty-four-minute jam called 'Sunsquashed'.

'Ira, it's twenty-four minutes long!' an executive complains.

'Yes,' he replies, 'but it only feels like seventeen.'

What a great bloke.

8) Murdering the classics

Throughout their career, they never forget their own fandom and maintain a strong commitment to the cover version. In fact, their knowledge is so encyclopedic, their enthusiasm so complete, that they even decide to raise funds for a local radio station by renting themselves out as the house band.

Listeners are encouraged to phone up and pledge for Yo La Tengo to perform a song of their choice live. They do this every year between 1996 and 2003, taking requests from listeners and covering songs as diverse as 'Downtown' by Petula Clark, 'Raw Power' by The Stooges and 'The Night Chicago Died' by Paper Lace.

During the cover of 'Rock the Boat' by The Hues Corporation, Ira forgets the words so just sings:

Our love is like a ship on the ocean
Got something something with love and devotion

I'll be honest, I'm not sure I've ever heard a band having so much fun in my entire life.

9) This week's album in fifty-eight words

I Can Hear the Heart Beating as One was released in 1997 and sounds like about ten different bands making one great album.

Personally, I like all of them, but my favourite song is 'Autumn Sweater'.

We could slip away, wouldn't that be better,
me with nothing to say, and you in your autumn sweater.

Take that Ray Davies.

10) My favourite band

It's now 2016, thirty-two years since Yo La Tengo were formed, and they're still going – an achievement to be celebrated. That's not because I think they're brilliant, or that everyone should like them, it's just that I admire the spirit that drives their career.

That's why they're my favourite band – not necessarily because of the music they've produced but because of who they are, or at least who I think they are. They're fans, they're what happens if people like me, Ruth and Iain Lee were to channel our inner music geek into actual sounds. It's an unbridled enthusiasm, a commitment to music that's so strong that it's hard to imagine them ever breaking up, or deciding it would ever be a good idea to stop being in Yo La Tengo.

The end game, the entire point of the enterprise, was just to be a band – the career and achievement summed up in one goal. Seems obvious but you'd be amazed how they're the exception – how their own fandom is the only agenda they ever had.

They called their first compilation album *Prisoners of Love*.

More than the 2,000 words I've just written, it perfectly sums them up.

So, over to you Iain. Why haven't you listened to it? WHAT'S WRONG WITH YOU?????

As you can tell, I like albums by bands that start with the definite article. *The* Beatles, *The* Beach Boys. When I was growing up in the eighties, I was really into *the* sixties. I became obsessed with *The* Monkees at a very young age and they kind of dominated everything for, well, pretty much all of my life so far. I tended not to stray too far from the formula.

I Can Hear the Heart Beating... by Yo La Tengo

Yo La Tengo never really entered my consciousness. This album came out in 1997. I was twenty-four and, well, I think I was getting drunk a lot. I thought I had heard of them before, when I saw the name on the list offered to me by Ruth and Martin's Album Club I was convinced I'd heard a reference to them in a John Hughes film, but I can find no evidence to back that up so I suspect I made that 'fact' up.

I *was* listening to some crazy stuff in '97 actually, Pizzicato 5 who are on the same label, so there is some crossover, but... oh no, hang on. I was in Pakistan for three months that year, working as a Christopher Lee double (actual true story) and I was discovering Hanson (again, true story) for myself.

I chose this album from the long and ever-changing list sent to me because I knew nothing about them. I knew nothing about a lot of the acts on there, but something about the name grabbed me. I honestly thought that with a name like that, they would be a fun, upbeat Spanish group playing world music in a similar vein to The Buena Vista Social Club. I have to stress here, I have never actually heard The Buena Vista Social Club, and I'm not sure if they really are a band or just a film, but I imagine if they are a band they make fun, bouncy, Spanish-type music.

I ordered a CD of it as I really wanted to invest myself in this by owning a physical copy. I'm not a huge fan of streaming, so actually purchasing something I could touch and feel, to me, is important if I want the music to mean something to me. It's a hard (and expensive) album to get hold of but I really, really wanted to like this.

I joke that I have enough bands and don't need any more, but actually, I'm aware that I am a bit of a gag myself because I always bang on about The Monkees and The Beach Boys. ALL. THE. TIME. *I Can Hear the Heart Beating as One* would be my sonic ticket into new, uncharted spheres of music. The tunes would enchant me, and I would be transported to sonic places I had never dreamed existed. I'd buy the entire back catalogue, and spontaneously purchase all the 'Customers who bought Yo La Tengo also bought...' recommendations on Amazon, because finally I would have found something new.

OK, well, let's just say, it didn't quite work out like that.

You've now listened to it at least three times, what do you think?

I didn't want to read anything about the group before I wrote this piece as I wanted the writing to be pure, based entirely on my musical experience and not any preconceived ideas I might pick up from Wikipedia. But I just had to have a look and see exactly which part of Spain or South America they were from:

'Yo La Tengo (often abbreviated as YLT) is an American indie rock band formed in Hoboken, New Jersey.'

Ah. Right. Disappointing. Well, let's see what happens when I listen.

The CD arrived and I played it in the car on the way to the radio show one night. I remember John Peel being interviewed years ago and saying he preferred to listen to new CDs in the car as, well, I can't recall the actual reason, but I do remember thinking that was a bit sad. Life, however, doesn't really give me much time apart from when I'm driving to listen to an entire album. Now that really is sad.

The opening track was totally not what I was expecting, which is, of course, not always a bad thing. A sombre instrumental, I quite liked it. It reminded me of a downbeat version of the theme tune to *The Kids in the Hall*, a Canadian sketch show from the nineties I was once briefly obsessed with. This was going to be brilliant! A moody opener followed by lighthearted, catchy and amusing pop songs from a quirky American band.

Then track two, 'Moby Octopad', kicked in and fuck me, it was shit. The sort of tuneless, 'artistic' drivel that the cool kids would listen to when I was at college and I would sagely nod along to as I didn't want to stand up and shout 'what are you all thinking? This is obviously bollocks! There's no tune. They're chancers and you've all been sucked in by it. The emperor is not only naked, but he's doing a massive poo at the same time and you're all applauding him!'

It really was that bad. Wikipedia had told me that Yo La Tengo were considered 'the quintessential critics' band' and this particular album 'received considerable acclaim from music critics'.

Music critics.

There's your problem right there.

Damn. I wanted to write a positive piece and look, I'm slagging off some people who made a record. I've never made a record. It must be hard. But some people do it so well, and Yo La Tengo, in my humble, worthless opinion, haven't done it very well at all here.

Let me try and find some positives, and there are a few. Yes, the cover of The Beach Boys' 'Little Honda' is an abomination, one that sucks all of the youthful exuberance of the original, throwaway ditty. And the ten minute and forty second instrumental 'Spec Bebop' is, and I say this as fact, the worst piece of music I have ever heard, but... but... but...

But. There are some gems tucked away. First listen I came away feeling angry. Angry with the band for making such a racket. Angry with me for not choosing Roxy Music from the list of albums I'd been offered. Angry that I had to listen to this twice more. I'm glad I went back though, because I did find some very sharp moments of sunlight amidst the darkness.

The songs that I liked were when the band dropped the noise and went soft. Soft guitars and soft vocals from the female singer. There was still angst and uncertainty and disappointment in the music, but it was actually quite beautiful.

'Centre of Gravity' is a fey, bossa nova love song. Dumb fifth-form poetry lyrics that were stunning in their naivety. A joyful celebration of the simplicity of being with someone who is everything to you, expressed in almost 'aw, gee, shucks' language. Absolutely brilliant.

Another highlight is their attempt at country. 'One PM Again' is a cracking tune. It may be a joke, I can't tell as it is so out of character with the rest of the record, but who cares? It's pitched perfectly. Beautiful harmonies and even a faithful pedal steel guitar solo in the middle. Stunning.

There are just enough of these slow, thoughtful, beautiful tunes, that by the third listen, I got angry again. Not because I felt I've wasted my time, but because I felt the band are wasting *their* time with the industrial noise that is the main thrust of this record. Yo La Tengo can obviously *do it*. They have the skills to make good music (by good music, I of course mean music I like). Instead of using their powers for good, they use them for evil.

I'm reminded of when I used to tape my sister's early R.E.M. LPs. I'd just record the poppier tunes and ignore the rest, so that worked out at about three songs a record for the first few albums. I'd have done the same with this back in the day.

It wouldn't have taken up much space on a C90.

Would you listen to it again?
What do you think? Really? You ask me that after what I've just written?

A mark out of 10?
3 (although 'Centre of Gravity' gets an 8).

20

Is This It by The Strokes

1. Is This It
2. The Modern Age
3. Soma
4. Barely Legal
5. Someday
6. Alone, Together
7. Last Nite
8. Hard to Explain
9. New York City Cops
10. Trying Your Luck
11. Take It or Leave It

First time listener – Anita Rani

Anita is an English broadcaster and journalist. You may have seen her on *Countryfile*, *The One Show*, or *Strictly Come Dancing* with a fella with a nice chest.

Anita's top three albums ever?

The Queen is Dead – The Smiths
Soundbombing II – Various Artists
Off the Wall/Thriller/Bad (all three) – Michael Jackson

Before we get to Anita, here's what Martin thinks of *Is This It*

Here's how The Strokes released a classic rock 'n' roll record while some people were listening to nu metal.

1) An early test

Julian Casablancas was minding his own business at college one day when a bunch of mates suddenly invited him to their room and shut the door.

Apprehensive, apprehended, Julian stood there and considered his fate.

The leader of the gang spoke – asking Julian to state his name, swear a loyalty to their fraternity, and declare his favourite sexual position.

As pivotal moments in the history of rock 'n' roll go, it's a big one. If Julian plays this wrong he could end as a frat boy for life or, even worse, a member of Blink-182. However, if he plays it right there's still a chance that the best album of 2000 will happen.

He considered his options.

Then he spoke.

'My name is Julian Casablancas. I don't want to join your fraternity and I don't know why I'm here.'

What a great bloke.

2) A gang

Having avoided hell, Julian then got some new mates and formed a band.

Let me quickly introduce the lineup:

On vocals we have the aforementioned Julian Casablancas.

On guitar we have Nick Valensi and Albert Hammond Jr.

On bass we have Nikolai Fraiture.

And last, but definitely not least, on drums we have Fab Moretti.

You'd be forgiven for assuming that some of these are made up, or from a rock 'n' roll comic strip, but remarkably they're all real. Put simply, they're the best five names of any five people ever and, without even hearing a note, you already know they're going to be better than a band with names like:

Liam Gallagher

Is This It by The Strokes

Noel Gallagher
Tony McCarroll
Paul McGuigan
Paul 'Bonehead' Arthurs

In fact, the only downside of the brilliance of these names is a tinge of sympathy for Julian Casablancas. In any other band he'd immediately hold the title of 'The One with the Coolest Name' but here he's denied that honour because he's in a band with a fella who has the best name ever – Fab Moretti.

Oh, and one last thing – The Strokes is a great name too. It's practically impossible to come up with a good 'The' name these days but somehow they managed it.

Just ask The Pigeon Detectives.

3) Phwoar!

Ok, they've got the names, it would now help if they also had the looks. The last thing The Strokes need is to look like a bunch of trainee vicars, or Radiohead (actually that's the same thing).

But fear not, The Strokes are probably the only band to achieve a 100 per cent 'I would' ratio – considerably better than The Rolling Stones (60 per cent), The Beatles (50 per cent) or The Who (0 per cent). Only The Monkees come close but I've decided they don't count because a) there's only four of them and b) they'd be too tired to have sex because they run around a lot.

Even modern boy bands, who are specifically put together based on their 'sex appeal', always have one who's a bit chubby and would rather be hugged or taken seriously – like that bloke in Westlife who looks like someone has drawn a good-looking person on a jacket potato.

The Strokes, however, have no such problem. To a man they all look like male models. Even the bass player who looks like a butler in a horror film looks like a *really* good-looking butler in a horror film.

And finally, while I'm being shallow, they complemented their good looks with an impeccable wardrobe. At a time when people were wearing hoodies and huge jeans with hundreds of pockets, they came along with a classic denim-and-leather look that was simultaneously timeless and refreshing.

Nick Valensi once told the rest of the band to 'dress every day like we're going to play a show'.

That's great advice to be honest.

Unless you're Genesis during that phase when Peter Gabriel played gigs with a massive flower on his head.

4) A guru

In our Pavement chapter you may remember that I referenced a book called *The Hero with a Thousand Faces* by Joseph Campbell.

'I didn't read your Pavement chapter, mate.'

'Don't worry, I'll quickly summarise it here.'

The book suggests that all mythical heroes essentially follow the same journey and points to the fact that there is always an older guide to help them along their way. For every Luke Skywalker there's an Obi Wan Kenobi, for every Frodo there's a Gandalf, and for every Terry McCann there's an Arthur Daley.

The Strokes were no different and had their own guru to point the way – J. P. Bowersock.

Bowersock's initial role was to teach Albert Hammond Jr how to play guitar but he was so knowledgeable that the rest of the band started to turn up to the lessons to hear what he had to say. He'd spend a lot of time talking to Julian about the craft of songwriting, collaborating on ideas and testing out different structures. He also played Nick Valensi a load of records he'd never heard which went on to massively influence his guitar style.

The whole band were mesmerised by him and he quickly taught them a comprehensive musical history that took in everything from Elmore James, to Link Wray, to the Nuggets compilations.

Such was his influence that his photograph was included in the album artwork, below the simple heading – 'Guru'.

Oh, and I hate to labour the point, but J. P. Bowersock is a brilliant name – considerably better than Dumbledore.

5) The Velvet Underground rule

During an interview in 2002, Julian Casablancas said The Velvet Underground are the only band that all five members of The Strokes like.

Along with the whole 'dressing like you're always going to play a show' thing, this is another great piece of advice that all bands should be forced to adhere to from the beginning.

Had it been a legal requirement there'd be no Red Hot Chili Peppers, half of Arcade Fire, that fella in M People who calls himself Shovel, The Rembrandts, that bloke out of The View who thinks it's a big deal to wear jeans for four days, Scouting for Girls, The Orb, Mani, Babybird, Ugly Kid Joe and John Cale.

Would Pete Best have liked The Velvet Underground?

No, and the rest of The Beatles knew it.

6) Rehearsals

With all the hard stuff in place, The Strokes now just needed to do the easy bit – become a decent band.

At the start of 1999 they diligently rehearsed in a tiny studio in the Hell's Kitchen district of Manhattan – the same place Madonna had rehearsed when she first arrived in New York. Starting at 10 p.m. each night and working through to 8 a.m., they financed the entire enterprise with a series of day jobs including selling frozen yoghurt, working in second-hand record stores and bar work.

Even Nick Valensi getting mugged three times in the same night by the same man couldn't put them off. They never missed a rehearsal and, crucially, they never thought they were ready until they actually were.

Six months after they started, six months of working through the night, they finally emerged and decided to play their first gig.

7) A live band

The Strokes' first gig was at a small New York club called the Spiral. The audience contained six people and Casablancas was so nervous that he threw up before going on stage.

Despite an inauspicious start, which left the band demoralised, they dissected the performance in minute detail and decided to soldier on – playing a series of local 'toilet' venues where Casablancas still used to throw up before taking the stage. One of these included playing a lobster restaurant in Delaware in front of a family of five who were trying to enjoy a meal.

Eventually they got bored of all these venues and decided to do what all great bands do – just find one venue and let the audience find them. They secured a residency at the Mercury Lounge in New York, just over the road from where they started out at the Spiral. Fifty people turned up for the first gig, which quickly became a hundred, and before long they had sold out.

They'd found their Cavern, quit their jobs, and developed into something like the band you hear on the first album.

8) The demo

By the time they entered the studio, everyone had stopped throwing up and they produced one of the best demo tapes ever, containing the songs 'The Modern Age', 'Barely Legal' and 'Last Nite'.

Geoff Travis at Rough Trade was halfway through listening to the first song and made an offer to their manager before it had finished. In fact, he was so impressed with it that he decided to release it in its current form.

How often has that happened? A 100 per cent strike rate with a record company and a demo that's so good it becomes your first single. It's tempting to view this as a remarkable chain of events but, in reality, Travis's response was entirely sensible and level-headed. When I first heard the chorus of 'The Modern Age' I thought it was the best thing I'd heard in years. When I later heard 'Last Nite' my head actually fell off.

Is This It by The Strokes

Had I been in charge of a record company, had anyone been in charge of a record company, they would have followed exactly the same course of action.

A few weeks after Rough Trade had signed them, Noel Gallagher was at The Strokes' first London gig, trying to crane his neck to see what all the fuss was about while probably wishing he didn't have a rubbish name like Noel Gallagher.

9) Is This It?

Yes it is, thank you very much.

We've all been taken in only to be let down by someone who turns out to be Babylon Zoo. Yet, whatever anyone thinks about The Strokes' later career, and the terrible bands they spawned, you have to give them the debut. I loved it at the time but I can safely say, listening to it all week, that I love it even more now.

More than that though, as if liking the songs isn't enough, there was a refreshing quality about it that belied its obvious influences. In 2001, I'd been listening to The Flaming Lips and Lambchop, both of whom I liked but only in that way people in their thirties like bands that make music for people in their thirties. I never thought they were exciting, or even cool. I just thought they were age appropriate and had a load of good songs.

Then The Strokes came along with no keyboards, a wardrobe of denim and leather, loads of packs of Marlboro Reds, and even better songs.

Just like The Velvet Underground, just like Television, just like The Jesus and Mary Chain.

So, over to you Anita. Why haven't you listened to it? WHAT'S WRONG WITH YOU?????

When I was a kid, music was my world. I remember singing Olivia Newton John's 'Physical' in the playground aged three at my day nursery. I distinctly recall trying to discuss *Top of the Pops* with the other kids in kindergarten, who probably had sensible bedtimes and weren't allowed to watch anything beyond *Rainbow*.

Aged eleven, I discovered New Kids on the Block and then woke up aged thirteen with taste, a die-hard fan of The Smiths. There followed a period of grunge, Pearl Jam, Nirvana, New Model Army, which morphed into dance and electronic music.

Once I began uni in 1996 my musical education exploded. I was soaking it up wherever I could. Discovering more and more. The beauty of opening one album and it leading into portals and portals of new genres.

I'd pop into Crash Records in Leeds on a weekly basis to hungrily listen to the latest drum and bass releases. Hours could disappear in Jumbo Records discovering bluegrass albums or hip hop compilations.

Back then I was a muso nerd and, along with it, a total musical snob.

I remember clearly when *Is This It* was released and exactly why I didn't listen to it. It was 2001 and I was twenty-one years old. I had landed a job for a TV company in London which specialised in music. I was finally leaving my beloved North. This was exactly where I wanted to be – working as a researcher, earning barely enough money to keep me in packets of cheap noodles, Encona chilli sauce and the odd pint or three.

I remember a conversation was taking place in the office on the brilliance of this new band The Strokes. Back then, the bits I heard did nothing for me. I wasn't going out to gigs in Camden, I was much happier in clubs in East London. I had such a wide range of taste but I couldn't hear what everyone else could hear in The Strokes, or maybe I didn't want to.

Inverted snobbery. If the crowd was telling me it was the best band ever or the *NME* had heralded them the saviours of rock 'n' roll, I'd dismiss them offhand and decide to listen in my own sweet time.

In this case fifteen years later.

Is This It by The Strokes

You've now listened to it at least three times, what do you think?

May 2016 I'm off to NYC, baby, to film a new project for the BBC. I figure the best place to introduce myself to this record is its birthplace. So on my first day I take a long walk from midtown to Chinatown with *Is This It* plugged into my ears.

It's strangely familiar for an album I've never listened to before. The dring dring dring dring dring dring of the guitar and Julian Casablancas' lazy vocals trigger a nostalgia that must have been formed via osmosis back in 2001. The album sounds timeless. It could be a New York band from the seventies or an album just released.

It does feel as though each song morphs into the other but what I may have seen as a sign of sameness back in my twenties now feels like a perfect continuous mix.

And then 'Someday' kicks in. 2001 comes flooding back. I have a flashback of jumping around to this record in some sweaty pub in Camden, or maybe it was King's College Union overlooking London. Suddenly I'm homesick.

This may be a band from New York but everything about their music says London to me and that's where I need to hear it. So I select Kendrick Lamar for the rest of my time in NYC and press play when I'm back across the pond.

It's an overcast, generic Monday morning back in London. I'm riding the tube at rush hour. It's grim but I'm in an alternate universe, fashioned by a bunch of greasy New Yorkers in leather jackets.

'Hard to Explain' seems to be carrying me through the crowds. I don't think my feet are even on the floor. The manic, repetitive guitar and Julian's casual vocals. I like that contrast: it's like my own relaxed inner world against the backdrop of rush-hour insanity.

'Trying Their Luck' slows down the pace as Julian's voice becomes more lyrical. Now this I like a lot. That lovely twiddly guitar solo. I'm absorbed in this now.

I must have mellowed a lot since 2001. Perhaps I'm less discerning.

Or free from the restraints of youthful cultural tribalism. I'm more open-minded and listening to this band now feels different. I get it now. It's a recording that captured the essence and vigour of youth. I might not have cared for The Strokes so much back then but it turns out that they were doing a good job of bottling my twenties all along.

I'm delighted I took the time to experience *Is This It*. It could have passed me by forever but listening to it has taken me back to early carefree days in London when music defined me more than anything else. I'm so pleased I've ditched the stubborn teens and now have the ability to listen with open ears.

Would you listen to it again?
The task was to listen to this album three times. This morning was the fifth play.

A mark out of 10?
8.

21

For Your Pleasure
by Roxy Music

1. Do the Strand
2. Beauty Queen
3. Strictly Confidential
4. Editions of You
5. In Every Dream Home a Heartache
6. The Bogus Man
7. Grey Lagoons
8. For Your Pleasure

First time listener – Richard Osman
That guy from that thing.

Richard's top three albums ever?
It's a Shame About Ray – The Lemonheads
Doggystyle – Snoop Doggy Dogg
The Stone Roses – The Stone Roses
(The more I've thought about this the more I realise I have really bad taste in music. At one point 'my Manics playlist on Spotify' was in my top three.)

Before we get to Richard, here's what Martin thinks of *For Your Pleasure*
As I'm writing this, 52 per cent of people have just voted for Britain

to leave the European Union and I feel some responsibility to try and cheer up those of you that didn't. So, it's with some relief that we're not doing *Berlin* by Lou Reed but, instead, an album where a well-dressed Geordie falls in love with a blow-up doll.

Let's go.

1) Actual best dad ever

You may have noticed by now that I hardly ever mention the parents of the artists we feature. Typically, they're either abusive or controlling dads who I have no interest in, or they're so inoffensive, invisible to the story, that they barely warrant a mention.

Then along came Bryan Ferry's dad, straight out of a Thomas Hardy novel.

Ferry Sr worked in the mines of Newcastle, looking after pit ponies, and had hardly a penny to his name. Despite this, he courted the love of his life in the most amazing manner – by riding to her on a carthorse, wearing a bowler hat, spats and a sprig of lavender in his buttonhole.

And he did this for ten years!

Eventually he saved up enough money to get married and the couple decided to mark their union by giving birth to Bryan Ferry.

A fitting end to the courtship, I'm sure you'll agree.

Ferry adored his dad so much that when he became a star he asked him to move in to his Surrey estate. Rather than winding down in splendour, or trying to control his son's career, Ferry Sr opted for a much more sensible option – he mostly rode around the grounds on a lawnmower wearing a mad hat.

What a lovely image.

Oh, and I've saved the best bit till last.

His name was Fred. Fred Ferry.

Cheered up? I know I am.

2) The childhood bit

Contrary to the St Moritz playboy image we now have of Ferry, he started life in his own version of Monty Python's 'Four Yorkshiremen' sketch. The family had no phone, no car, no TV and, in the backyard, a tin bath hung on the wall.

'We were so poor I couldn't even afford air for my blow-up doll.'

Still, the early signs of a desire for decadence were there and Ferry has since spoken of feeling 'out of place' as a child. On Saturdays, he worked at a local tailor's and pored through magazines showing impeccably dressed men stepping out of sports cars. He dreamt of being an actor, a mountaineer and even a cyclist winning the Tour de France.

Yet the defining moment came in 1968. The young Ferry hitchhiked to London and saw the Stax/Volt Revue – Otis Redding and Sam & Dave taking the stage in some of the best suits he'd ever seen.

'It was just what I wanted to see and hear,' he said.

3) The first attempts at stardom bit

Fresh from his experience in London, Ferry returned to Newcastle and formed a band with a terrible name – The Gas Board. Mike Figgis, future director of *Leaving Las Vegas*, was also a member and claimed that Ferry couldn't really sing. Others also questioned his commitment, saying he never rehearsed and just had a habit of turning up at gigs with a couple of girls on each arm.

Not really sure what sort of lead singer The Gas Board were after to be honest.

Anyway, Ferry was subsequently sacked and moved to London to further his career, initially making do with a series of day jobs including van driver, antiques restorer, and, best of all, ceramics teacher at an all-girls school in Hammersmith. His approach to education was as follows:

'If they wanted to talk about their boyfriends, I'd talk about their boyfriends. If they brought records in, I'd play them.'

Obviously they sacked him.

With The Gas Board and the school board now in the past, he then attempted to infiltrate an even more frightening organisation – King Crimson.

Fortunately, he failed at that too and couldn't get past the audition. So, tired of everything and everyone, he acquired a piano, started to write his own songs, and went looking for the rest of Roxy Music.

4) Sliding doors

First up, Ferry places an ad in the *Melody Maker* and recruits a fella called Andy Mackay – a trained saxophonist and oboe player.

Good start Bryan, every band needs one of them.

A short while later, Mackay was on the tube on the Northern line and, unbeknown to him, a friend was waiting on the platform at the next stop. As the doors opened, the friend had the choice of the two carriages – an empty one and the one that Mackay was in. He opted for the latter, saw his friend, and was quickly recruited into the band.

His name was, wait for it, Brian Peter George St John le Baptiste de la Salle Eno.

Whereas Mackay played terrible instruments, Eno couldn't play any at all. Instead, he owned thirty-two tape recorders, a little black book of 'ideas', and performed experiments like recording a pen hitting a tin lampshade and then slowing it down to see what it sounded like.

Obviously, it sounded like someone slowly hitting a tin lampshade with a pen.

Remarkably, though, these were the credentials that led him to become the band's 'sound doctor' and, subsequently, hero to many – a non-musician who was short on technique but big on ideas. In fact, many other people doing this intro would probably dedicate the whole thing to his 'genius' and his 'influence'. I get that, but I still think that Ferry sums him up the best:

'With Eno, there were always wires everywhere.'

Ferry finds the rest of the band but, unfortunately, the recruitment process is relatively boring so I won't go into it here. The only thing of note, and remember I'm trying to cheer people up, is that they had a bass player who used to be in a band called Mouseproof.

5) 1971

The band needed a name and exclusively narrowed it down to a list of old cinemas, places of classical grandeur and ornate interiors where the public would go to forget about everything outside – Odeon, Gaumont, Essoldo.

They settled for Roxy, a name both mundane and evocative, and then expanded it to Roxy Music after finding out an American band, undoubtedly awful, had got there first.

With a cool name and a collection of mostly amateur musicians, Roxy Music spent most of 1971 as a 'behind closed doors' project that eschewed the traditional route of gigging their way into form. There were so many disparate parts that no one quite knew what direction they were taking – a revolving door of bass players and guitarists, that fella on the oboe, a Geordie that people thought couldn't sing, and Eno being Eno.

You can see why they kept themselves to themselves; you can't really imagine them supporting Badfinger, for example.

So instead, Ferry tried something else.

He put together a tape of the band's songs, added loads of stickers of little aeroplanes flying over tall buildings skywriting the name 'Roxy', and sent it to a journalist at the *Melody Maker*. The journalist loved it and phoned up the number written on the back of the tape.

In the subsequent interview, Ferry was quoted as saying:

'We've got a lot of confidence in what we're doing and we're determined to make it in as civilised a way as possible. The average age of the band is about twenty-seven, and we're not interested in scuffling. If someone will invest some time and money in us, we'll be very good indeed.'

What a gent.

6) 1972

There are a couple of quotes about Roxy Music in 1972 from two of my heroes that have always intrigued me.

Michael Stipe of R.E.M. once affectionately referred to the band as 'the car wreck that was Roxy Music in 1972'.

Stuart Murdoch of Belle and Sebastian wrote the following line in their song 'Me and the Major':

> He remembers all the punks and the hippies too
> And he remembers Roxy Music in '72

1972 is the key year then. So what happened?

Well, firstly they released their debut album, which contains a brilliant song with a car number plate for a chorus.

Secondly, they finally left the house and started playing these chaotic gigs where Ferry would be acting weird at one end of the stage and Eno would be doing his best to match him at the other. With the tension between them already palpable, they divided the fans' affections and created a 'Bryan camp' pitted against a 'Brian camp' – one half of the audience migrating to Ferry and the other half to Eno. By all accounts, the gigs were haphazard and raw but refreshingly different. While Bowie and Bolan were glam versions of a musical heritage, Roxy Music, for better or worse, were making it up as they went along.

Thirdly, they released 'Virginia Plain' and appeared on *Top of the Pops* looking like a band that had been shipped in from another planet to play in front of an audience of tank tops and Keith Chegwin haircuts.

But more than all this, their attitude and image was different – a combination of excess and refinement that set them apart from their glitter contemporaries, the status quo and Status Quo.

Ferry said in an interview at the time that 'while other bands wanted to wreck hotel rooms, Roxy Music wanted to redecorate them'.

As usual, he's put it far better than I ever could.

7) For Your Pleasure

The crowning moment of all of this: a genuinely brilliant album that often gets overlooked and ignored by a modern audience that has convinced itself Roxy Music were never *this* good.

But they were.

'In Every Dream Home a Heartache' is simultaneously unnerving, funny, gothic, postmodern and spectacular. Not just because of how it must have sounded then but because of how it sounds now.

Trust me, nothing quite prepares you for the introduction of the doll.

'Beauty Queen' proved that Ferry *was* a singer and 'Editions of You' is obviously the best punk song ever written.

For an album that was released over forty years ago it somehow feels preserved, rather than dated. It creates its own images and doesn't let early seventies nostalgia get in the way. Morrissey said it was the only truly great British album he could think of.

In response to Morrissey's kind words, Ferry said:

'I believe that sort of sad chap, Morrissey, is a progeny of mine. Though I don't think he is nearly as virile.'

I know. He's done it again.

8) A final word on Ferry

The future has been a little unkind to our hero.

While Eno's brilliance has diverted a lot of the critical acclaim away from Roxy Music, and on to him, you can't help but feel Ferry has been slightly overlooked. It now seems forgotten that they were *his* band and *his* songs. Instead, he's been thrown under the bus and lumped in with a load of eighties groups like Johnny Hates Jazz – a soundtrack to some terrible wine bar that has since closed down.

And when you're down on your luck, making comments about how cool the Nazis looked and having a son who campaigns for fox hunting probably doesn't help the situation. It adds to an overall suspicion of Ferry, a sense that he's anything but a working-class hero and he's betrayed his roots. You can get away with being earnest and dressing down, apparently, but being aloof in a great suit is a hard act to pull off.

But that's the problem with it not being 1972 anymore. You look at him now through the prism of everything that's happened since and you scratch your head a bit.

Whereas in 1972, it was a different story – a classic about a kid who took the best from his dad and went to the big city for an adventure.

Aren't they the stories we all love?

So, over to you Richard. Why haven't you listened to it? WHAT'S WRONG WITH YOU?????

Roxy Music utterly passed me by, and if I thought about them at all I just had an image of a guy in a suit singing in a weird voice about things I wasn't interested in, so I never felt the need to get involved. I think in my brain the words 'Roxy Music' were entirely represented by Kevin Eldon singing 'Virginia Plain' on *Big Train*.

I was interested to know if I was missing out on something, so I texted my brother 'Mat from Suede' – who has utterly unimpeachable taste in music – to tell him I was doing Ruth and Martin's Album Club.

'I'm listening to some iconic Roxy Music album. I chose it because I've always instinctively hated Roxy Music and I don't know why. But I think you're a fan?'

He replied instantly.

'Wait, you don't like Roxy Music?'

I know my brother well enough to know how to wind him up next.

'I liked "Jealous Guy".'

His measured reply:

'You're dead to me.'

And so, headphones on, let's Roxy.

You've now listened to it at least three times, what do you think?

On my first listen I have to say I was feeling vindicated. I liked some of the songs, but I just couldn't get past Ferry's mannered voice, with its quivers and quavers. I hope I speak for many of us when I say that often when I listen to music I like to pretend that it's really me singing and all of my friends and exes are watching me on stage and saying 'Wow, I didn't know Richard was such an amazing singer! And apparently he wrote this amazing song himself too!' Even if I'm doing 'Gin and Juice' by Snoop.

If I imagined them watching me singing 'Do the Strand' I knew they'd be saying, 'Why is Richard singing in that weird voice? I'm glad we split up.'

Again I texted to enlist the sage advice of Mat from Suede.

'Why does he sing like that?'

'Partly a pop-art affectation, spoofing fifties crooners. Partly adenoids.'

'Why don't the rest of the band say "we've written some really great songs, why are you spoiling them by not singing properly?"'

'Because he's one of *the* great British voices, and because they come from art school backgrounds and an ultra-styled surface is important.'

My brother is cleverer than me, as evidenced by my reply.

'I honestly get embarrassed listening to his voice. I'd rather listen to The Fratellis.'

Mat doesn't take the bait and instead sends me an essay about why Brian Eno is a genius.

OK, round two.

On second listen I start to be reeled in, firstly by 'Beauty Queen', which I don't think is supposed to be the best song on the album, but seems like a fabulous tune to me, and then by 'Editions of You' which Mat had told me was the prototype for most of British punk.

I had secretly hoped that I was going to end up loving this album, but then stumble over the final three songs on the album, 'The Bogus Man', 'Grey Lagoons' and 'For Your Pleasure'. Each has the odd little bit that would be a good middle-eight in a Killers song, but these three songs go on for twenty minutes. 'The Bogus Man' is nine minutes long, which I felt inexcusable. I started noticing Bryan Ferry's voice again.

OK, stop getting angry about that Killers reference. Third listen.

Well wouldn't you know, I love this stuff. 'Do the Strand', which I'd sort of dismissed as a novelty song for some reason, is clearly a pop gem, and 'Beauty Queen' has now taken residence in my head. 'Strictly Confidential' is a bit 'Anthony and the Johnsons B-side' for me, but 'Editions of You' and 'In Every Dream Home a Heartache' get us back on track.

I'm not ever going to get on with the last three songs on this album, but it was the 1970s, I understand that. Perhaps I would have written a nine-minute-long song if Viennetta hadn't even been invented yet.

I texted my brother.

'I really like this album.'

He took a while to reply, but I thought he'd be impressed by my newfound taste. He finally answered.

'What? Even "The Bogus Man"?'

This is a guy who knows his music.

Would you listen to it again?

I don't think I would ever choose to listen to the whole album again, but I am very grateful to have been introduced to the four songs I particularly love, and I think I have been cured of my fear of Roxy Music. I am delighted to have found another great band, and ashamed it has taken me so long.

I still think I might prefer Roxy Music without Bryan Ferry though. Please supply your own 'Brexit' joke here.

A mark out of 10?
8.

22

Violent Femmes by Violent Femmes

1. Blister in the Sun
2. Kiss Off
3. Please Do Not Go
4. Add It Up
5. Confessions
6. Prove My Love
7. Promise
8. To the Kill
9. Gone Daddy Gone
10. Good Feeling

First time listener – J. K. Rowling
I write novels and screenplays. For light relief, I get into rows about politics on Twitter.

Jo's top three albums ever?
1. *Revolver* – The Beatles
2. *Broken English* – Marianne Faithfull
3. Changes daily. Yesterday it was *White Light/White Heat* by The Velvet Underground. Today it's *Hozier* by Hozier.

Before we get to Jo, here's what Martin thinks of *Violent Femmes*
I was talking to my friend Ben about this album the other day.

'Did you know most of these songs were written by a kid in school?' I asked.

He didn't.

Like most normal people, he probably assumed that one of the best debut albums ever was written by an adult – someone who had matured and deleted all his teenage drafts. For example, when Kurt Cobain was in high school the best he could come up with was a song about Spam.

Yet Gordon Gano, future lead singer and songwriter for the Violent Femmes, somehow managed to do something incredibly rare – he created the definitive account of being a teenager, by a teenager.

Ben and I talk about this. The sheer madness of writing songs in school, sat at the back of class, or in between homework and football practice. What are the chances of that being any good? If Gano can write 'Blister in the Sun' at school, then how good were his English essays?

'He must have been the most popular kid in class!' Ben says. 'It's like Ferris Bueller released an album!'

I see where he's coming from, except he's wrong. Because everyone loves Ferris and the whole school rallies around him just because he has one bloody day off sick. They even made a film about it.

'No, this isn't "Ferris Bueller: The Album",' I reply.

Ben tries again.

'You're right, it's more like an album made by his mate Cameron – the weird one.'

I don't tell Ben he's wrong again because, frankly, he'll just keep going with the Ferris Bueller comparisons before probably moving on to *Diary of a Wimpy Kid*. So I laugh and agree.

'Yeah, it's as if Cameron made an album.'

But it isn't. Because at least Cameron had Ferris and Ferris is the most popular kid in the world.

Gano, on the other hand, doesn't have anyone, so ends up writing stuff like:

And I'm so lonely
I just don't think I can take it any more
And I'm so lonely
I just don't know what to do
And I'm so lonely
Feel like I'm gonna crawl away and die
And I'm so lonely
Feel like I'm gonna
Hack hack hack hack it apart

Fast forward a couple of years in the life of Gordon Gano.

It's 1981, he's found a couple of mates, and they're now busking outside a Pretenders gig in Milwaukee – singing those same songs he wrote in school. It doesn't feel like a launch pad for success but, of course, in this story, it becomes exactly that.

James Honeyman-Scott and Chrissie Hynde from The Pretenders walk past the bedraggled trio and are so impressed that, rather than throwing them a couple of dollars, they offer them a slot on their show that night. Within an hour they go from the street corner to playing in front of 2,000 people.

It is, without question, the most successful piece of busking ever.

From there, they secure a record deal and, in the summer of 1982, enter the studio to record their first album – *Violent Femmes*. And the best part is they change *nothing*. It's the same old songs, the same sound they made on the street, and the whole album is largely played out using just an acoustic guitar, an acoustic bass and a snare drum.

Only on the ninth song, 'Gone Daddy Gone', do they make a concession to the fact they're now in a studio and they're not busking anymore – they use a xylophone.

All they need now is an album cover.

Enter Billie Jo Campbell, a three-year-old who is walking down the street with her mother in California.

A stranger approaches and asks the mother whether he can photograph the girl for an album cover he's working on and pays her $100 for the privilege. He then tells the girl to look into a derelict building where he assures her there'll be loads of animals roaming inside. So, without posing or even really knowing what's going on, she gets on her tiptoes and peeks through the window, trying to see what she's been promised.

After a while, she pulls back from the window.

'There are no animals in there,' she says.

And she's right, there aren't. But by that point the photographer has already got what he wanted and moved on.

Violent Femmes is released in the summer of 1983 to minimal fanfare and poor initial sales. When it was recorded, Gordon Gano was just eighteen years old.

Fast forward to 1989, to my own life.

I'm eighteen years old and mooching about the Venue in New Cross, an indie club from a golden age before The Red Hot Chili Peppers released 'Give It Away' and ruined everything.

During this particular evening, a song comes on I've never heard before – a thin, whiny voice asking why he can't get JUST ONE FUCK! Immediately, it cuts through the twee and gothic melodrama that I was used to and grabs my attention.

That voice again – 'THERE'S NOTHING I CAN SAY WHEN I'M IN YOUR THIGHS.'

It was exactly what I wanted – a song about someone who couldn't get laid and then, when it finally happens, they're unable to talk. What eighteen-year-old wearing a second-hand cardigan can't relate to that?

After it finished, I approached the DJ.

'What was that song you just played mate?'

'"Add It Up" by the Violent Femmes.'

Obviously, should a situation like this happen today I could have mainlined Spotify on the way home and listened to it on repeat. But this was 1989, you couldn't just listen to a song whenever you wanted to. So, faced with the prospect of waiting a whole week for the possibility of hearing it again, I decided to take the only sensible course of action open to me – I went to a record shop the next day and handed over £10.99 for an album on the strength of one song.

It looked amazing, but it sounded even better. The whole thing, from start to finish, blew my head off. That voice, the simplicity of the lyrics and the way it seemed, in places, like a rough draft scattered with annotations and unfinished thoughts.

'Third verse, same as the first.'

'Eight, I forget what eight was for.'

Who cares what eight is for? I didn't.

Yet for all its angst and triviality, there was something else that I admired. It seems weird to focus on it now, but *Violent Femmes* was released at a time when albums had sides that couldn't be shuffled or disorganised. You had to get the order right and I've always thought (well, since 1989) that no one has ever done it better than them – two sides of five songs where the first two are fast, the third slows you down, the fourth picks you up, and the fifth provides a finale.

Put simply – you can't put these ten songs in any other order and make them better than *this*.

It became a staple, an album I haven't gone six months without listening to since I discovered it in 1989. And, during Ruth and Martin's 2016 summer break, I was horrified to realise that *we* hadn't even done it!

If it wasn't for J. K. Rowling I'd probably still be repeatedly punching myself in the face.

Fast forward, one last time, to 1997.

Billie Jo Campbell, the girl on the cover, is now eighteen and the Violent Femmes have slowly made it. In various times, in different places, people have found this album that was quietly released in 1983 and it's now sold millions of copies. At the end of the film *Grosse Pointe Blank* its credits roll to 'Blister in the Sun' while Minnie Driver and John Cusack drive off into the distance.

The songs have reached a new audience. They're being played at college parties and Billie Jo Campbell is hearing them for the first time.

How does she feel to be reminded of her three-year-old self and the photograph that she was tricked into? How does she feel when it came back to her as an eighteen-year-old?

It's tempting to think that she would have been like any other teenager – simultaneously energetic and anxious about what the future holds. If that's true, then maybe she identified with the same qualities in the album that I did when I was eighteen, the same sentiments that drove Gordon Gano to write it when he was in high school.

Who knows? What I do know is that Billie Jo Campbell decided to pursue the best option open to her.

She became a massive fan of the Violent Femmes.

She framed the album cover and put it on her wall.

She used the fact that *she* was the girl on the cover to help boost her confidence and meet boys.

And in 2008, she married one of them.

Roll credits.

So, over to you Jo. Why haven't you listened to it? WHAT'S WRONG WITH YOU?????

I'm not quite sure how the Violent Femmes passed me by. I turned eighteen the year this album came out, but I was obsessed with The Beatles at the time. Of contemporary bands I really loved, the standouts were The Smiths and The Psychedelic Furs. I loved any band with a great guitarist. I played guitar myself, mostly alone in my bedroom.

It's possible that I heard the Violent Femmes but I've forgotten. They could easily have been part of the informal seminars on alternative music I received from the muso I dated in my late teens. His parents were Dutch and we hung out mostly at his house, because we were allowed to smoke in his attic bedroom. I've got happy memories of sunlit wooden rafters and smoke rings and walls covered in black and white pictures he'd clipped out of *NME*, while The Dead Kennedys, Jah Wobble or The Birthday Party blasted out of the speakers. Setting aside the fact that I had a pair of very long-lived goldfish named after Guggi and Gavin of the Virgin Prunes, I never became a whole-hearted convert to his favourite bands. Much as I adored him, I didn't share Muso Boyfriend's attitude to music: his scorn for the accessible and tuneful, the baffling mixture of irony and obsession with which he regarded his favourites, and his conviction that if the herd hates something, it's almost certainly brilliant.

The *NME* was Muso Boyfriend's bible and it took a hard line on nearly anything commercial or popular, talking about bands in the top ten with the kind of contempt most people reserve for child abusers. A few real gods could be forgiven commercial success, obviously – people like Bowie or the Stones – but the likes of Nik Kershaw might as well have been Thatcher herself as far as *NME* were concerned.

When The Stranglers released *Feline* and it went to number four in the album charts, an *NME* journo went into meltdown, ranting about the fact that people who'd never heard *Rattus Norvegicus* were now calling themselves Stranglers fans. You could almost see the flecks of spittle on the page. (I'd bought *Feline*. I didn't own *Rattus Norvegicus*.) And I still vividly remember an *NME* interview with Gary Kemp from Spandau Ballet, a band I never liked, though I admired Gary's chutzpah in agreeing to talk to them. The interviewer's disapproval of Gary and everything he stood for reached a glorious peak with the phrase 'this whorehouse called success'. I never made much headway arguing about this sort of thing with Muso Boyfriend, though, so after a bit of snogging I'd cycle home and listen to *Rubber Soul*.

My first live gig and my first music festival were both with Muso Boyfriend. We saw Big Country at Dingwalls in Bristol (supporting act: John Cooper Clarke, the punk poet). We spent my eighteenth birthday at the Elephant Fayre in Cornwall, hitching there from South Wales. I'd told my parents some whopping lie about how we were getting there, probably that Muso Boyfriend's older brother was driving us. Half an hour of unsuccessful hitching later, it suddenly occurred to me that my parents had said they were going shopping later. This meant they might soon be driving past us, so I kept diving for cover every time a Honda Civic came into view.

We finally got a lift, thank God, so I survived to enjoy my birthday at the Elephant Fayre. We pitched the two-person tent by a marquee full of Rastas selling tea and hot knives and saw The Cure, who Muso Boyfriend was weirdly keen to hear, in spite of the fact that they'd actually been on *Top of the Pops*. The only other act I remember well from the Elephant Fayre is Benjamin Zephaniah. He did a poem about having the shit kicked out of him by a policeman. Twenty-odd years later, I was on a team with him at a kids' book quiz at the Edinburgh Book Festival.

You've now listened to it at least three times, what do you think?

I didn't Google the band or the album before listening, because that felt like cheating, so I knew virtually nothing about them except that this came out in 1983. When I told my friend Euan which album I was going to review he assured me I'd like it, but his favourite album's by The Cramps, so that wasn't entirely reassuring.

Wanting to concentrate, I go outside to my writing room in the garden, which has a wooden ceiling. This, unlikely as it may seem, is relevant information.

So I put on *Violent Femmes* and hear a catchy acoustic guitar riff and I think, this is great! I'm going to love them! I'll get a Violent Femmes T-shirt, buy the entire back catalogue and bore everyone rigid with my new obsession!

But then the vocalist kicks in and I have an immediate, visceral response of 'no, scratch everything, I hate this'. The change of mood is so abrupt my mind goes blank. I try to analyse why I moved from appreciation to intense dislike in a matter of seconds, but the best I can do is 'I've heard voices like that before.'

Violent Femmes by Violent Femmes

By the time I reach track seven, all I can think about is the Toy Dolls' cover of 'Nelly the Elephant'. I'm not proud. I know this says more about me than about the Violent Femmes.

After I've listened to the whole album once, I look down at the place where I was supposed to be making notes and all I've written is: 'his upper register sounds like a bee in a plastic cup', which the professional writer in me recognises as 'not 500 words'. Feeling glum, I postpone a second listen to the following day.

It's raining next morning and I can't be bothered to go and find shoes, so I don't take the album into the writing room, but stay in the kitchen. With minimal enthusiasm, I put on the album again.

This is weird. The vocalist is actually, um… good. Where did the bloke I heard yesterday go? Now I'm not busy hating him, I notice all the great hooks and how they sometimes sound like a manic skiffle band. There's a nice bit of bluesy slide guitar and an actual xylophone on 'Gone Daddy Gone'. Plus, when he half talks, half sings, Gordon Gano (I checked the album credits) sounds a bit Lou Reed, and I love Lou Reed. Apart from being the vocalist, Gano also happens to be the guitarist I fell for yesterday.

I can't understand why he grated on me so much first time round. Beneath my wooden ceiling, he was the Ur-voice of all those *NME*-approved punky bands I never liked: nasal, whiny and brash. Today, sitting beside my kettle, he's raw, catchy and soulful.

Only then, staring into a mug of tea, do I have the little epiphany that you, clever reader, saw coming a mile off. Listening to an album that reeks of 1983, in a room that bears a passing resemblance to that attic of long ago, was a mistake. It wasn't Gordon Gano who was the problem: it was me. I was listening with a ghostly eighteen-year-old ex-boyfriend at my shoulder, and behind him, a chorus of snarling early eighties *NME* journalists, all ready to jeer, because even if I like the Violent Femmes, I'll like them in the wrong way.

So the sun came out and I took the Violent Femmes back across the wet lawn into the writing room, telling myself that it's not 1983 anymore, and this is between me and the Violent Femmes, nobody else. On the third listen, I realised that I loved the album. Before I knew it, I was listening to it over and over again. Only then did I let myself look at their Wikipedia page.

The Violent Femmes, I read, were 'one of the most successful alternative rock bands of the 1980s, selling over 9 million albums by 2005'. Yes, the Violent Femmes ended up in that whorehouse called success, and you know what? It only makes me love them more.

Would you listen to it again?
Yes.

A mark out of 10?
8.5/10.

23

The Village Green Preservation Society by The Kinks

1. The Village Green Preservation Society
2. Do You Remember Walter
3. Picture Book
4. Johnny Thunder
5. Last of the Steam Powered Trains
6. Big Sky
7. Sitting by the Riverside
8. Animal Farm
9. Village Green
10. Starstruck
11. Phenomenal Cat
12. All of My Friends Were There
13. Wicked Annabella
14. Monica
15. People Take Pictures of Each Other

First time listener – Peter Hitchens

Author and journalist, currently columnist for the *Mail on Sunday*, born 1951.

Peter's top three albums ever?

Beethoven's Seventh Symphony

Concerti Grossi – Arcangelo Corelli
Messiah – G. F. Handel

Before we get to Peter, here's what Martin thinks of *The Village Green Preservation Society*

So here we are, the final chapter, and I'm over the moon it's The Kinks.

Let's go.

1) Ray and Dave

Everything started so well for Ray.

Born in 1944, he was the youngest member of the family and star of the house. Six older sisters would take turns mothering him, reading him stories and playing records to send him off to sleep.

Sounds like the perfect life. But then Dave was born.

'I fucked it up for him,' Dave said. 'He was the baby of the family, the centre of attention for three years. Then I came along and stole his thunder.'

Great start then – a baby is born and, with that act alone, he's already ruined his brother's life and set in motion a rivalry that lasts to this day.

2) Opposites

The brothers would grow up as very different children.

Ray was insular, thoughtful, and would often go for long periods without speaking to anyone. He also suffered from insomnia and, when he did finally get some sleep, he was prone to bouts of sleepwalking. His parents became so concerned with Ray's subdued behaviour they sent him to a child psychiatrist for counselling.

Dave, on the other hand, was hotheaded and enthusiastic – determined to get as much fun out of life as possible. He threw mud at his neighbour's washing lines and, on his third day at school, he threw some plasticine at his teacher because she shouted too much.

Basically, he was good at throwing things.

Despite these personality differences, though, there's an interesting story that explains the strong connection between them.

When Ray was ten years old he was admitted to hospital for an operation and, at one point, it looked as if he might die – only an emergency tracheotomy saved him. Meanwhile, back at home, Dave suddenly awoke in the middle of the night, covered in sweat and gasping for breath. He hurried into his parents' room, gesturing to his throat and, in between his erratic breathing, pleaded for help. His mum calmed him down, wiping away his sweat and giving him glasses of water until his breathing was under control again.

She would later discover that Dave woke up from his sleep at exactly the same time the hospital was performing the tracheotomy on Ray.

Spooky.

3) Thwarted ambition

Ray had looked into the future and decided he didn't want the mundane life that his parents lived in Muswell Hill. He wanted to be a leader, a star.

He threw all his efforts into sport and became a talented footballer, athlete and local boxing champion. A star of track and field, until he injured his back by falling awkwardly on a goalpost.

Next up, a girl passed him a note during class and said he'd been voted 'Best Bum In School'. A nice compliment, one of the best, but in 1960 that wasn't the career move it probably is today.

And Dave? What was he up to?

When he wasn't throwing things, he spent a large portion of his childhood building a papier-mâché mountain in his room that got so big he couldn't get it out of the door.

Now put yourself in the position of their parents for a moment.

They've spawned a nice bum with a bad back and an early version of Richard Dreyfuss in *Close Encounters of the Third Kind*. What would you do? Probably the same as them – buy them both guitars and hope they stop mucking about and become one of the best bands of the sixties.

Ray of course played his guitar thoughtfully and artistically, leaning over the instrument and picking out Spanish-style arpeggios and complex chord arrangements. Dave, on the other hand, just cranked up the volume and played a load of power chords as powerfully as he could.

Course he did.

4) The Kinks

I'm going to rush through the whole 'forming the band and getting signed thing'.

All you really need to know is they recruited Peter Quaife on bass and a succession of drummers until they settled on Mick Avory. That just left a vacancy for a singer, which was temporarily filled by a young Rod Stewart and a variety of others, until one of them smashed his mouth on a microphone during a gig and exited the stage to tend his wounds.

Without a ready-made replacement, Ray stepped up, and that was that.

They were subsequently signed to Pye and given the opportunity to record three singles to prove themselves.

No pressure.

5) The third single

The first single was a mediocre cover of Little Richard's 'Long Tall Sally'. It reached number forty-two in the charts.

The second single was a Ray Davies original called 'You Still Want Me?' It fared even worse – failing to chart at all.

With one single left to save their career, Pye were already considering dropping them.

Ray then comes into the studio and plays the opening bars of 'You Really Got Me' on a piano, originally thinking it would be a nice, relaxed tune that might give them a chance in the charts.

Whether he was right we'll never know, because as soon as Dave hears it he realises it would sound better sped up, through an electric guitar. Not only that, he also thinks it would be a good idea to take a razor blade to his amp so it sounds 'different' and then adds one of the great solos to top it off.

'You Really Got Me' went to number one.

It was Ray's song, but Dave, by being Dave, had saved The Kinks.

6) Meet The Beatles

The Kinks and The Beatles came face to face on 2 August at the Gaumont Cinema in Bournemouth.

As The Kinks' support slot drew closer and closer, Lennon was hanging about on stage basking in the adoration of an audience that was there for him. Ray Davies watched him mark his ground and felt anxiety at the prospect ahead – supporting The Beatles, the biggest band in the world.

Still, he walked up to Lennon and said, 'It's our turn. You're on after us.'

Lennon, the absolute Scouser, immediately put him in his place.

'With The Beatles, laddie, nobody gets a turn. You're just there to keep the crowd occupied until we go on.'

Laddie? I'm surprised Dave Davies didn't throw something at him from the wings.

Chastened by the experience, The Kinks meandered though their set while a Beatlemania audience chanted for their band. They then finished with 'You Really Got Me' and the place went nuts.

'Later I watched The Beatles play and actually heard some fans screaming, "We Want The Kinks",' said Ray.

London 1, Liverpool 0.

7) Singles 3–8

I have a theory about these early Kinks singles – they all tell one story.

In 'You Really Got Me', Ray is madly in love. He doesn't know what he's doing, he can't even sleep at night (he never could to be honest) and says 'See, don't ever set me free. I always wanna be your side.'

He continues in 'All Day and All of the Night'. Still desperately in love, he now wants a twenty-four-hour companion and the only time he feels all right is by her side – 'I believe that you and me last forever.'

He then goes through the ups and down of a fragile romance. Impatient and fed up in 'Tired of Waiting for You', followed by one last optimistic plea to her in 'Everybody's Gonna Be Happy' – including you and me my love.

But then he throws the towel in for good.

In 'Set Me Free' he literally tells her to do just that and, in 'See My Friends', he declares that 'She is gone, she is gone and now there's no one left.' He ends by telling her he'll probably be OK because he's got loads of great mates that lie around in rivers.

Finally, in 'Till the End of the Day', he validates everything by saying 'Baby I feel good, from the moment I rise, feel good from morning till the end of the day.' He's back on that twenty-four-hour thing again and tells her that they're both free and their life can now begin.

There you go, over the course of a few singles, through a continuing narrative, Ray writes himself out of the boy/girl love song.

8) The Ray Davies wedding story

Really short this, but worth including.

Ray got married and Dave was the best man. Ah, that's nice. They've finally realised that blood *is* thicker than water and put all their differences aside for Ray's big day.

However, when the time came for Dave to do his duty and give a speech, no one could find him. The sisters organised a search party and eventually discovered him upstairs having sex with one of the guests.

I told you it was short but, I think you'll agree, definitely worth including.

9) The best band fight story ever

A lot's been said about the rivalry and explosive relationship between the two brothers but, arguably, the biggest fight was the one between Dave Davies and the drummer, Mick Avory.

It all started in the hotel, the night before a gig. Dave and Mick had got into an argument and Mick, the tallest drummer ever, had punched Dave in the face – giving him two black eyes. The next night, Dave goes on stage wearing sunglasses to hide his defeat.

Suddenly, in between songs, he turns to Mick and says something.

Mick immediately leaps from his drum kit and hits Dave over the head with his drum pedal, leaving him unconscious on the floor.

He actually thought he'd killed him and, with his own preservation in mind, he ran out of the venue and tried to lie low – a difficult task for someone wearing an Edwardian hunting jacket and a pink frilly shirt. Still, he managed to find sanctuary at a friend's house and nervously passed the time away with all the anxiety of someone who thinks he's just murdered the lead guitarist of The Kinks.

Of course, he hadn't. Dave awoke in hospital covered in blood but lived to fight another day.

So what had Dave said to him during the gig? What could be so bad that it would lead to such an altercation?

During a break in songs, Dave had turned to the drummer and said, 'Hey Mick, you'd be better off playing the drums with your cock, mate.'

As last words go, they're up there with Nelson's if you ask me.

The band would continue to fight at nearly every opportunity and were eventually banned from playing America after a chaotic tour where they beat everyone up.

10) Singles 9–13

Having freed himself from the love song, and an American audience, Ray then wrote a series of English character studies: 'Dedicated Follower of Fashion', 'Sunny Afternoon', 'Dead End Street', 'Waterloo Sunset' and 'Autumn Almanac'.

What sets these songs apart is the lack of broad brush in the storytelling. The attention to detail, to the minutiae, holds sway and Ray produces little vignettes of living with cracks in the ceiling, men in frilly nylons, and a couple that are so in love they imagine Waterloo *not* to be the grimy train station that it undoubtedly was, but a sun-drenched vista that solves everything.

My particular favourite is 'Autumn Almanac' – the best song Blur never wrote and a pre-emptive strike against the chaos of Sky Sports' kick-off times.

I like my football on a Saturday,
Roast beef on Sundays, all right.

Dave Davies may have saved The Kinks, but it was now Ray's eye, and his imagination, that took them in another direction.

11) *The Village Green Preservation Society*

And this is where it took him. This is where we end.

Like all nostalgia, it's a con, an outright lie – a symptom of someone with an active imagination who isn't happy with the present day.

Yet, like all nostalgia, it's seductive in what it promises and careful in what it avoids.

Was there ever a Merrie England of village greens and cheerful cricketers? Was it ever this bright? This clear?

I'm not sure it was and I'm equally sure that throwing our lot into 'preserving the old ways' is a recipe for disaster. We all have our own imagined past but those that shout the loudest about theirs are often those who are most unhappy today.

That, more than anything, worries me – an Unmerrie England that takes refuge in its past.

So I take two things.

The songs are great, the songs are really great, but it won't be God, or even The Kinks, that save the little shops.

**So, over to you Peter. Why haven't you listened to it?
WHAT'S WRONG WITH YOU?????**

What's wrong with me is a puritanical desire to be serious, and an actual inability to take popular music seriously. I pretty much gave up listening to pop music round about the time Radio London (Big L, 266 on the medium wave band, not the BBC one) went off the air in 1967, and absolutely gave up soon after I crashed my motorbike in the late summer of 1969, an event that strengthened my wish to be serious.

I'd been listening to Tin Pan Alley, I can now work out, since about 1963 (*Pick of the Pops* on Sunday afternoons was eventually permitted by my boarding school headmaster who until then had insisted nobody could listen to the radio unless he could make his own set, which a couple of my schoolfellows did, so subverting the ban). So I was in on the beginning of it, and it was all catchy, memorable singles which quickly came and quickly went, and the waters closed over them. I don't think anyone ever expected to hear them again once they'd dropped off the charts, and it was amazing how quickly singles vanished from the shops once they had stopped selling.

As a result, they're great memory-joggers, instantly taking me back to certain long-ago moments. But most of them are pretty artless. I never thought it was anything more than an ephemeral pleasure, and I still don't, though one or two singles, e.g. 'We've Gotta Get Out of This Place' and 'Meet on the Ledge', appealed to my gloomy instincts more than the rest.

It seemed to have run out of energy and originality, and after Big L, BBC Radio 1 was impossible to listen to, for some reason. I saw the whole thing as entertainment, ice cream for the mind, except for Bob Dylan, which was something separate anyway, and I kept up an interest in him until *Blood on the Tracks* in 1975 (I'm surprised, on looking this up, to find out that this was so late. My lying memory would have put it four or five years earlier). Even then, I suspected (and still suspect) that Dylan was having us on, most of the time. Who was going to dare to laugh, however pretentious and obscure he got? Mind you, I get the same feeling about *The Waste Land*.

A schoolfriend urged early Pink Floyd on to me, but I just got bored. And then, though utterly musically uneducated, I found out about Beethoven, whose music is like a cathedral, whereas this stuff is like an asbestos youth club hut.

You've now listened to it at least three times, what do you think?

Bored. Bored. And bored again. Did you think I was a nostalgist? Common mistake. The past is dead, that's the point about it. I quite liked 'Days', which has a faintly elegiac, plangent tinge to it, especially if you can't make out the words properly. I have heard it somewhere else, long ago, without having any idea who was singing it (this is quite common for me – once you stop listening systematically you have quite a lot of these half-memories and then discover that everybody else knows what they are called and who sang them. This can be quite funny sometimes). Mostly, the album (as we must now call it) reminds me of that early Pink Floyd, especially something which began 'I've got a bike, you can ride it if you like...' – and these were grown men, singing this nursery stuff. And then more boredom. And then even more boredom. I looked up the lyrics, to see if there was anything there either. Banality, and a feeling of someone trying to fill up an LP (as this must have been when it started life). It's a search for meaning, but it doesn't find anything. But by then I'd found revolutionary socialism, which had plenty of meaning, even if it was all a mistake.

HANG ON A MINUTE! SHOUTS MARTIN

So, I received Peter's piece and, while I liked it, I wanted more. I hadn't really got to know him through his writing and felt a little brushed aside – like one of those fellas in the *Question Time* audience who has made a cheap point just for the applause. But no one applauded.

An over-sensitivity on my part? Always.

Still, I did want more. It's the final entry in the book and I wasn't happy with it being left there.

With that in mind I contacted Peter. What follows is the correspondence we had on a bank holiday some time ago. It wasn't intended for publication, it was just two fellas emailing each other, but once I realised it gave me everything I was after, I approached Peter and he kindly agreed for me to use it here.

Here it is.

Martin: Hi Peter. Thanks for your piece and apologies for not getting back to you sooner. Had a crazy weekend with Tim Farron listening to N.W.A. for the first time – you know how it is.

Anyway, I love it.

If you have anything to add then please do as, if anything, it's a little short.

The second part may be hard to expand on as you have nothing really to say about the album other than what you've said. Except maybe, did you have a memory of The Kinks from the sixties?

The first part is fascinating though. I could have read so much more. You were the right age in what people often say is *the* right decade to be the right age (I wouldn't know, I was born in 1971). Yet there seemed to be a clash and you didn't want ice cream. In fact, you hated ice cream so much that you haven't ever tasted it since.

Don't you miss ice cream? On a hot day?

Appreciate I'm imposing on you to do more and you've already done enough by giving your time for free. But it's only because I know me, the readers, and the ice cream makers – we all want more.

I probably overplayed the ice cream analogy there – forgive me.

Peter: I'll take another look in a week or two, and if I feel the urge, I'll add. But not for the moment. Ice cream's a thing for the young. I didn't hate it. I just reckoned I was too old for it. I used to like corned beef sandwiches and Corona fizzy drinks, too, but I don't now. These days ice cream hurts and rots my teeth and makes me fatter.

If I remember anything about The Kinks from the 1960s it is

the words '...to the end of the day'. I can't recall what came before or afterwards.

To be 'the right age' you had to have experienced the world before pop culture. I wasn't sure it was a good thing, and now I'm sure it wasn't.

Martin: Firstly, delighted you're carrying on the ice cream analogy. I feel much better about the whole thing now.

Secondly, I've always been more than a little annoyed that the sixties is now told through its stock footage – miniskirts in Carnaby Street and everything's swinging all over the place. I'm sure it wasn't like that, it must be a lie. Mustn't it?

Our club is about trying to tell different truths, to come at things from other angles. The sixties as a concept now seems overplayed to me, but it's still incredibly pervasive. So I guess I'm just interested in hearing a different take for a change.

It can't have been fab and groovy in Darlington, and it sounds like it wasn't for Peter Hitchens. Not that I'm comparing you to Darlington – I've never actually been.

But, yes, only if you feel the urge and have the time.

Peter: I was mostly in non-university Oxford (and non-university Cambridge, oddly enough). There was definitely something going on, a kind of shiver through the landscape, a feeling of weakened authority and infinite possibility. Take a look at the original film of *Far from the Madding Crowd* with Julie Christie and Terence Stamp (so much better than the recent remake, and now available on DVD), or Antonioni's *Blow-Up*, and you'll get a hint of how thrilling it was. Those girls! The feeling of a summer morning and an endless blue day coming (like almost all English days, it clouded over quite quickly, of course).

But the ordinary world carried on often quite obliviously, while all this gestated in the middle of it.

There's a lovely YouTube film (a tiny bit of Carnaby Street but lots of more normal London) in which B. Dylan singing 'Don't Think

Twice, It's All Right' (that's how to find it) is played as background to a series of scenes from London as it was in about 1965.

It was *exactly* like that.

Martin: Did you ever see Bob Dylan in the sixties? My imagination tells me it must have been brilliant but that's the problem with my imagination – it's endlessly cheerful. In reality, I suspect I would have had to sit next to a beatnik who wore a beret and smoked Gauloises all evening.

It's interesting that you use colour to describe what was happening.

As someone who wasn't there and has only seen it on the TV it always strikes me that the sixties is about a transition from a supposedly black and white world to full technicolour. Then I remind myself that I'm being misled again – i.e. people actually live in colour. There were no black and white lives, just televisions.

Yet, there was a promise, or at the very least a suggestion, of an endless blue for you?

Just to touch on a previous email. I had some corned beef recently and was reminded of how nice it was. It's the beef that works best with vinegar I think.

Peter: No, never saw Dylan. Too young and too broke to do the necessary travel, I think. In any case, I think you'd have had to be around in the early sixties, and in the USA, to see the real thing, before he went electric. There's a wonderful YouTube of him singing 'Tambourine Man' (one verse missing) at Newport, before he was a megastar. You can see the wind blowing in the trees.

My wife (a Londoner) did see Mick Jagger in his dress at the Hyde Park Brian Jones benefit. Of course that time was lived in colour, though in fact the colours of clothes, cars, buses, advertising billboards etc. were different (and cruder) in that largely pre-synthetic age. And it was a lot shabbier and more run down, even in the parts that were supposed to be OK. But now it somehow seems more real in black and white, which underlines that these events are impossibly unreachable, and the people you can see in them are irrecoverably altered or dead.

Here's an odd thing, coincidental for me but for nobody else.

I think you noticed my recent interest in Sandy Denny. This isn't especially musical, though I think her voice in 'Meet on the Ledge' and 'Farewell, Farewell' is fit to break your heart if you were alive then, and know what happened to her later. Notice how Irish, or at least Gaelic, she gets, in 'Farewell, Farewell', and that strange skirling yell she lets out in 'Meet on the Ledge'. Ancestry coming out, I think.

Well, I'd never heard 'Farewell, Farewell' until about a year ago. And now I have, I cannot get it out of my head and I am quite sure it was about that terrible crash they had in early 1969, and I know why Richard Thompson never sings it any more. I didn't know about that then.

But I had my own crash later that same year in which, by the grace of God, I hurt nobody but myself. And, my goodness, that was the end of the blue day. From then till now, I'm set apart from everyone who's never been in such a thing. The veil comes right off, you feel real fear, and real pain, and then real remorse, and the old naked skull is there grinning at you, as he does on all those old tombstones. I've never been the same since, though I have to walk about ten miles before the old broken bone begins to ache, and the scars aren't where anyone can see them.

Poor old Sandy wasn't in the Fairport crash, of course. She had a different kind of crash later. But look at her little happy face, with the big red scarf, in that picture of them all in the midst of a load of hay, and you'll see what the sixties were like at the beginning. Then look at the later pictures of her (not the posed, glamorised ones, the ordinary ones, a bit bloated and sagging) and you'll see what happened later. We all thought we were playing harmless games in a safe suburban garden. And we were in a jungle.

Martin: That's incredible, Peter. I hope the after-effects of the crash continue to lessen. I've never really had my Fairport Convention phase yet, although I know I will. All these things are about timing don't you think?

I mean, if you weren't there, absorbing it at the time, then you have to choose wisely when approaching 'the great works'.

Catcher in the Rye, *Portnoy's Complaint* — best appreciated when adolescent I suspect.

Blood on the Tracks — well, that's probably a different thing. For me anyway.

And *Village Green*? Well, probably anytime other than when it came out, in 1968.

So, I think so much of what's in the past is probably ahead of me. Sandy Denny, Beethoven, and *Lawrence of Arabia* — a film I try every ten years and still can't grasp.

Yet people say you had to be there. So much of any generation teases future travellers as if their time and works of art can only be enjoyed in that context. But I'm never sure that's as vital as the personal — the place that *you* exist in when approaching the past.

Throughout the last year and a half of running this club it's the thing that's struck me the most — there is no objective good or bad, of course there isn't, there's just people colliding with things at different times, with different sentiments.

Peter: Oh, I'm very grateful for the crash. It did me very little harm, killed or seriously injured nobody else, and did me a great deal of lasting good, though it could explain why so many things seem obvious to me that are baffling to others, and why I am such a physical coward.

I had no Fairport phase or moment. I was just thrilled by 'Meet on the Ledge' at the time, and amazed long years afterwards to find it had become a sort of classic. I also intuitively understood it at the time, in a way I now recognise was more or less accurate. The poor things (well, some of them) were already doomed when they sang it, in their various ways.

Films are very personal. And when *Lawrence* first came out, in an era of 405-line black and white TVs with ten-inch screens, there probably was no more powerful aesthetic experience available. Though I'm surprised it doesn't resonate at all, as David Lean was a genius

(*Great Expectations* was far better, but never mind) and I can instantly recall several scenes, from 'no prisoners!' to Lawrence bringing the Arab boy into the officers' mess in Cairo after Aqaba, and the filthy hospital in Damascus.

Beethoven, well, just listen to the slow (second) movement of the seventh symphony, with no distractions to hand, through headphones, preferably at twilight. Do it three times. You won't regret it. Then you can move outwards from there.

And there is an objective measure, though few of us know how to use it.

> Thou, silent form! dost tease us out of thought
> As doth eternity: Cold Pastoral!
> When old age shall this generation waste,
> Thou shalt remain, in midst of other woe
> Than ours, a friend to man, to whom thou say'st,
> 'Beauty is truth, truth beauty'—that is all
> Ye know on earth, and all ye need to know.

Acknowledgements

I'd like to thank the following people for helping with this project and offering encouragement: Neil Atkinson, Lucy Bailie, Rich Collings, Chris Deerin, John Gibbons, Mike Girling, Rob Gutmann, Danny Hugklestone, Kate Forrester, Catherine Jackson, Euan McColm, Kate Musgrave, Helen Milburn, Brian Scanlan and Jeremy Thomas.

Ruth Lockwood for never forcing me to listen to Bright Eyes in the first place.

ToykoSexwhale for his brilliant illustrations.

Clare Newstead who gave the best advice throughout and Jessie Ramplin for her invaluable editing and support.

Finally, I'm hugely appreciative of all the guests that gave up their time to contribute to this project.

Unbound is the world's first crowdfunding publisher, established in 2011.

We believe that wonderful things can happen when you clear a path for people who share a passion. That's why we've built a platform that brings together readers and authors to crowdfund books they believe in – and give fresh ideas that don't fit the traditional mould the chance they deserve.

This book is in your hands because readers made it possible. Everyone who pledged their support is listed below. Join them by visiting unbound.com and supporting a book today.

@frauxirah
@WearsTheFoxHat_
Gabrielle Ackroyd
Anne-Marie Adair
Karen Adamson
Phil Agius
Glenn Airey
David Akroyd
Andy Aldridge
Moose Allain
Graham Allerton
Jo Amsden
Casey Amspacher
Ian Anderson
Liam Anderson
Richie Anderson
Mark Anderson-Flynn
Ian A. Archibald

Robert Armiger
Matthew Armstrong
Rob Armstrong
Sergio Miera Arnaiz
Ross Arshad
Carl Ashworth
Steve Askew
Neil Atkinson
David Austin
Jim Auton
Jeremy Aves
Clare Axton
Chris Azotea
Cam Baddeley
Lucy Bailie
Ed Baines
Jon Baines
Sol Baish

Scott Bamber

Christopher Barbour

Kristy Barker

Alice Barnes

Charles Barry

Jeff Bartrop

Dan Base

Vernon Baseley

Ian Bateman

Adam Baylis-West

Andrew Beasley

Joe Beattie

Lee Beattie

Sean Beattie

Janine Bedford-Livingstone

Mark Bell

Gareth Bellamy

James Bennett

Julian Bennett

Daniel Benoliel

Steven Bentley

Russell Berrisford

Chris Bertram

Gavin Best

Ian Betts

Matthew Biggs

Michael Biggs

Allan Bilsky

Brian Bilston

Stuart Bishop

Fiona Black

Ian Bleakley

Michael Blencowe

Adrian Bloxham

Oliver Blumfield

Rob Blundell

Stephanie Boland

Colin Bolster

Cin Bono

Chris Boor

Alan Booth

Jon Boulton

Nathan Bown

Derek Bracken

Steve Bradley

Paul Brattisani

Ian Brennan

James Brennan

Michael Brennan

Paul Brennan

Steve Brennan

Rob Brewer

Ross Brierley

Matt Frost Bright

Melissa Briski

Ian Brock

Sam Brocklehurst

Marc Brooker

Martin Brookes

Joanne Broom

David Brophy

Alastair Brown

David Brown

Matt Brown

Matthew Brownnutt

Keith Brunt

Lee Bryer

Liz Buckley

Joshua Buergel

Nic Bullen

Stuart Bunby

Phil B Bundell

Simon Burgess

Daniel Burke

Matt Burleigh

Rob Burley

Zoe Burnett

Girvan Burnside

Tim Burroughs

Richard Bushell

Marcus Butcher

Nick Butcher

John Byers

David Byfield

Neil Cadman

Ian Caine

Ben Cameron

Mouse Campbell

Giulio Canetti

Scott Cann

Simon Carberry

Lisa Carey

Jonathan Carr

Martin Carr

Steve Carr

Paul Carroll

Sean Carroll

Joseph Cartlidge

Nathan Carver

Brendan Casey

Francis Cassidy

John Cassidy

Steven Cassidy

Lauren Castagni Mote

Christopher Cates

Daniel Chapman

Richard Chappel

Sarah Chappell

Paul Child

Joe Churcher

John Clark

Kay Clark

Nancy Clark

Alan Clarke

Mick Clarke

Philip Clarkson

Steve Clarricoats

Lucy Clayton

Mathew Clayton

Steve Clegg

George Clerk

Garrett Coakley

David Coates

Ian Coburn

Mark Cole

David Collier

Andy Collins

Ben Collins

Peter Conneely

Christine Connolly

Joe Connolly

John Connolly

Daniel Cooke

Lisa Cookson

David Cooney

Karl Coppack

Nick Coppack

Wayne Corben

Darren Corcoran

Ali Cordrey

John Raymond Correll

Toby Cotton

Conrad Cotton-Barratt

Matt Cox

Matthew Cox

Ryan Cox

Steve Cox

Ian Coy

Fiona Coyle

Joe Coyne

Jason Crimp

Phil Crinnion

Connor Crofts

Lorna Crombie

Dave Cross

Michael Cross

Lewis Cubbin

Carl Cullinane

Shane and Catherine Cullinane

Cathey Cullum

Stephen Cunningham

Claire Curran

Vickie Curtis

Jo D'Andrea

Liam Daly

Mark Davies

Paul Davies

Stephen Davies

J Davies Porter

Alice Davis

Louise Davis

Simon Davis

Tom Dawkins

Celia Deakin

Karl Dean

Jo deBank

Mary Delaney

Tim Dellow

Steve Denison

Claire Denton

Chris Devaney

Max Deveson

Neil Dewhurst

Ann Dillon

Rosie Dimont

Robbie Dinwoodie

Josh Dipple

Thomas Docker

Ryan Doherty

Paul Doran

Sonya Douglas

John Dovey

Andy Dowling

Laurence Downes

Paddy Downey

Gregory Doyle

Carolyn Drake

Benny Duggan

Supporters

Bryan Duggan

Graham Dumble

Rachael Dunstan

Valerie Duskin

Paul Dyson

Sarah Eden

Hilary Edgcombe

Ben Edge

Iestyn Edwards

Janine Edwards

Louise Edwards

Mike Edwards

Owain Elidir

Stu Emerson

Carl Engleman

Steve Eustice

David Evans

Paul Evans

Will Evans

James Everington

Håkan Fält

Amy Farrant

Graham Faulkner

Tim Ferris

Oliver Fetiveau

Richard Fitz-Thomas

Chloe Fitzpatrick

Kenneth Fleming

Mark Fletcher

Stu Fletcher

Tony Flynn

Keith Ford

Steven Foreman

Kate Forrester

Graeme Forward

Clare Fowler

David Fowles

Chris Fox

Liz Fox

Anne Fox-Smythe

Aldo Framingo

Ann Frank

Alex Freeth

Dean Friedman

Ben Fry

Francisca Fuentes

Rob Fuller

Simon Furnivall

Craig Fyffe

Ben Gallivan

Enda O Gara

Adam Garbutt

Rebecca Garnham

Annabel Gaskell

Richard Gatrell

Frankie Gault

Emily Gay

Mark Gelder

Chris George

Sharon Gerrard

John Gibbons

Jane Gibbs

John Gibson

Andrew Gifford

Donald Gilbert

Gerry Gill

Mark Gillies

Tim Gillions

Mark Ginns

Mike Girling

Kenny Glover

Travis Glover

Sam Goodwin

Helen Gordon

Paul Gordon

Greg Gormley

Jenny Gower

Linda Grant

Miles Gray

Simon Green

Jonathan Greener

Phil Greenland

Hayley Griffith

Geoff Griffiths

Mark Gudgeon

Barb Guiney

Kristian Gunn

Nik Gupta

Robert Gutmann

Jacky Guy

Dunstan Hadley

Adam Hall

Alan Hall

David Hall

Tony Halpin

John Halton

Kev Hamer

Roddy Hamilton

Barry Hammond

Brendan Hammond

Ian Hanham

Donna Hanley

Emma Hardaker-Jones

Tim Hardy

Jason Hares

Frank Harkin

Graham Harley

Simon Harper

David Harris

John Harris

Kim Harris

Nick Harrison

Paul Harrison

Richard Harrison

Sean Harrison

Andy Hartley

Ian Hartley

Jock Harvey

David Haskoll

Jon Haskoll

Justin Hatch

Ben Hayes

Jane Haynes

David Heales

Kathryn Heaphy

David Hebblethwaite

Keith Hector

Chris Hencken

Christopher Hennessey

Alan Hepburn

Iain Hepburn

Antony Herbert

Ben Herbert
Tim Hewett
James Hewison-Carter
Chris Hewitt
Sean Hewitt
Gwyneth Hibbett
Brent Hickman
Steve Hicks
Darran Higgins
William Hill
Gerry Hoban
Gavin Hogg
Sophie Holborow
Luke Holland
Jœ Høllåñd
Graham Holliday
Adrian Hones
Graeme Hood
Debbie Hoods
Alan Hope
Laura Hopkins
Jamie Horn
Tomasz Hoskins
Alistair Houghton
Theresa Houlihan
Richard Howat
Lesley Hoyles
John Hudson
Ray Hughes
Simon Hughes
Nick Humfrey
William Humphreys-Jones
Derek Humphries

Andy Hunt
James Hunt
Andy Hurley
Richard Hurst
Robert Hutton
Christopher Hyde-Wyatt
Matthew Ingate
James Inman
Christopher Irvine
Lindsay Isaacs
Sean Isham
Linda Isles
Shun Ito
Dr Jan Ives
Catherine Jackson
Luke Jackson
Gareth James
Louis James
Peter James
Helen Jeffery
Henry Jeffreys
Joe Joe
Andrew Johnson
Ben Johnson
Chris Johnson
Lola Johnson
Jonah M. Johnson's dad, John K.
  Johnson
Traci Johnston
Steve Johnstone
Simon Joiner
Ben Jones
Fiona Jones

Leo Jones

Lois Boogaloo Jones

Nonny Jones

Owen Jones

Phil Jones

Rob Jones

Simon Jones

Shirley Judd

Greg Kane

Nayan Karanth

Edward Kearney

Phil Kedward

Gavin Kelly

Jon Kelly

Martin Kelly

Simon Kelly

Al Kennedy

Rachel Kennedy

Paul Kerr

Rob Kerr

David Key

Dan Kieran

Rich King

Steven King

Richard Knight

Alex Koschier

Peter Koukoularides

Jane Raffaele Krause

Peter Labella

Mo Lambe

Paul Lancaster

Colm Larkin

Michael Lasley

Chris Latimer

Peter Latimer

Marcus Laughton

Dani Lawrence

Geoff Layne

Yann Le Coz

Sean Leahy

Dean Lee

Dickey Lee

Fran Leighs

Ian Leslie

Kendra K. Levine

Craig Lewis

Oliver Lewis

Matt Lewsey

Scott Liddell

Mark Linnett

Tom Lionetti-Maguire

Paul Livingstone

Geoff Lloyd

Quentin Lockwood

Rob Long

Gill French Lorimer

David Loughlin

Alastair Love

Andy Lowe

Catrin Lowe

Edward Lowe

Iain Lynn

Brendan Lyons

Mathew Lyons

Calum Macaulay

Bill MacKay

Supporters

Colin MacKenzie

Jamie Macrae

Koa Maddock-Bradley

Chris Maguire

Jonathan Maguire

Julie Maguire

Daniel Maier

Lewis Malin

Sarah Mann

Mike Mantin

Simon Manuel

Luis Maquez

Patrick Marber

Stuart Marker

Eben Marks

David Marples

Peter Marshall

Luke Marshall-Waterfield

Paul Martin

Sarah Marwood

Jonathan Mason

Alex Massie

Stu Mather

David Matkins

Miles Matthews

Matthew Mawdsley

Nicola Mayell

Nicola McAlley

John McAllister

Ruth McAllister

Grant McBain

Luke McBratney

David McBride

Fergus McCann

Gerard McCann

Charlie McCartney

Ben McCausland

Euan McColm

Paul McCormack

Alan McCredie

Andy McCrorie-Shand

Bruce Mccubbin

Niall McCurdy

Michael McDonnell

David McGonigle

Kevin McGregor

Darren McGurrin

Peter McKay

Anthony McKenna

Iain McKinney

Alastair McLellan

Peter McLoughlin

Andrew McMillan

Stuart McNair

Phil McNicholas

David McVerry

Gerry McWilliams

Alec Meadows

Andrew Meldrum

Adam Melia

Sam Menter

Richard Merrett

Paul Merrey

Michael Meyer

Jana Michaelis

Helen Milburn

John Milburn

Peter Milburn

Scott Millar

David Miller

Paul Miller

David Millicheap

Sean Milligan

Jon Milloy

Joseph Mills

Lee Mills

Rich Mills

Margo Milne

David Milton

Alastair Mitchell

Richard Mitchell

John Mitchinson

Stuart Moffatt

Stephen Moir

Anthony Molloy

Jim Monteath

Ricardo Monteblan

John Moore

Kathy Moore

Liam Moran

Neville Morley

James Morris

Russell Morris

Phil Morton

Richard Moseley

Chris Mott

Tim Mouncer

Iain Mullan

Humphrey Murphy

Jonathan Murphy

Ewen Murray

Tim Murray

Kate Musgrave

Ollie Mustill

Sachin Nakrani

Michelle Naughton

Carlo Navato

Chris Neagle

Graeme Neill

Sandy Nelson

Caishnah Nevans

Peter Newlands

Ed Newman

Richard Newman

Rosie & Greg Nice

David Nicholas

David Nicholas

Matt Nicholson

Harriet Noble

Liam Nolan

Steve Nolan

Ashley Norris

Phil Noyce

Maria Nunn

Lorraine Nutt

Dave O'Brien

Matthew O'Carroll

Donal O'Connor

Eddie O'Connor

Seainín Ó'Donnagáin

Martin O'Donnell

Paul O'Donnell

Supporters

Aodhán O'Donoghue

Catherine O'Flynn

John O'Hare

Mark O'Neill

Paul O'Reilly

Georgia Odd

Hugh Odling-Smee

Charlotte Organ

Mark Owen-Ward

Martin Oxnard

Scott Pack

Thomas Packard

Jason Palmer

Tim Parkin

Andrew Parsons

Ian Partington

Satch Patel

Keith Paulin

Tony Payne

Russell Peake

Marcus Pearce

Stuart Pearce

Ian Pearson

George Peebles and his
     Vinyl Nights

James Pennock

Rachel Percival

Matt Perdeaux

Claire Perry

Pete & Claudia

Paul Phillips

David Pichilingi

Jonathan Pinnock

Bryan Pitts

Maureen Plumpton

Justin Pollard

Neil Pollard

Malcolm Porter

Chris Porton

Tracy Powell

Peter Pratt

Neil Pretty

Richard Newell Price

Nathaniel Pryce

Niamh Puirseil

Lesley Purcell

Emma Pusill

Roger Quimbly

Mark Rae

Kate Ramsay

Nicola Ranger

Ian Rankin

Jon Rans

Ronald Rashbrook

Joad Raymond

Martin Rayner

Bethan Rees

Phil Reilly

Steve Renals

Chris Rice

James Rice

Donna Richards

Glyn Richards

Joel Richards

Shane Richmond

Olly Ricketts

Bill Ridgers
Derek Ridgers
Simon Ridley
Ed Riordan
Huw Roberts
Matt Roberts
Paul Roberts
Adam Robinson
Simon & Rachel Robinson
Tim Robinson
Hannah Rochell
Mark Rochell
Mike Rodger
Steve and Gill Roffey
Paul Rogers
Susanne Rogers
Marc Rooney
Matthew Rooney
David Ross
James Rossiter
Mark Rostron
Anthony Round
Charlie Rowlands
James Rowling
Matt Charles Ruscoe
Dave Russell
Isobel Russell
Ian Rutherford
Martin Ryan
Robbie Ryan
Matt Rycroft
Matt Rynn
Annie Saha

Ian Salmon
Kay Salmon
Selina Sammi
Kevin Sampson
Paul Samuel
James Samuels
Sally Sanchez
Robert Saunders
Daniel Savage
Brian Scanlan
Paul Schofield
Derek Scobie
Mark Scorah
Bill Scott-Kerr
John Seal
Alan Searl
Richard Seldon
Steven Semple
Rob Shalliker
Ian Sharp
Matt Shaw
Clare Shepherd
Sean Sheridan
Martin Shiel
Barry Short
Tom Simmonds
Neil Simmons
Paul Simper
Graeme Simpson
Ian Simpson
Joe Simpson
Tim Simpson
Harinder Singh

Supporters

Sandip Singh

Jamie Sitzia

Skirky Skirky

Iain Slack

Keiran Smart

Alastair Smith

Alex Smith

Cameron Smith

Ciaran Smith

David Smith

Iain Smith

Mark Smith

Paul Smith

Peter Smith

Richard Smith

Stuart Smith

Dave Smither

Jake Snell

Malcolm South

Tim Sowula

Andrew Spencer

Graham Spencer

Anthony Squires

John Stack

Andrew Staniland

Chris & Gill Starmer

Chris Stead

Aidan Stennett

Richard Stephens

Scott Stevens

Tracey Stevens

Adam Stewart

Brett Stewart

Mitchell Stirling

Mark Stobbart

Keith Stoddart

Bill Stone

Simon Stone

John Stothard

Brad Stott

Andrew Straughan

Ian Straughan

Ben Street

Laura Stringer

Paul Stringer

Tom Strong

Richard Suchet

Robert Sugden

Martin Sullivan

Rob Summers

Graeme Sumner

Paul Sutcliffe

Graham Sutton

Peggy Sutton

Helena Sweeney

Steve Sweeney

Will Sykes

Michael Sylvain

Kaelan Taggart

Martin Talbot

Ewan Tant

Aaron Tap

James Taylor

Matthew Taylor

Graham Terris

Adam Terry

The Rider Podcast
Eric Thibault
Graham Thom
Andrew Thomas
Joseph Thomas
Andy Thompson
Helen Thompson
Alex Thomson
Irene Thomson
Matthew Thomson
Otto Thoresen
James Thornett
Andy Thornley
Chris Thornton
Gary Threadgold
Ronan Tierney
Tim & Jenny
Peter Tomlinson
Austin Toone
Alex Towers
Emma Townshend
Andrew Trace
james.travis@internode.
    on.net Travis
Damian Treece
Paul Trenell
Alexi Tsonopoulos
Kate Turgoose
Ian Turp
Scott Turton
Andy Tutt
Paul Hamilton Tweedale
Chris Tyrrell

Nicola Tyzack
Charles Ullman
Steve Van Riel
David Vaughan-Birch
Ben Ventress
Seb Ventura
Steve Vickers
Paul Vincent
Ian Wacogne
Andreas Wadd
Michael Wadding
Andy Waghorn
Philip Walberg
Steve Walker
Yvette Walker
Stephen Wall
Derek Walmsley
June Walmsley
Nick Walpole
Jonathan Walsh
Kevin Walsh
Shaun Walsh
Tom Warburton
Galina Ward
Robert Washington
Andrew Watson
Richard Watson
Tom Watson
Neil Weatherall
Adam Webb
Paul Webb
Michael Webster
Mike Weeple

Supporters

David Welsh

Alice Wenban-Smith

Steve Westwood

Gary Whalley

Bethany Wheatley

Matthew Wheeler

Stephen White

Barry Whiting

James Wickham

Gary Williams

Mark Williams

Mike Williams

Richard Williams

Rob Williams

Zoë-Elise Williamson

Iain Wilson

Kirsten Wilson

Mark Wilson

Sam Wilson

Stuart Wilson

Peter Winter

Chris Withers

Mark Woffenden

David Wood

George Wood

Peter Wood

Darren Woodyatt

Noel Woollard

Christopher Woolley

Ben Woolmer

Stuart Woolsey

The Woozle

Chris Wright

Martin Wrightson

Kristian Wyatt

Chris York

Andrew Young

Matthew Young